Unwrapping Me

Unwrapping Me

With Some Help from My Friends

The questions & answers that helped me to discover self-love hidden beneath sickness, sadness, and self-loathing.

A.P. Morris

Synchronistic Books
Gilbert, Arizona

Unwrapping Me
With Some Help from My Friends
The questions & answers that helped me to discover self-love hidden beneath sickness, sadness, and self-loathing.

Copyright © 2013 by A.P. Morris

All rights reserved.

This book may not be reproduced, transmitted, or stored in whole or in part by any means, including graphic, electronic, or mechanical without the express written consent of the publisher except in the case of brief quotations embodied in articles or reviews.

The author has represented full ownership and/or legal right to publish all the materials in this book.

ISBN: 978-0-9854893-1-1

Published by:
Synchronistic Books
Gilbert, Arizona
www.synchronisticbooks.com

PRINTED IN THE UNITED STATES OF AMERICA

To Changing Woman…
I know your spirit is very much alive.

Thank you.

Contents

Introduction 3
1   Desperate for Change 9
2   The Questioning Begins 13
3   Opening Up 27
4   Going into My Heart 37
5   Filling in the Holes 47
6   Seeing in the Dark 57
7   Letting Go 65
8   It All Begins with Self-Love .85
9   Meeting Changing Woman .101
10 Digging Deeper 107
11 Finding Compassion for Me 121
12 Beneath the Pain 143
13 It's All Judgment 167
14 A Pain in the Back 183
15 Giving Away My Power 199
16 Remembering Who I Am 217
17 Finding Faith 229
18 Nitty-Gritty Details 243

19	Resolving Pain	257
20	Trusting My Intuition	271
21	Unexpected Surprises	293
22	The Magic Continues	317
23	Back to Reality	323
24	One Year Later	337

Acknowledgements

Thank you Mary Ellen, Ricky, Robert, Toni, Cassandra, Amber, Karyn, family, friends, and each and every person I've ever met. You have been my greatest teachers.

Thank you to all of the amazing authors, speakers, and teachers that I have not met personally for generously sharing your experiences and insights so that I could learn from you.

I also can't forget to thank the universe, divine spirits, angels or whomever you are that continuously find people, statues, numbers, songs and all the other avenues that you share your messages through. You are so very clever and I am so grateful.

You have all been great teachers, motivators, guide posts, cheerleaders, friends, and comfort when I needed it. I believe more than ever that we all make it with some help from our friends.

Introduction

MY NAME IS AMY. ON paper I suppose, in the USA, I would be considered an average girl from a lower middle-class upbringing whose early years where probably a bit worse than the average kids, but probably far from the worst stories out there. I'm average height, weight, and intelligence. I received average grades in school and although I did graduate with an average Bachelor's degree, I do not bare any remarkable letters behind my name. I am not a doctor, a spiritual guru, or a scientist. I am simply a girl who wanted so much to live a life free of pain—physical, mental, emotional, and spiritual—that I searched and searched until I found the answer.

I was given many diagnoses from different doctors over the years such as: fibromyalgia, chronic fatigue, depression, bipolar, anxiety, PTSD, ADD, irritable bowel syndrome and numerous others labels for physical maladies. After taking more than a few medications, going through therapy many times over, trying an assortment of alternative treatments even spending 10k on a strict program run by a neurologist chiropractor, I still felt tired, sick, unhappy, and like something was 'wrong' with me. Don't get me wrong, the natural methods helped a lot. Eating a healthy diet and supplementing with whole-food supplements did help along with employing many natural healing modalities. During this time, I was able to eliminate all of the medications that I had used to treat the above mentioned array of issues. So I can't say nothing helped, it did, but even after addressing nutrition, exercise, and supplementation something still wasn't right. This is when I turned to energy work or looking more at the spiritual aspects of health.

After a medical doctor was unable to figure out why I didn't feel well she suggested that maybe I needed to see a psychologist. At the time, I was so angry because I thought that she was insinuating that something was wrong with me psychologically and that my physical pain was not real. I already went that route multiple times and even delved into alternative psychological work utilizing EMDR and other cutting-edge therapies to help heal childhood traumas. I knew something was wrong but I knew that it didn't involve any psychological labels that could explain away why I wasn't happy.

It has been a few years since then and I can say that I no longer resent her for telling me that it wasn't a physical problem. Since I now believe that our emotions are the root cause to most physical ailments, she did me a huge favor by directing me to energy work and therapy. That was the beginning of my inward journey to discovering the cause of my problems.

I could not afford to go to multiple schools to learn, nor could I afford fancy seminars from well-known gurus, but with the help of many books, YouTube videos, TV shows on OWN, and unpretentious people that were great healers and teachers—Robert Taub with ascension/healing work and Mary Ellen Foust with Bodytalk Therapy, I finally realized that although I was helped greatly by them and their talents, I needed to do more on my own. I needed to ask myself what was wrong and how to heal. With their guidance, I began to really look inside. I couldn't work with healers every day nor every week so I decided one day when I was in a great amount of pain, to sit myself down, meditate, get really centered and ask myself what the problem really was.

I learned how to look inside myself. Then and only then was I able to see what nothing else could teach me—**that not only did I not love myself but that I actually loathed myself.**

What a gift this last year has been discovering that I am whole, loved, beautiful, complete, perfectly imperfect, gifted, and everything that I had been searching for. Because what I found is that me, you, and every living thing is already infused with the power, beauty, and wholeness of the universe. We are all one.

It took me many years of pain, yearning, searching, and learning but I found it. And when I did, it made me smile at how simple it is. It was always there, yet I just hadn't seen it.

To my amazement when I began to sit quietly after meditating, I received written answers to the questions I had. At first as you will see in the pages that follow, I just worked on trying to 'hear' the answer to a general question of something I struggled with. The answers I received through writing were beautiful, poignant, and enlightening responses, so I took them.

Who was 'answering' me? I don't know.

What I **do** know is that I never knew what the answers were going to be, although they always contained things that I understood to help with explanations. I also know they always came from a place of love, kindness, and compassion. That was enough for me. So whether 'they' are ascended masters, guides, angels, God, my higher self, or Elvis, I don't feel concerned with figuring out who was giving me the answers. Maybe one day I will, but during the time that I wrote all of the questions and answers that is how I felt.

After beginning to trust that I was getting real answers, I kept meditating and asking more detailed questions. Each day for over nine months I approached meditation and my question-and-answer sessions with curiosity as to what I would learn next. I was never quite sure what would happen but as you will see, as my meditations and writings became stronger I trusted more, asked more, and thus learned so much more.

The first few questions and answers were more to test myself to see if I could really ask and get an answer. As time went on, I really opened up to the deep and painful issues that I had previously buried. I know I didn't make up the answers for a few reasons, one being that I'm not that smart. I'm not belittling myself, I'm just sure that I didn't know the answers because if I had, I wouldn't have been in such pain. Another reason I know it wasn't me making up the advice is because I'm not one for mantras or repeating positive affirmations, but as you will see this is a common theme in the answers.

Why did I choose to share these very personal questions and answers with you?

Because although some of the problems may be different from yours and you may not have an issue with many of the things I did, the answers are so enlightening, so loving, and so universal in their messages, that I felt who was I to ***not*** share it with whoever is searching.

May reading some of my questions, struggles, and the answers I received help you to avoid much of what I went through. I wish you an easier path and a smoother ride filled with more fun so that you may quickly get to what it took me decades to find. That all you ever wanted, needed, yearned for, wished for, hoped for—you already have that and more than you can imagine just waiting for you to recognize it. **All that you have to do is to love yourself, for then you will see that you are everything and everything is a part of you.**

Finally, I have to say this is not only about my questions and answers. This is also about a journey of learning to see the synchronicities that the universe places in front of us all the time. Not just the ones that we physically see and speak to, but the ones that we don't see. I can say definitively now that we only thrive in this life with a lot of help from our friends. Without them, my journey this past year would not have been possible.

If I can be a friend to you, a tiny part of pointing you towards seeing your own infinite well of self-love, I am grateful.

Desperate for Change

IT WAS A COLD CRISP mid-December morning in rural southeastern Pennsylvania. Pausing for a moment to take one last look at the empty townhouse that we had called home for the last four years, I shut the door and climbed into the driver's seat of my car. It didn't take long for the heater to warm me up and I began to relax into driving mode. Besides Ricky's taillights, there weren't a lot of drivers on the road at 4:30 a.m.

As we entered the highway, I could hardly believe that we were doing what we had talked about for so long. Ricky, my love and partner of eleven years, and I packed all of our belongings that we hadn't sold into two cars, and were driving across the country to begin anew in Arizona. It seemed almost unreal that it was actually time; we were finally getting to move west as we had dreamed of for so long. I was looking forward to seeing the sun daily and saying goodbye to the rain. Kind of a metaphor for my life or at least what I thought about my life.

The last few years felt like a big ball of struggle and disappointment for me. Actually not just the last few years, but most of my life. Don't get me wrong, there were some unbelievably beautiful moments with my daughter Cassandra when she was a young girl. And although my marriage to her father didn't work out, I felt truly blessed to have found Ricky. I can honestly say that he was the first person that ever made me feel completely loved and supported. His love is kind and gentle and constant, even when he is disappointed. But, just as is true with most relationships, even with great love we had our own issues to work through.

Here we were on the road, together, ready to start a new chapter in our lives out west. I shivered with anticipation topped with a sprinkling of self-doubt. *Was I doing the right thing?* I sure thought I was for Ricky and me, but I was driving away from my daughter. Not really, but through my mommy eyes I wasn't sure.

Technically she had left over a year ago, and for the last few years she was not the little girl I once knew. I still couldn't believe that it had turned out this way. I mean I had dedicated myself to being a good mother, the best mother I could possibly be. I never wanted her to have to feel unloved or abandoned the way mine had made me feel. I wanted so hard to give her all that I didn't have, so much so that I went overboard. Growing up she had health issues that kept me busy. I'd spent the last year wondering if it was all wasted effort. Although my therapist assured me that no acts of love and dedication are wasted, I still didn't fully believe it.

I had spent so many hours researching and trying natural and holistic therapies, not to mention the financial cost, to heal her arthritis. I'd been there for every single parent/teacher conference, every school activity, every holiday, every karate test, every doctor, test, and physical therapy appointment, every tear and every hurt feeling, and *what did I get when she turned sixteen?* She wanted to go live with her father who had been there occasionally for a few of the aforementioned moments.

At first I refused, but after a year of weekly counseling her therapist told me there was nothing else I could do. And although she had never seen someone try so hard to be a good mom *(her words not mine)* that at sixteen, Cassandra could choose where to live. Which seems kind of unbelievable that the courts would allow teenagers to make that type of decision. I could have fought it and possibly won based on having full custody because of her father's lack of parenting in the past, but I didn't have it in me. Emotionally or financially.

So she had left almost a year ago. I had tried to have visitation like her father had when the roles were reversed, but she refused and he didn't care. So I saw her one to two days a month. I was begging for crumbs and putting our plans to move on hold to sit there wishing she wanted to see me more. Eventually, we decided to leave a year earlier than planned.

Ricky's sister and her family lived in Arizona as well as my half-brother. Longing to be near her and her daughter, Ricky had spent the last five years flying back and forth to build his business so that when we did move, he already had a presence and income in the area.

Hopeful and ready to live a different life, we drove over two thousand miles to sunny Arizona. During those five long days of driving, I thought about letting go of my anger and sadness at what my life had brought me. For once, probably the first time ever, I was trying to take a healthy approach to focusing on myself by working on getting over things that I could not change, finding out who I was, trying to heal, and find some sort of joy.

On the last day of our trip at a rest stop in New Mexico, I came face-to-face with a Native American man who, unbeknownst to me at the time, set the tone for the upcoming year. Growing up on the east coast, I was not accustomed to strangers speaking to one another so I was taken aback when he looked me in the eye, bowed his head, and said a pleasant hello as we passed each other. I thought about the brief and seemingly uneventful interlude as we drove past an Indian Reservation.

I had read Drunvalo Melchezidek's first two books recently and I loved hearing him speak of his experiences with the Native Americans and indigenous people around the world. It really piqued my interest, which kind of surprised me because I'd never really felt compelled to learn more about their history or culture before now. As I drove on, for a long while I couldn't seem to shake the curiosity I had about the Native man in the rest stop. There seemed to be a deep pool of wisdom swirling in his eyes. Thinking that maybe I was making too much of it and was just excited to be starting my life in Arizona, I let it go.

2

The Questioning Begins

OUR FIRST FEW MONTHS IN Arizona flew by in a frenzy of domestic duties like finding a home to rent, changing tags, licenses, insurance and addresses on bills, creating a home, and getting into a routine that took me into February.

We love winter here. Low 70's, sunny, and pleasant is the norm for an Arizona winter day. Not too hard to love. We also found that people are so much happier here. I'm not sure if it is because of the higher levels of Vitamin D from the ever shining sun, or the mild temperatures that allowed people to move more slowly instead of rushing in to escape the cold. Whatever the reason, the smiles and conversations in most stores, restaurants, or just about anywhere you go is a pleasant way to be.

Sadly though, even with loving our cute, little home and the welcoming spirit, I found that my pain had followed me here. I still didn't feel well a lot of the time, and my easily exhausted and easily angered disposition remained intact. I continued working with Mary Ellen Foust, a Bodytalk Practitioner in Pennsylvania, over the phone and I found a lot of comfort and healing during our sessions. The problem was that I only talked to her once a month and I found that within a week after our appointment, I was always met with something that would knock me out of balance again. Something I thought, or something that someone did or said would upset me, and I would feel my peace unraveling. And the worst part is that I would get angry at myself for not being able to control myself. I was miserable again, albeit with much better background scenery.

One day when I was feeling particularly low, I decided to sit and meditate. I wanted some answers about why I felt this way and how I could do things differently. This became my daily ritual and work. It was tough at first. It seemed as though I had to strain to get the information, like I was trying to listen to a conversation through a wall, but I refused to give up. I was thrilled when I went back and read the answers because I knew I wasn't making it up. Although they seem logical to me now, when I was in pain and asking I couldn't fathom an answer to my problem. There were days that I sat in meditation in front of my computer waiting for an answer with tears running down my face.

It eventually became easier to hear or more accurately 'know' the answer to type it, but the answers were never easy for me to get without writing them. Really it was as if, and still is to an extent, I can allow answers to flow to me through writing that I can't get otherwise. And really, I didn't absorb the answer until going back to read it at a later time. This is also why I know that I did not make the answers up because when I read them it was as if reading them for the first time. Even within subjects that I've written about before, and if I'd been asked this question by someone else, I wouldn't have used the same analogies or been able to see the answer so clearly from such a higher perspective.

This particular day I was feeling lonely and began to think about missing my brother and mother that passed away many years ago. I'd come to terms with their passing and that their spirits still existed, but I wanted to feel a connection to them that was real to me on a physical level.

Here is where I began with my first question—

Q: *Although I've come to terms with the death of those I've loved, how can I live without them in their physical body and feel happy and know that they are always with me?*

A: We have adopted the word death to mean gone. Finite. The end of the existence of your loved ones when this is not so. **As humans we have based so much of our reality on our physical senses.** If we do not see them, they do not exist anymore. If we do not feel them or smell them, they are just gone. How untrue this is.

As long as you think of those you love as there and you are here, you will feel pain. But when you go into meditation or close your eyes or go in your temple, you see them, you feel them, and you know them. They are still alive. We have to reach beyond the boundaries of physical touch. It is so flat and non-reaching, look at it as 3D.

All the things that you didn't think were possible are. Suspend all thought, all that you think you know. Pretend as you say. Pretend or make believe. Make up the world you want, the scenario you want and then go into that. That is not denial, it is awakening. You are not hiding, you are opening your eyes, your heart, and your mind. You are stepping into what is real.

For so long you have based what you think is reality as what you can touch with your senses. If you can see it with your eyes or feel it with your hands, it is real. That is not so. There is so much beyond that child-like seeing-is-believing mentality.

What you can believe you will conceive, create, and become. You create your reality. *Why not make it the one you want?* You deserve it. You are not dirty or undeserving or a sinner. You are perfect as is everyone else. You are just learning. Choose to have the joy you want right now.

It is not a crutch to use music, meditation guidance, and props like a waterfall, chanting, or singing bowls—whatever it is that gets you in touch with that place. Your place—who you really are.

When you are there you will feel lighter, you can breathe better, and there is no impediment in your comfort, joy, or being. Everything feels somewhat light and magical like you are a million sparks that are alive with perfection. That is who you really are.

Sit in that every day. You do have time, bask in it. The more you do, the more you can merge who you are with your so-called reality. You will be living heaven on earth. You will be fulfilled, whole, and in a state of bliss.

It may take practice, but *what is better than practicing to find yourself?* Nothing. It is perfect. You are…now experience it.

My first book, *They're NOT Gone*, was all about reconnecting with spirits that crossed over through Psychic Medium Ricky Wood, so although I felt like the answer I got was different from that, I still wasn't sure if I was making it up or really receiving some guidance. But, my curiosity was peaked so I asked some more questions.

Q: *It is my mission to find my bliss and share it through words that allow people to feel. For when they feel they can understand and when they understand it allows them to comfortably find who they are. Who am I?*

A: A small piece but magnificent. No more or less important than every other piece. For each piece is an integral piece of the puzzle. Without one it is incomplete. Together we are whole.

The Questioning Begins

Repeat—*I am imperfectly perfect. I am beautiful because of my scars. I am love regardless of who loves me or not. I am everything at once. Full yet seeking. Hungry yet satisfied. Sad yet happy. I am everything and nothing. I am old but young. I am complete yet searching. If only I could see the big picture I would quit forgetting who I am.*

Q: *How do we heal our pain from abuse & betrayal? Why are we screwed up?*

A: *Who screwed us up?* Our parents, teachers, siblings, friends, children, mate, etcetera. There is always someone to blame about why we are the way we are.

But the first step to 'fixing' yourself or more accurately finding peace, wholeness, true happiness and bliss is to take responsibility, to take ownership, and to realize that you are in charge of you. No one else.

Repeat—*Past hurts, abuses and loss can no longer determine who I am, who I want to become, or what I can do in this life. I am not at a lesser starting point or have less available to me because I was homeless or lived in a trailer or had poor parents.* They did what they knew how to do at that time in their lives.

Maya Angelo said, *"You did the best you could do with what you knew at that time. When you know better you do better."*

Now you know better. You know that you are the reason you are where you are. You are an adult. You are free. You are no longer that hurt, scared little one who was hungry, or abused, or unloved. Because now you have the only thing you need to change your life. Your own love.

Yes, we need each other for growth, lessons, and mirrors, but all that you need to fix yourself is you. Too often we rely on a child to fix our own failed childhood dreams, or a mate to fix our own lack of self-love. **No one can make you love yourself.** No one can make you see the light and beauty inside, only you can. And only you can when you have cleared the clouds of self-loathing, mistrust, hurt, and open wounds from your vision. When you have cried and let go of those who hurt you, when you have let the wounds ooze and scab and heal into beautiful gleaming scars. They are not there to focus on, rehash, or use as a crutch, but appreciate as glistening beauty marks. They were pointers to your salvation. To finding who you are inside. To seeing the beauty that is buried below that skin.

For under that skin, we are all the same. No matter your color, hue, or undertone, we all possess the same beautiful light that comes from the same perfect source of all things. We are all beauty, we are all perfect, and we are all one.

So, whose job is it to love you? You and only you. Stop blaming everyone else. Forgive them and let them go. It is not helping you find the one and only person, source, and light that can give you all that you have been searching for. You. Your higher self. The pure and perfect you that has always existed but that you've forgotten. That you couldn't see because you were looking with your eyes. **Our beauty cannot be encompassed by our eyes, our ears, or any of our senses, for the beauty that lies within each and every one of us has and always will be there and everywhere, it is infinite.** No matter how many sins we have committed or had committed upon us, it can never touch that beauty, that fountain of eternal love that flows through each and every person.

Do you want a pointer to see a speck of what exists in you? Stare at a flower, a drop of rain, a bird, a leaf and you will eventually feel a pureness and perfection in that. That is merely a speck of the grandness that lies within you my friend. **Do not feel that you are being pompous or arrogant by basking in your glory because it is**

The Questioning Begins

yours. Feeling and being one with who you are is not only your right, but your responsibility.

Is it wrong to embrace the music that flows through you by expressing it in a beautiful song? Is it wrong to allow that perfection that is you to come out in melodies while singing? Is it wrong to show the magnificence of who you are by heaping affection and love onto a child? No, these are all expressions of your spirit. Who you are, what you are, and what we all come from. What we all are. We are all one. This is why we find so much joy in melodies that touch our souls when a singer belts from their toes and their expression of spirit brings tears to your eyes. *Why?* Because you recognize the beauty of your soul by seeing it in another, the one you so long to reconnect with and that you are. Embrace any and all expressions that help you get in touch and feel who you really are.

Stop wanting everyone else to love you the right way. Stop wanting everyone else to fix your problems. Stop wanting circumstances, jobs, or money to fix you and make you happy. You are perfect. You are bliss. Tap into that. Once you allow your expressions of beauty and spirit to run through you, you will filter it to create your own perfect sound, words, or craft. What you have to offer to the universe as your happiness. You will freely express your love, which will not only help everyone else, but yourself. Your happiness, your fullness, your satisfaction will become your reality.

In reality you are all that is beautiful. You are perfect. You are whole. All you must do is allow yourself to discover it.

Although I'd heard it before, this was the first time in my life that I really got that I needed to let go of my story and look inside myself to find the answers I needed. I definitely knew now that this was not me making stuff up because I'd never thought of it that way. This just motivated me more to continue asking.

Q: *Why are we always trying to reach perfection? Or at least I am.*

A: To know you is to know all. *Seems too simplistic?* But it is not. You are a microcosm of the whole. You possess all that is. Do not believe the fear some religions teach you. You are not dirty. You are not imperfect. You need not repent for being alive or making mistakes. **You cannot learn who you are without making mistakes.** Stop trying to be perfect. No need to try for you are already perfection.

The mistakes are merely a pointer to letting you see this. You do not need to learn to be perfect. You do not need to repent enough to be perfect. You do not need to practice for hours to become perfect. You are.

The only thing you may need to practice is letting love flow and letting your connection flow. As you let it flow, you will stop interrupting the flow and your masterpieces will come easier, more fluidly, and more clearly.

And when you are thinking about being great at something it is merely practicing to become better at a task. Basketball, painting, skating and so on all take practice to allow you to flow in this activity. The key is not to practice for perfection sake but for allowing you to let it flow.

Practice does not make perfect. You are perfect. Practice is to learn to let your perfection flow.

And each of us has a predisposition to certain things. That is why we are drawn to them. You may love something or prefer doing it. Then do it. Do not try to force yourself to do something you do not like. Only do those things that bring you joy. Then you are aligned with your perfection. Then you are allowing it to flow out. Not only will you reap these rewards but so will all those who behold what you do. And if only you find joy in it, then that is all that matters because the only person you must impress is yourself. You need to feel good. You need to feel your perfection, for when you do you will have experienced perfection—your perfection—which is all that there is.

You are all there is all wrapped up inside of you.

Amen

Q: *Most days I don't feel well, how can I feel better?*

A: It has nothing to do with trying harder, struggling, or pain. It has everything to do with allowing, relaxing, and letting in what feels good to you.

You struggle and bear down to try so hard to eat right, exercise, know everything you should. **When what you don't know enough of is you.** You are here to learn, grow and be for others. But you are to experience joy. Feel joy. Share Joy.

Who do you see the most joy in? Children and animals. *What do they have in common?* **They live in the now.** They have fun. They see the magic in the little things. A dandelion, a caterpillar, a piece of chalk and what it can create. They play make believe a lot. They are who they want to be—a pirate, a princess, or whatever they want. They know that if they believe that, they are that.

It is that simple. We should take notes and watch children play. Or better yet play with them. Let go of what you should be doing, how you look, or if it is silly. Let a child teach you how to live today. Laugh, make stuff up, and laugh some more. Run, jump, and giggle.

Let the beauty of life flow through you...for when you do your life will be as you wish.

You may not have had a childhood that you wanted. You may have been hurt and felt pain. You may wish it could have been different. It is gone. Let it go. Be happy today. It is never too late to live your childhood over because *are you not that little girl inside still? Do you not feel as she did?* Give her love, fun, and joy. Or better yet, let her show you how.

There is more power in one tiny finger than all of the armies in the world. For one touch of a child's love will send out a ripple that will change everything.

Love is in the simple things. Happiness begins with loving yourself, loving that little girl. She is not separate from you…she is you.

Now play little girl. Play.

Q: *How do I play? How do I act as an adult & have the mind of a child?*

A: Have an open mind. Allow joy to flow. Do not worry about adult things or how to be a child because then again you are holding yourself to a standard. A child-like awe of the world is a pointer and example of the way to approach life. It wouldn't make any sense to regress in the things you've learned. We don't mean that.

We mean when you are doing something, do it fully, giving one hundred percent of yourself, your mind, body, and spirit to it. Do not think of other things or you will miss the magic in that moment. There is magic underlying every moment, we just generally miss it.

We also mean believe that what you are playing or want or can conceive is a part of your reality. What you conjure up and want to be, you can. You just first have to believe and be ready for the next step.

Don't care what others think or say. Take on the child-like approach where they don't care who is watching them run or jump or explore because they are so engrossed in what they are doing that they don't care what the others are doing. Only what they are doing at that moment is important.

Truly allow yourself to feel what you are doing. Use your senses touch, smell, feel it on your skin. This is the portal. These senses are a gift, pointers to the bigger one—feeling it with your soul. The physical senses are a small inkling of the immense and grand way you feel or experience with your soul.

For you Amy, this automatic writing does it for you at this moment. You allow yourself to relax. You forget about time, what bills are due, or what you must do even fifteen minutes from now. For now, this energy is flowing and you are riding it, like a surfer in Hawaii. You feel free like there are no limitations, no road blocks—only freedom to breathe in all of life.

It is beautiful. That is heaven. That is why it is good to meditate each day to stay in connection with this. With life. With all that is greater than you. With your soul which is huge and minute at the same time. It is as grand as the universe yet only a thread. A great dichotomy that is. Enjoy your day.

Namaste

Now I am hooked! There is nothing more important to me than sitting down, meditating, and getting these answers. It feels like for once I can find out whatever I need to know.

One day a while back during a Bodytalk session, Mary Ellen said with unwavering conviction that she loved herself. This made me pause because you could hear it in her voice that she really meant it.

My previous therapist Toni had told me to look myself in the mirror each morning and say, "*I love you,*" to myself. I had tried it, but I knew I didn't feel it and didn't mean it. I knew I was hurt, angry, and shut off from others and myself.

Q: *How do I allow my heart to open?*

A: The heart speaks. Let it flow. See it opening with its bright pure green illuminating everything. See through the green. Like rose colored glasses but these are green, the color of the heart chakra. Everything feels softer, *does it not?* It feels serene and beautiful because when you see through the heart you see it without fear, without judgment, without sadness, and you see the grand scheme which is all enveloped in love.

All is love, all comes from love. Struggles fall away. Struggling never brought you anything and it won't. The heart does not need struggle just openness, acceptance, and motivation from a loving pure heart. You have this dear. We all do. It is whether you choose to see and work from this place. When fear, pain, and sadness are the motivation, it does not come from this place.

So now that you understand how to relax and let all that flows come from this place—the real work can begin. **You can only heal, grow, help and feel all of the joys you want when you come from an open heart.** It is the beginning, middle, and end to everything and everyone. It is life.

It can feel foreign; *do you feel that ache you have where your physical heart is?* That is because you harbor pain and sadness there. Allow it to release, let go…do not fear it. It is freedom. Open your hands and arms wide and allow the pain to flow out as the love swells. Breathe, deep, in and out allowing it to open up. You are safe and loved. You are giving yourself a gift allowing the energy to swell. You deserve to feel this joy; it is your innate wisdom. It is your gift. Don't deny yourself. You deserve it for just agreeing to be born to come here and be you.

Humans are not perfect. You are here to learn and grow. Do not allow others short comings and not knowing to affect your life. **Your love is yours, give it to yourself. Only you can.** Allow it to be your guide. Feel it. *Yes, do you feel that release of the old stuck sadness? Feel the butterflies in your heart?* There is love. There is you. There is the true you. You always had it my dear, you just didn't know. Now you do, let it flow and share it with others.

Amen

3

Opening Up

THE HIGHLIGHT OF EACH OF my days is asking another question and getting another answer. It is becoming easier and it seems that I am able to stay tuned into the flow of the information for longer periods of time. There isn't any rhyme or reason to what questions I ask. Whatever I am struggling with when I sit down is what I ask.

Q: *How do I let go of the physical pain?*

A: You are not good or noble by holding onto it and suffering. The misnomer that Jesus was perfect because of his suffering is false. He was perfect and beautiful because he was. Just like we all are. He suffered before death as he did not suffer in life. It was a full circle. **We spend much if not most of our lives suffering…it is not noble. It is not holy. It is not Christ-like. Being open to our heart and loving others is.** No matter what you do, who you are, or how much you have…you are just as perfect, whole, loved and important as he was. *Isn't that beautiful?*

Let go of the suffering, it does not make you pure. You are already pure. No matter what you did to or with your body, you are pure. No amount of drugs, sex, or anything else can touch that. It is infinite, it is intangible, it is the real you. **Nothing can ever tarnish the beauty of your true essence.**

Stand back from a mirror. Do not focus on the color of your skin, eyes, or hair. Look out of the corner of your eye and only see the outer edges. They will glow pure perfect bright light. This is your true self—your spirit, your essence. If you look by opening the cloak of your body, you will see glowing beautiful colors radiating spinning light. It is pure magnificence. Perfection.

There is nothing you have to do or be to have this. You already are. Everyone is. You can cover it with more skin or fat or tans or tattoos. You can be small or big, dark or light, but we are all this pure beautiful light.

The question is, will you allow yourself to see the true you?

Q: *Is it wrong for me to want money?*

A: You are waiting for me to speak of your manifestation of money as you are in a bad way. Or you think you are. Large sums of money are needed to pay to the government. It makes you feel petrified, scared, paralyzed…*yes?*

It is just money. Yes, easy for me to say, because it is true. **It is merely a physical manifestation of your thought.** *Do you need or think you need or want money?* Yes, than put your hands out and thank the universe for delivering this to you. Now put your hands down and do this…

See it there in your hands. Be grateful. Feel it. Feel grateful for it. Know it. Do not wish; be thankful that you have it. It will be yours if you believe from the bottom of your heart that it is so.

The money and things you need are easy to conjure, but they are not what is important. Love is. Sharing it, giving it freely, wanting to help and doing whatever little thing you can do that day is your mission. Be love. Feel love. Give love. Receive love.

The cycle is complete because all there ever is, is love.

I am really confused about how to let go and believe this flow of information, as well as, how to let go of what I've always known. I detest feeling the way I do, but I just don't know how to be different. I've never fully trusted anyone, including myself so letting go of the past and letting a different energy come into my life is petrifying.

Q: *How do I let go? I feel this urge to hold on like I'm falling…how can I let go in joy and relax and allow?*

A: It may seem simple but start with your breath. That is why yoga is so loved. It focuses on breath. You hold your breath a lot. Think about it…if you breathe you are allowing the air in slowly and out slowly. Immediately you feel more relaxed because you are allowing.

It is that simple. You do not need to brace yourself. You are not falling. You will not gain anything by sitting at attention ready just in case something happens. Relax. Just start with the breath.

Just sit and focus on your breath—as slow and sure and full that you can. So inhale slowly and fill your body with air. Slowly let it out. Keep doing it until it becomes second nature and it feels wonderful. It feels natural; you are not fighting it or forcing it. It just is. It may take a few minutes or many minutes. But this is important…stay focused on nothing else except reaching that place where it flows, you are in a rhythm.

When you realize that you have reached this place. Do not stop focusing just ease the focus. Relax it. You know it is there and it isn't going anywhere so step back just a little from it. Just enough where you feel comfortable. Don't jump back and pull yourself out completely. If you do that just pull up close again concentrating on the breathing. Then when you are comfortably in a rhythm slowly ease back. You are not sneaking away, you are not on high alert, you are slowly releasing and allowing.

As you step back you realize how vast the air is around you. It is still and simple yet twinkling with so much. There is that dichotomy again. There is nothing but everything. All that you need is already here, already within you. **Just as you believe in love when you can never see it, just as you believe in the spirit although you can't see it, believe in you. Because all that is, all that ever was, all that can be potentially, exists in you already.**

You just have to let go and allow it to unfold. Trust you. You are your best friend and you have all that you need.

Q: *Why do I feel the need to have someone love me to feel OK? Like I need someone to complete me?*

A: **You are complete, you are whole, and you are all that you will ever need.**

This is not something made up by lonely people who don't have someone. This is not something to appease those who are alone and are wishing for the love-of-their-life. This is the truth. Men and women commune because it is a pointer to completeness and a way to procreate. It is also one of the biggest catalysts to waking up, because it calls into play so much feeling. It points to what is in you or what you are lacking to see within you.

You do not need anyone to feel whole, to feel loved, or to feel complete. You already are. **And until you stop trying to find yourself in others: lovers, friends, parents, children, deceased loved ones or inanimate objects—money, alcohol, shopping, drugs, drama, or whatever, you will never be happy.**

Because all your spirit wants is for you to see it. Love it. Acknowledge it. Feed it. Enjoy it. All of the other relationships, joys, pain, sorrow, ecstasy are just pointers to what is already inside of you waiting for you to align with it.

You don't need your daughters love to be complete. You don't need your mom to physically come back to life and hug you and say she loves you. You don't need a man to look you in the eyes and tell you that you complete him, because he cannot.

You need to get to know you, feel you, and love you. That is all.

That is the biggest mistake we make as humans—looking outside of ourselves for fulfillment. Blinded to the fact that we are searching around in the dark for all of the things we want. When all we have to do is close our eyes, where it is not dark, it is light because you cannot see it with your eyes or touch it with your fingers, you must feel it inside. And when you do, you will realize that there is more there than you could ever have imagined.

You will wonder how something so simple, and perfect, and easy was something that you struggled with for so long. Because you cannot struggle, suffer, push, pull, or force. It just is. You just are. You are perfect, full, complete right now, always and in all ways.

On a particularly difficult day when I was in a lot of physical pain, I found myself pondering my lack of will and lack of interest in being physically alive.

Q: *I know I don't want to kill myself, having lived through that pain of losing my brother that way. But sometimes, I'm in so much pain, I really do understand why people do it. How can I stop feeling this way?*

A: Although you may feel like you want to die, escape the pain and be done, killing yourself will not give you this because your spirit is what holds the pain—that is where physical pain comes from. So if you take out a gun and shoot the physical body, it will die. Your spirit will leave it, but your pain will go with you.

So now you are a spirit in pain with regret. You see your loved ones crying and sad and struggling. In your jest to rid yourself of pain, you not only did not do this but you created more pain, deep pain for those you love. The last ones you would want to hurt.

So suicide is not the answer. And those who have done this are not evil; they do not get cast out and made to suffer for all of eternity by some higher power. Their suffering may get worse because they were already suffering and now they added more to it when they see that they have indeed caused more pain to those whom they love. They are not punished by anyone but themselves. Even without the body they are the same.

The only way to fix this suffering is to do the work—which is to let go, release, forgive and let go of the suffering and the pain you hold. And it may be easier to see this in the spirit world. It all begins with the spirit—heal it and all will transform. Love yourself enough to give yourself that gift. You deserve it. You are important. You are perfect and when you release the pain, you are freeing your spirit to see itself, be itself, and be love.

Opening Up

There is no escape through physical death, only through spiritual freedom.

The spirit wants to be free and commune in love. That is all it wants is love. But only you can give it that by freeing it. It cannot be filled by someone else, only when you allow yourself to see its beauty will you be free.

Although I know that this is definitely information that I'm getting from somewhere, it sometimes feels like I'm half way between being the regular me writing and just out of my grasp is this information. Like if I stop concentrating it vanishes as quickly as it comes.

Q: *Why can it feel so difficult sometimes to get into a deep meditation?*

A: You may be wondering why you can't or why it is so hard or what the secret to meditating and getting in touch with the real you is because you are making it something that is untouchable, hard, difficult, or only for those who are enlightened. All of which will stop you from doing the easiest thing there is which is sitting and allowing the true you to come through.

It doesn't matter if you like music, or rhythmic noises, or chants, or bells, or monks singing, or birds chirping or if you like to sit cross-legged or straight-legged or stand on your head.

You are not cheating or not doing it right. Whatever it takes to allow yourself to relax and experience the real you is right for you. **Life is not a test, life is not one big struggle; it is merely your job to remember or reconnect with the authentic you.** Yes, it is that simple. And once you do, you will easily take action through your heart and from your highest self and things will unfold beautifully.

So sit down, breathe, turn on whatever you like to make you feel good to listen to or look at, and go deep within. Where you on the outside may look as if you are barely there, but on the inside you will feel as if you are freer than you ever thought possible. You are soaring with love, possibility, joy, and peace.

All that you need is your breath and giving yourself the time each day to connect. It is just as important as the time you require for eating, sleeping, exercising, and fun. It will only support all of those things. So, do not put it aside any more than you would food or sleep, it is one of the most important things you can do for you.

I'm getting a little frustrated and feel like I keep coming back to this question. I know I've asked before but I don't feel like I'm getting it.

Q: *Why do I struggle with physical pain so much? I eat very well, I work out, and I take quality wholefood supplements, maybe not as much as I should, but I try to live a healthy life. Why do I still struggle with physical pain? I.e.-back pain, neck pain, pain in joints.*

A: Simply, pain is a block within your 'system.' Physical pain is an unresolved energy, generally sadness, which gets stuck in your energy field. Your energy field is much larger and more than your physical self. When energy is stagnant or not moving it slows down and stops, becoming lodged in your physical body. It did not begin there, it ends there. To get rid of physical pain you must release the block. This is the simplistic explanation.

How do you do that you might ask?

With energy work, either by yourself or with the guidance of an energy healer. That is the name you give them although they are not healing you, you are. Or more accurately your energy is. They just know how to facilitate the movement of energy.

Remember the block is caused by stagnant energy. Introducing clear, flowing energy will help to get it unstuck. This is why you feel so much better after an energy healing session. Your energy is moving again and you feel the life force alive in you.

This is also why it usually does not last. Energy healers are facilitating the movement of your energy by helping you in this way. **But if you do not change how you approach life and your own energy, you will continually go back into pain.** It will continue to get stuck, and you will need to go back to the energy healer or many of them until you learn to do this for yourself.

This is where you come in my dear with your diligent drive to find out why and get to the cause or crux of the matter. You want to help heal, share information, and although you knew there was validity to much in the alternative energy healing world *(you have seen and experienced it working)*, you wanted to go deeper. You want to find out how to heal yourself and share that so people can learn to heal themselves. What is that infamous saying by Anne Isabella Ritchie—*"Give a man a fish, he eats for a day, teach him to fish, he eats for a lifetime."* This sums it up completely.

You have wondered *why it is that you have suffered so.* You wonder *why you are so drawn to the spiritual world.* And why you want to see or learn more than just how to be an energy healer. This is why. Your curiosity will help you learn how to empower yourself, heal yourself, and share this so others may learn this as well.

For to heal the earth it must begin within ourselves—one person at a time. **Teach man to heal thyself; it will help heal a nation, a continent, a world.**

This feels powerful and like there is nothing else I am supposed to be doing right now. I can't explain it, it doesn't even really make sense to me. I just know that it is imperative that I put my pain into questions, ask for answers, and heal myself. Wanting to be led to knowledge that will help assist me I ask—

Q: *How do I know what path, teacher, book, or class that I need?*

A: Our answer is yes. Funny but true. You are drawn to so many different teachers, books, and healing techniques because no one is right or wrong, not one is the key. Each shows or uncovers another piece so that you may put them together collectively like pieces to a 1000 piece puzzle. It will take a while and you will have to try many things, but you will eventually see the big picture, the solution. And it is simple, yet complex. Easy when it is complete, yet evasive when lying in a 1000 different small pieces that look so similar.

Embrace every day, each one holds another piece, or a clue to your picture. Each person's journey is different because each person needs to see different things to 'get it' for them. This is why no one religion is more right or wrong than another. No one class, healer, form of study, or guru is better or correct for all. Each needs something different depending what day, situation, or person the information is being given to.

We are all unique and require a unique perspective. Embrace yours. Follow yours. Love yours. It is waiting for you.

The right people, information, tools, books and all that you need will present themselves to you. All you have to do is be ready, willing, and awake enough to receive it. We are all one.

Amen

4

Going into My Heart

I BEGAN READING *LIVING IN THE HEART* by Drunvalo Melchizedek. Mary Ellen had lent his first two books to me a while back and I'd found him fascinating. He refers to himself as a spiritual scientist and in his first two books he intricately demonstrates the relationship between sacred geometry and all living things. And although they were pretty interesting, I'm not a big science or math kind-of-girl so my attention span didn't last very long for that. Somehow though, Drunvalo knew just when to change gears and share his personal experience with stories about traveling around the world. What he learned from his interactions with indigenous and the native people enthralled me along with his deep trust and ability to listen to his angels and guides

This third book of his seemed different at first glance. And it was. Once I started reading it, I couldn't stop. One night after reading more than half of his book, I found myself awake at 3:00 a.m. hungry to learn more. I noticed that I was in a lot of physical pain but I pushed it aside and read on. The only time I would stop was to try the exercises he would describe about going into the heart space.

Before I knew it the birds were singing and welcoming the sun as it rose. I walked outside and watched it all. While sitting there I noticed that I felt wonderful. Not only did I feel amazing physically and a welcomed rarity it was, but even more astounding was that emotionally I felt just as good.

It was as if I was seeing a sunrise and nature for the first time; like I'd never really seen or felt or listened to the perfection of the beginning of a new day. Everything looked and sounded like the most exquisite gifts I'd ever beholden. It was like watching a symphony of lights and sounds led by an invisible conductor. I remember having rare glimpses of such beauty when I'd sat on a beach and watched the sunrise a few years ago while on a vacation. But now, here I was, at home on a typical day feeling as if every little thing was absolutely perfect.

I didn't want it to end, but eventually I had to get on with my day. I did seem to float through that day and the next. Between writing and reading more of his book, I'd found my heaven on Earth. This gave me hope that I was on the right path. After a couple of days, just like a feather I gently floated back down, but I did not forget that euphoria. I wanted more of that and felt even more determined to continue on this journey.

I wanted to live, feel, and operate from that place on a consistent basis. Although it didn't last, the memory was still so vivid. I believe I'd been given this glimpse so I knew what I was shooting for. I wanted to know more and feel that way again, so I asked—

Q: *How do you retrain yourself to think, act, & be in your heart all of the time?*

A: You know you need to live from your heart now. You know that the only way to your own salvation is through love. But you find each day when you awake, there lingers that physical pain and the tendency to be in the negative—*"I don't feel well, I just want to lay here, I have so much to do, I don't feel like it,"* and so on.

It is easy to fall back in this trap of old patterns of thinking. But the great news is that you have the power to be, have, and do anything you want today. You can become frazzled when something goes wrong to your standards or you can take a deep breath, release your resistance, and look for the message or even gift it may be bringing to you. *How do you know that it is not a gift?*

You may be thinking—*Well, having a flat tire so I can't make it to my appointment is not a gift, it is a pain is the ass.* Did you ever think that maybe that flat tire stopped you from driving to the appointment that on the way an overly tired truck driver may not have seen the red light and would have t-boned you, which would have seriously injured you causing you to have to go through years of therapy? *What a gift that flat tire is now, huh?*

You never know how the universe is working, what circumstances they set up for your good, what person you may meet that day that could be just the key to changing the trajectory of your life. Approach each day like those books you so loved as a child. You know, the hard board ones that had the shiny 3D pictures on the front that you loved to sit and just turn it so it looked as if it changed. Holographic.

You know that is an example of the life you are supposed to have, right? One small change and the picture could change.

All you have to do is believe. No, that is not esoteric crap, it is true and simple. Wake up and no matter how you feel, take a deep breath or as many as you need. Let go of those negative emotions, feelings of pain, and focus on what you do want.

Use the tools you are given by your mentors and teachers. Feel it deep within you as you say it, *"I am that I am, and what I am is perfect."* That is not cocky that is the truth. Each of us is a piece of the divine, God, or whatever you prefer to call it. Here is a non-denominational spiritual way that is simple for you to remember.

Each of us is born and always holds, no matter what, a piece of perfection. It is a light, a ball of light within your heart that is untouchable. It is perfect, it is sacred, and it is divine and everlasting. It is a tiny piece of all that it is. It is a piece that everyone and everything possesses. No more than another, no matter who you are, how rich you become, how enlightened you are, how smart you are, or how many initials appear behind your name.

Each of us has the same important piece, equally.

You will never lose it, tarnish it, or throw it away, you can't because it is the very fabric of who you are. It is the center of your spirit or soul.

When you recognize that, honor that, sit with it, get to know it, and everyday align yourself with that, you will be free. Free of pain, sadness, hardship, and grief. You will know when you connect with it, although that is not correct because you are always connected to it, you just forgot. But when you live through it, with it in harmony, you will know who you are and all the other things will fall into place.

Your life will seem to begin to flow in harmony with everything else. It won't feel like a struggle. It won't feel like you have to fight or crawl your way to the top. You won't worry about the race or winning because when you touch and bathe in the sacredness of your being you will know that you are already all that you want. You are complete. You are not broken.

You are full, you are loved, and you are one with all that is. Then you will know joy, peace, and love. Now stop typing and sit with yourself—that beautiful glowing ball of perfection.

Repeat—*I am that I am.*

Now that I am beginning to see some peace within myself at times, I want to have this in my relationships with others. I'm not sure why it seems so difficult to do this. It is definitely not from a lack of love or effort. I must not understand though because it seems neither of those changes the outcome. I asked—

Q: *What is it you would like me to know oh spirit of mine? I feel sadness about the state of my relationships. I feel it is not easy to communicate with my significant other, my daughter, or my family. Why is it so hard?*

A: Simply, because you come from a place of fear, hurt, resentment, and righteousness. All of which will lead to disharmony, not only in your relationships but with yourself. And remember it all starts with you. If you are balanced and come from you heart in your communication, you give your loved ones a space to come from their heart.

Your so-called struggles or difficult communication issues are merely you feeling that you are either misunderstood, underappreciated, or unloved. Again, all of these things are an illusion to your core, your heart, and your soul. These all come from a lack of place, which will only breed more lack of mentality, frustration, and sadness.

It is not, let me repeat that…**it is NOT your spouses, your daughters, or anyone else's job to make you feel loved, appreciated, or understood. It is your job, period.** Once you take that responsibility, all the rest will fall in place because only you can love yourself like you want. Only you can appreciate the perfection and beauty inside of you that you are craving, and only you can understand yourself fully.

You are expecting someone else to give you what you need— to feel loved, appreciated, and understood. This is why you are unhappy. They cannot give that to you, only you can.

When you fully understand this by making yourself your number one priority, and you love yourself like you deserve, you will no longer need or crave this from others. Then and only then can you have healthy relationships because you will come to them full, whole, and from a place of love which is the only way to do it successfully.

In a state of self-love you will then be able to look at them with eyes of pure, unconditional love. You will love them, flaws and all. You will love them regardless of how much love they bestow upon you. You will love them regardless of how they make you feel, you will love them simply because you love them. Without any conditions.

They don't need to make you happy, give you anything, or offer you all of their emotional love. Because you are not wanting unconditional love from them, you want them to feed you and your lack of love. That is not their job, it is yours.

Once you see this and step back from all of your relationships knowing that you have been looking at them inaccurately, you will realize those that you love are perfect just as they are. When you don't need them to be this or do that for you, you can then enjoy and appreciate the mere fact that they love you. And that will be enough, and then will you know contentment, truly reciprocal love and true unconditional love, which is the only love that lasts.

When you love you enough, you will stop seeking to feel whole from others.

Q: *How do you love yourself so you are full and don't need it from someone else?*
A: Easy, love yourself.
How?

By giving yourself the love, time, attention, affection, fun, pampering, and growth that you crave. All because you are you; you need no other reason. You are born perfect, and you stay that way forever.

How do you specifically love yourself?

Heal yourself, let go of the pain, sadness, abandonment feelings, anger, resentment, disappointment that you have in your parents, your siblings, your children, your friends, your family members, your abusers, your molesters, strangers, teachers, and anyone else who you feel ever transgressed against you.

Forgive them. Forgive yourself. Then you will be free.

Think of it this way...*you usually try your best with your loved ones right?* You think of them, plan for them, do for them, love them the best that you know how. *Right? Isn't that why you feel slighted, taken for granted, because you feel that you have given more than you've gotten?* Step back from that and look as if you were an onlooker. You gave your all and so did they.

Now you may say, *"Well, no they didn't because they would have done this..."* Stop. They gave their all. It may not have been what you wanted, wished for, or would have preferred. But they gave you all they could at that time, period. So they gave you all that they could.

Be grateful for that. Appreciate that they tried to give you their all. Do not hold them to a standard that they cannot reach. That is not fair to them and it will do you no good. Appreciate that you have people that are willing to try to love you the best they can. Then you will have realized how grateful you should be.

Remember, it is your job to love you to fullness and peace. Not theirs. They are simply there doing their best. Appreciate them, give what you can to them, and bask in the beauty of that because that is all there is.

We are all here learning, giving and trying, and we all deserve to be loved for who we are, where we are at, no matter what and without condition. Give that to yourself and then you can give that to others.

A friend, a lover, a parent, a child, a psychic medium, a healer, a doctor, and a pet cannot heal you. They cannot take your pain away. You and only you are your salvation. That does NOT mean you are alone. They are here to teach you, to commune with you, to guide you, and to hug you, but it is your job to heal you and love you.

We are always trying to give that job away and keep becoming disappointed when no one does it right. They are not wrong, they just can't. It is not their job. It's yours.

So you might as well take it on and love it because otherwise it will never get done.

I find it difficult at times to put into practice being OK with what I get from others. When I am hurt or disappointed because of an interaction I had with someone, I feel like they have some sort of responsibility in our communication. Like it takes two. I guess I get upset when I'm hurt by someone and then I'm told just because I feel a certain way doesn't mean that is how it is.

Q: *I don't like the statement, 'Feelings are not facts,' because my feelings seem very real to me.*

A: It is not because they aren't real to you and because they are not real pointers to what the issue is. They are. But your feeling towards something, someone, or a situation is not what makes it so. It is about you. **Your feelings are about your inner workings not about someone else's actions.**

Too often we go into a situation and what someone does makes, or we think makes us feel a certain way. Then we judge that situation, person or place as good or bad depending on whether we felt good or bad while there, which is completely inaccurate.

If we felt good or bad depends upon ourselves. For example, think about if you went into a coffee shop and the clerk was kind and attentive and smiled before, during, and after your order. Then the gentleman behind you picked up your change as it fell on the floor while getting money out to pay. You would get your coffee and think…Wow this is great coffee, a great shop, it is high quality and I'm going to tell everyone this is the best place and they should go there.

Do you know that they may use the worst quality coffee ever? Do you know that there may be rats running around the back room? The counters may not have been cleaned and harbor many dangerous germs.

You were responding to the people's energy around you. You liked feeling welcomed, appreciated, respected, and treated with kindness. That is what you loved, that was your positive experience.

On the flip side, you could enter a high-end swanky coffee shop that was brand new, full of beautiful furniture, art, sparkling clean, and had the best grade coffee available—organic everything. You are stunned by the immaculate beauty glistening around you. Then the inattentive barista shortly clips, *"What can I get for you?"* as she looks down at your shirt where your baby had spit up and you had tried to wipe it off but there was a faint ring left. You feel dirty, unkempt. Then you are thrown off and you can't remember if you wanted a cinnamon dolce or mocha latte. *What size did you want?* Then you hear a lady behind you sigh loudly like you are the slowest thing on the earth who has now messed up her entire day by failing to fire off your order with the precision of a drill sergeant.

Once you get your coffee and step outside, you can't get away fast enough from the negative energy that was bombarding you. The coffee is good but you don't feel great and you don't really care if you come back again.

That is the difference in energy. That is the difference energy makes in business, life, relationships and how you feel about any particular person, place, or thing.

So as you see, feelings are not facts. Energy changed how you felt about a place, people, and a product. It is not about 'it' as much as it is about how it 'made you feel.' The fact is energy is what affects how you feel about everything. Once we let go of pain, suffering, anger, resentment, bitterness and all other non-productive feelings rooted in unresolved pain, we can go into every day with positive, clear, healthy energy. Not only will we feel better but many more people, places, and things will feel better.

This is how we change our world. **This is how we change how we feel by being responsible for the energy we bring to ourselves, others, places, events, and life.** It starts with each individual and will grow into a new norm, a new way of living, and a new consciousness.

Peace.

5

Filling in the Holes

I'VE LEARNED SO MUCH IN a short period of time and I see so much more than I used to. I guess I'm still frustrated though because this is not the beginning of my journey. I've worked with Mary Ellen for over a year now with Bodytalk, and before that I worked with Robert Taub with healing and ascension work many times over a year period. Even before that I read Eckhart Tolle's books—*The Power of Now* and *A New Earth*—which both really changed how I looked at things, as well as many other self-help books. I'm upset that I seem unable to 'get it' after having spent years already trying to see things differently.

Q: *Why is it that I have been doing this 'work' for many years now but I'm still often feeling so much pain—physically, emotionally, and spiritually?*

A: There are a few reasons as you say, but to put it simply, because you choose it. I know that probably angers you as you say, "I do not choose this. I do not choose pain. I did not choose for those *awful things to happen to me. I am begging for you to help me not hurt anymore!"*

Right? Smile.

You chose to come here in this body, in this life. To feel these experiences and to remember who you are. So you may wake up and know who you truly are. When you do, you will realize that you have the power. You do not need to kneel and beg for God or angels or whomever to heal you or release you from the pain.

Because you will know that only you can do that. You are all that you need.

As far as it taking so long, that is how long you need to get it. Not because you are being punished, but your belief system is such that you think it takes a long time. You think that it is hard work. You believe that you have to struggle and know everything before you can let that 'stuff' you call pain go.

You do not. The only thing you have to do is believe.

Believe what?

That you are perfect, whole, and deserving because you are, you just don't believe it. And what is impeding you is the depth of these beliefs. They are ingrained, deep, and slow to fill in.

Choose today to say out loud and accept it into your heart. You cannot do this through your mind. You cannot eat a certain thing or take a certain supplement and that will change it. It can assist and is a good choice, but ultimately the final puzzle piece that you have been searching for all these years has been right there waiting patiently for you to see. Close your eyes and put your hand on your heart. Put all of your focus on it. Just sit quietly until you feel, know, and see what you truly are.

It is magnificent. You are. We all are because we are all one from the same source. You do not need anything—any one healer, love from anyone else, any accolades, any one religion, or any specific blessing. **All that you need is to discover the love and perfection that you**

are in your heart. It holds the key. When you finally allow yourself to see who you truly are, everything will fall into place.

You will naturally follow what is best for your health with what to eat or take. You will naturally follow what is best for you in all areas of your life. You will be living your authentic self, your authentic life, and it will be as you wish.

Q: *I understand now that I have all that I need inside. I've experienced it and I know it many times over. Then why do I feel like each day that I wake up, I have to 'get it' again—like it is a struggle to get back to that sweet spot. Why can't I be like that at all times regardless of what is going on?*

A: This happens to you dear one because you have such deep trenches of sadness dug inside of you. You see your way out of them when you meditate or spend time in nature. You feel that peace in the space of knowing that you are already perfect and no matter what you've done or how low you've felt that, you have all that you need inside of you.

But then you come across another ditch that you created when you were asleep. No not sleeping at night, but asleep in that you were not aware of your magnificence and perfection that you discovered.

It is like this. You've taken many years of pain, suffering, and holding onto things to create the turmoil that led you to this point of awakening. The pain was so unbearable that you would have rather died than continue in the life you were leading. This is what allowed you to surrender to what is. **And what is, is that you are already all that you need. You already possess all the love that you need to feel complete. You already are everything you wish for.**

Now you know, but there are some residual holes left that the sadness dug. Your job is when you fall in one, feel sad again, or feel pain, to go to your heart. Revisit—"*I am that I am,*" and know that you are already perfect. That is the piece of you that is real. That is the piece of you that is perfect for it is a piece of God.

Just as an artist paints each day and just as a writer you write each day, **you must each day practice knowing who you are**. Eventually the peace will last longer, the time between being in the sweet spot and going back to falling in the ditches will grow. Then one day you will realize that it has been a week since you felt the pain, then a month, and so on.

Have patience. Have faith. Keep going to your heart and reveling in the beauty of your true self. Soon you will have filled all of those crevices with pure love and it will be smooth sailing!

I've found that over the last year and with help from my geographical move, I was able to distance myself from people that I know are in a different place. I no longer want to spend my time gossiping about other people's stuff, judging them, or waste time talking about them. It seems though that once one situation falls away, another appears and now it involves people that can't be so easily avoided.

Q: *I've learned to separate myself from people who thrive on drama. But it seems when it ends with someone, it begins with someone else. I do not want to abandon them. I do not think I'm better than them, I just feel so disconnected when I'm around the drama. How do I show up for those I want to support and offer what I can without feeling that out of balance and wired feeling that drama feeds. I want to remain calm in the storm, but I find it so difficult. What can I do?*

A: You have been lucky with your work that you can separate yourself and you have been able to retain your peace and learning that way, but that is not the way of the world. We must interact and you are being forced to learn this because your love is stronger than your need to protect yourself from the energy of pain, drama, and turmoil.

You have read through many of Lee Carroll's Kyron channelings about being a lighthouse. How they still shine and remain strong and standing no matter if the waters are rough or calm. They are the same. This is how you can visualize and model yourself during these times.

Feeding into someone's problems or drama is not helpful to them. Remaining calm, peaceful and showing up with light does. *Why?* Because it will shine light in their life, light they desperately need and are unable to see on their own at the moment.

You are looking at it as if their stuff is tarnishing you. No, not because you think you are better but because you are scared that you are not strong enough or bright enough to not fall back in the trappings of living through fear, drama, and pain. It is too late for that. You live from light, the light within. No amount of drama can extinguish that because it is from source, it is everlasting.

It is now your job to shine that for those you love. You never know it could make all the difference in their life. So do not run or hide from it. Lovingly stand next to them shining your light allowing them to see more clearly because of it. This is your job, all of our jobs, to help one another. Success will not come from you standing on your own two feet and pushing your way through. **True success will come when you do your best and offer what you can on a daily basis to those around you.**

When you were in the dark, did you not meet a teacher, a friend, or a healer that shined light for you so you could see? Did they not hold up a mirror and help you to see the real you. Did the words that someone wrote from love touch your heart and bring tears to your eyes?

Yes, because they gave of themselves, they shined their light and allowed you to see the magnificence of you. We all share that magnificence. We are all one. We all need one another at different times in different ways to help us remember that beauty and perfection inside.

Being here on earth is not a test of your individual strength, prowess, or genius. It is to help you see that love connects us all. It is the thread that ties us all together. You are not alone. You are not expected to do it all by yourself.

And know that the more you shine your light for others the happier you will be. For giving to others is a gift to yourself more than anything because that is your purpose and it will bring you all that you ever wanted.

Now go and open your cloak and allow others to bask in your light so they may see their own light, so they can see who they truly are. It is a gift to you and to them. It is the circle of life. It is all there is.

Go forth in love.

I read a quote on Facebook today speaking about the subject of how it only matters what's on the inside. I agree that is important but it seems that people are always bashing one thing or another. *Is it wrong to care about looking good on the outside as well as developing what is on the inside? Do you have to let go of caring what you look like on the outside to embrace your beauty on the inside?*

Q: *Why is it that there is such a dichotomy spoken of 'pretty on the outside and ugly on the inside,' or 'ugly on the outside and beautiful on the inside?' Can't there be both? Can't one have both?*

A: Yes, there can be both. There are examples of both. But people usually embrace or covet one or the other. They see the young and physically beautiful as stupid and shallow. This is because they are babies just learning. They are not stupid just naïve. There is beauty in that because they are learning and growing and on their adventure to see their true beauty.

There is nothing wrong with admiring outward beauty. It is pleasing to the eye and the senses, and that is good. The resisting, the struggle, the anger, the pain…this is what damages the outward physical beauty. By the time most see their inner beauty the outward beauty has long gone according to what your society's guidelines for beauty are. We do not see lines, wrinkles, scars and such as ugly or signs of the old and unattractive, but beauty marks acquired along a road of learning, growing, and ultimately remembering who you truly are.

This is where these sayings come from. But it is not how it has to be. If more people awaken and learn how easy it is to see the beauty inside while the outward youth is still intact, they can become one. It is not all or nothing, one or another. It is what you choose. But what you are comparing outward beauty to is youth. Youthful beauty has its place. So does mature beauty.

Don't you wonder why when you see the pictures of the 71-year-old vegan woman and how beautiful she still is physically? It can be for everyone. She just learned how at a younger age and embraced it. That is not to say that a vegan diet is the only way. It works for her. She eats from love and does not eat angry, abused, and fearful animals. She exercises gently and most importantly loves herself and her life.

This slows this physical aging process. She is not withdrawing from life in fear, she is embracing it in love which keeps her young in all aspects. This is how she maintained the physical beauty that she merged with the light of knowing her inner beauty.

Q: *Why is it that people who 'see' loved ones who've passed over, see them looking well and youthful and vibrant?*

A: Because that is the natural way. Aging and shrinking down and decaying is not allowing life to flow through you and it is evident.

Embrace love. Embrace you. Know who you are. Love everything and everyone. Believe, have faith. Let your innate wisdom lead your food and lifestyle choices and you will be healthy. You will be youthful in appearance. You will shine and stay physically attractive.

This is OK. If this is your desire it is not wrong or counterproductive to seeing your inner beauty because all beauty was given for you to enjoy. There is beauty all around you. *Why would it be 'wrong' for you to want to feel and look beautiful?* Whatever that means to you.

It is not a sin. The only so-called sin is that you fear one thing will take away from another. And by the way that is not a sin, it is just naiveté, no matter what your age. *Wink*

Have a blessed day!

Q: *I'm frustrated. I eat pristinely with organic whole foods, no sugar, no white flours and very little grains, tons of leafy greens, veggies, and a little fruit. I do not exercise as much as I should, it makes me feel so tired and run down. I know I should embrace yoga, tai chi, or a softer type of exercise. Why can't I lose weight? And what can I do to lose it?*

A: The main reason is because you are focused on 'not being able to lose weight.' What you focus on persists. It really is that simple. I know that you do not want to hear this as you are rolling your eyes. But what you focus on, say, feel, and believe is what you get. You have seen this in the manifesting of your new writing work. *Have you not?*

Well, it is the same for your health, relationships, and everything you wish to see another way. Focus on what you do want. Be grateful every day for what you do have.

You want examples. OK, so when you are cleaning your organic fruits and vegetables to make a smoothie repeat—*I am so grateful for these healthy foods. I with gratitude feed this to my body to nourish it and I feel great. I am satisfied and full of nature's goodness. My body loves it and is so healthy, lean, and strong. I love my body. It looks perfect, feels perfect, and I am so grateful for it as it is a miraculous tool that I am so lucky to use in thousands of ways each day to bring me joy. It is perfect, I love it, and I treat it with great love and respect.*

Yes, it may seem over the top or a lot but it is what your cells crave—to be acknowledged, loved, and appreciated. When you are not paying attention to the roll on your stomach but the beauty of how your fingers type these words, or how your ears hear this meditation music, or how your eyes behold the beautiful blue sky, your body comes into balance. When it is in balance, all of the hormones and chemicals are at peace and work in conjunction with everything in perfect harmony. Only your thoughts—the angry, frustrated or unhappy ones, mess up that balance.

This is why you hear so much about meditation, yoga, and all of the new age type activities as you label them. Because they allow your body, mind, and spirit to become one healthy functioning team. When there is peace and harmony there is complete health. Superior health results in you feeling great, looking great, and feeling ultimate happiness. This feeds gratitude which begets more of the same. It is a cycle. It is all connected. It is perfect. You need not fight or torture or beat yourself into submission. You merely need to turn into it. Embrace it.

Think of it as a breeze blowing your hair into your face and a small turn into the wind blows it back and away from your face. And then you close your eyes and feel free. That is all it is... quiet, gentle, and simple.

There is such wisdom in the meek for they are quiet, listen, and know the simplicity of being one with all that is. There is no need to boast, force, or push for what you want. Power is in the simple, easy steps to peace.

Open your fists, turn your palms up, and feel the beauty in all that is. When you simply let go of resistance, it will be there waiting for you my friend.

Let it in.

6

Seeing in the Dark

AS I GO DEEPER INTO this, I begin to explore the darkest and coldest parts of me. Like I am a scuba diver purposely swimming into the deep dark depths of the ocean. In these hidden and dim areas of my soul, I am so sad. I'm hoping that I can receive answers that assist in my healing by bringing light to these areas. I know I am safe to do this here, but it hurts nonetheless. At times, it feels almost unbearable like there isn't enough oxygen. Out of desperation, I dive and sometimes become so disoriented it is difficult to see any light.

Q: *Why is it that my defense mechanism is to be angry and filled with rage? I don't want to be filled with this, throw things, or say words that I cannot take back. Why is it that when I am the most scared and most hurt, I act out? Why can't I sit quietly and just accept it calmly and let what is supposed to be come next?*

A: Because you are acting out of fear and you are reacting as a little child who is scared and vulnerable. You still believe that you are that hurt little girl who doesn't know what to do. You still see through the eyes of that toddler who doesn't know when she will get her next meal and she is hungry now. You still feel as though you don't know where you will be sleeping that night and if you will be safe, even from your own mother.

You are vulnerable and vulnerability scares you because you feel helpless. But you are not. *Did you ever starve to death as a little girl?* No, you may have been hungry more than you wanted to, but someone always came in and fed you. You may have been scared but someone always stepped in and protected you. Even if you did not see them or know it, divine intervention was there.

Now you know that all is possible and that you are protected. All that you have to do is know this and just be. For if you believe, it will come.

Once you look at the other side of your pain in those young years and realize the good, you will see things differently. Although you were hungry, you were always fed. Although you were afraid, you were always protected. Now you can see the divine that intervened.

Know that when you feel as though your life is falling apart because your partner says he doesn't want this with you anymore that it doesn't have to be the end, but perhaps the spawning of a renewed and better relationship then before. And if it is the end, know that you will be OK—you always have been.

Do not fear change, it is not bad or scary. Change is the way of everything. Look around you, this is how you learn and grow. You should have learned that from your childhood. No matter how horrible that moment was, it always changed and there was always something better. It is never the end.

You learned that through your study of dying. That it is a fallacy because although you may leave your physical form, you do not die. You cannot. That change is not bad; it is just a different way of existing.

Resistance is what causes most of your pain. Let go of resistance, stop digging your heels in and lift up your feet and

know that you are going to not only be OK but be better than you were. When things shift and change, you will rejoice in life.

Pain is merely a side-effect of not going with the flow, not accepting and stepping into the wind. If you fight against the wind or surf you struggle, you are tense and feel beat up. If you go with it, it carries you.

Let divine guidance carry you. Do not react out of fear. You are not a scared little girl who is defenseless. The only thing that you need you already have, and that is the knowing that you are loved. You are divine. You are perfect. You will always have the ability to go with the flow of change.

*You want change with certain things…*better relationships, more money, success for your writing, a vacation. Well then you know that change is good. Embrace it and the rest will follow.

Q: *I am not happy with my relationships right now…with my partner or with my daughter…but I feel so low that even if they were going well, I don't know that I'd be happy either. How do I fix this deep sadness in me that seems like it is innate as I do not ever remember feeling happy on a consistent basis?*

A: Be sad. Yes, I am telling you to let yourself be sad. You are taught that depression is bad and that sadness is a waste of emotion and to just be happy. Well, if you see sadness as bad you are always fighting against it. You are not allowing the sadness to just be in you. You are not resigning yourself to the fact that you had a lot of things that you would rightly feel sad about.

You so badly want to be happy and enlightened that you are not allowing yourself or giving yourself permission to be sad. Yes, living in this forever is destructive as you saw with the slow suicide of your mother and the quicker suicide with your brother. From this pain you learned that you do not want to kill yourself, as you know that it does not fix your problem.

You want to transmute the pain, resolve the sadness and get on to the happy times. **This is great and commendable, but what you are missing is that you are allowed to be sad.** When you relax your shoulders, and unclench your fists and allow yourself to be sad. *What happens?*

Try it now.

Yes, your feel it wash through you and tears form in your eyes. You feel the lump rise in your throat. You are filled with the sadness in every cell *are you not?* Let it be for as long as you need.

Now slowly, what happens? You feel it recede like a low tide, it washes in less, then it goes away some. You may feel it again but it is less now. Each wave is less overwhelming. It as if the sadness is evaporating *is it not?*

You may feel tired; you may feel like resting after this. Then do! This is how you release sadness. Not by force, not by willing it, not by repeating mantras or faking it. **You release sadness by feeling it, by accepting it, by crying, and by allowing yourself to feel this pain.**

It may seem counterproductive to feel it, like you are allowing yourself to sink in quick sand but it is not. You have heard the phrase by C.G. Jung, *"What you resist, persists."* And this sums this up perfectly.

Stop resisting the sadness, stop resisting the pain and allow yourself to relax knowing that it is temporary. That it is your job to feel it, accept it, be OK with it, then it will release on its own.

That is how you become happy by letting go of the sadness. You can't let it go until you have accepted it, felt it, become one with it—until you have acknowledged it.

Being sad or depressed is not wrong. It is not weak, it is not failing. It is human and you are human while in this body. It is harder to 'see' things as they are. You must use the gifts of your senses and 'feeling' is the ultimate one. **You cannot stifle the feelings that come up. You cannot ignore them, or hide from them or numb them with alcohol or drugs because not only will they be there when you sober up, but they will be worse.** They have festered and grown and wrapped themselves around things. So do not hide from or fight your feelings. They are there, feel them, allow them, and do not resist them.

When you do you will finally find freedom, peace, and ultimate happiness. **The goal is not to live in perpetual bliss; it is to allow all to flow so that it does not become blocked, so that you are not fighting it and making it worse.**

When someone does something that hurts you, be hurt. Feel the hurt, allow it to be. It will recede unless you resist it, then it will become stronger. Know that the person that 'hurt' you was in pain themselves. They did not mean to hurt you. This does not mean you lay there and keep allowing them to, it just means you feel it then release it.

Explain to them the pain it caused. If they continue to treat you this way, you may need to distance yourself from them. Maybe they need this to look at their pain. It is so easy when we are intertwined with people to blame our problems on them and to blame our sadness on them.

Only you have the power over your happiness. Not by controlling or grinning and bearing it, or by ignoring it, but by allowing it to transmute and learning what to allow in your life. You are the keeper for your happiness. Treat yourself kindly and with love, like a sweet little innocent baby. You are still one inside. Love that little baby enough. Tell her it is OK to feel sad. Hold her, pat her, and allow it to go. Then help her by recognizing where to be or not to be to find her happiness, at least most of the time because along with interaction with every human you will have to feel emotion that is caused by their own pain. Unless of course you live alone on a mountain top but not only would that be lonely, it would not help you to realize who you truly are.

Your job today is to lay with the sadness, feel it, accept it and tell it you understand. Then quietly let it recede at its own pace. The more you allow, the more quickly it will go. Then reward yourself for a job well done. Take yourself to a favorite meal or to buy yourself a new dress—anything to reward yourself for taking the time to love yourself. You deserve it, we all do.

Let everything begin and end with love.

Q: *I'm allowing myself to 'feel' the pain as you said above, crying and trying to accept it but I'm so depressed and in so much pain. I guess I don't understand. What am I doing wrong?*

A: Think of it like this. You are turning the faucet just a touch. You are not turning it on. You are letting it drip slowly. You are feeling it in slow motion. It is painful to allow yourself to be in the sadness or grief, but by only putting your toe in you are making the process much worse.

You know how when you get into a pool ever so slowly how painful the cold water feels on your upper thighs, your stomach, and your chest until you're submerged but when you just get in, the pain is gone in a few seconds? It is the same for this. You do not want to feel this pain and sadness because you feel that you will become one with it again. You will fall into depression and complacency. You will be it. But you won't. You know that you do not want that anymore so you will not relapse as you think of it.

You are different now. You have lived that deep depression and you know that you no longer want it. So do not fear regression and just get in the pool all the way, quickly. The more quickly you do, the more quickly it will dissipate. Let go and let it flow. That is not a new age saying for the sake of sounding fluffy. It is what you need to do—let go. Jump in the water. It will be gone before you know it. By dipping each piece you are creating more pain for yourself.

Now go lay down. Feel the pain in your body. Put yourself there and just be with it. You are safe; you will not fall back to where you do not want to be. Feel it and it will evaporate quickly. Do not anticipate, overthink, or believe that ignoring and suppressing it will help. Do not think that one feeling at a time, mulling it over, feeling the pain slowly will help. It will not as you are seeing. You feel nauseous because you are holding onto it. It is unreleased.

Now go. Lay down. Repeat—*Pain, I hear you. I will now allow you your time. Come forward, let me feel it. I'm sorry I pushed you down and did not listen or acknowledge you before. Come tell me your sadness.*

Let it come and your higher self will transmute it for you and will see it for what it is. Not real, temporary, just a made up pain to mask the real issue that you do not feel loved. You do not feel worthy of love. That you feel alone.

These are all false. You are loved. You are worthy of love. And you are never alone.

Let this be your job today. Now go and be free.

Amen

Q: *Why is it that I did the thing above with allowing the pain but it is worse? I feel so low that if I did not know the pain that suicide caused loved ones I may have considered it. If I thought it would get rid*

of this pain, I would consider it. But I know that it won't. So, I let it come up, I feel it, and I feel like I'm drowning? Help…

I couldn't seem to hear anything I was in so much pain. I called a healer, Mary Ellen Foust, and she was able to help me see that all was not as bad as I thought.

This taught me that although we do have the answers within, we all need each other. We share our talents and gifts with each other for a reason. Because on this day, at this time, those words were the ones I needed to hear and feel at that moment.

Thank you Mary Ellen for sharing your gifts, lessons, insight, and helping me to see who I really am. Thank you for showing me that we are not alone. Thank you for showing me that moments of pain are not all consuming and that just by looking at something differently, the way one day started is not the way it ended.

Thank you for being my angel this day.

7

Letting Go

I ALWAYS THOUGHT THAT IF ONLY something in my life was this way, or if only I could do this or that, I would feel better. Yet no matter what has or has not happened, I still don't feel OK with what is. I want to, I really want to, it just seems I don't know how.

Q: *I wake up feeling overwhelmed most days. I know I'm lucky that I get to make my own schedule by working from home so I should feel relaxed and happy and let it flow. But I don't. I feel stressed, overwhelmed, and anxiety-ridden. Why? And what are some tools I can do to change this?*

A: First of all, no matter how you wake up, you can change how you feel. There is nothing more important. There is absolutely nothing more important than realigning yourself with the energy you wish to live in that day.

So if you do wake up feeling stressed, overwhelmed, or anxiety-ridden, stop. Use your mantra that Candy Hough gave you in your session with her—"*I am perfect and loved just as I am. I do not have to be, perform, do, or create anything to be worthy. I am already, just as I am."* And really say it to yourself and mean it and feel it. Go to your heart space where you feel whole and welcomed and perfectly content and bask in that. Do whatever it is that you need to do to re-center yourself in that light. You need to do it before taking one step into the day. If this means setting your alarm fifteen minutes earlier, do it.

It is more important than food, hygiene, exercise, or anything else that you deem the most important. There is nothing more important than beginning, ending, and living every moment of your day in your heart energy, and from a place of self-love and joy. Otherwise nothing else you do will be as you want it. Nothing else can make your day better, so it must be your top priority.

Now you ask, *"Why do I wake up feeling this way?"*

There can be many reasons but the most abundant would be because the old patterns and ways of thinking are so deeply ingrained that you gravitate back to that each time you are not aware. So, your homeostasis if you will is to be in a place of self-loathing instead of self-love.

This is your biggest job, your most important job, the only thing that will change your life to how you want to live it. Change your resting nature to joy, self-love, and self-acceptance. Realize that you are perfect exactly as you are at this moment. Yes, with stomach rolls, with dimples on your thighs, with unkempt hair. You are perfect, for perfection is not the aesthetic beauty your society measures beauty, joy, and happiness by.

Do you see joyful happy children dancing and singing and exploring life with perfectly coiffed hair? Do you see them dressed to the standard of sexiness or perfection or high heels? No, you see them running barefoot, hair wildly flying around, with their arms in the air full of the joy of nature and life. They have no worries about whether they are wearing what is cool to wear or what's in style. They only know that all is perfect when they are in joy and one with love.

Letting Go

That is how you should model your perfection by imitating the children. That is how you should measure your success by the joy that fills your soul.

Go forth today, in joy, in simplicity, and putting the most important thing first—you. You are perfect just as you are. You are most beautiful when you are one with your own never ending pool of self-love, joy, and knowing that you are perfect just as you are.

Amen

And I go deeper into the anxiety...

Q: *I feel like every time I quit worrying about money for a few days and choose to just know it will be there and feel relaxed about it (it feels so good), something comes up—an unexpected bill or expense and then I'm right back to worrying again. Why is this and how can I change it?*

A: Some bills and expenses are unexpected, that is the nature of the world you live in at this moment. **You cannot change that, only your response to that.** You said it yourself above, you relax and then a bill comes and you are back to worrying. *Why?* There is no reason. Just as you relax and believe that all of your regular bills are paid, relax and know that all of the unexpected ones are paid as well.

Be happy and grateful that you had the money this morning to pull out and pay that bill. Yes, you would have liked to spend it on something else, but instead of being upset and going into worrying mode, be content that you had the money and the bill is paid. That will bring you more of the same, so every time you have an unexpected bill you will have the money ready and available to pay it.

As far as wanting to spend that money on something fun, get to work on imagining that the money is there for your recreation, your vacation, your furniture, or whatever it is that you are wanting. You do not hide money away for that which you want, get upset when you have it to pay a bill, and feel scared again.

Celebrate! You paid a bill today and had the money for it! *Do you see the difference?* **Happiness and gratitude will show the universe you like having the money to pay these bills.** Now look at that beautiful tropical water and feel that same gratitude that you have the money to go there. Then you will.

It is not about forcing yourself to go and get an additional job that will cause you pain just to earn those small pennies to save to get what you want. It is about ushering in the feelings, the passion, the gratitude and the happiness that you have what you are wanting. Then expand that to include the things you dream of. Believe you have them and are planning that beautiful getaway with your loved one. Like begets like, joy begets joy. Feeling gratitude for being wealthy begets more of the same.

This is the law of attraction. Not just saying the words. Not just wishing, but being proactive every day in all that you do. Start with the small things and say things like—*I am so grateful for the money I always have to put gas in my car to drive to the store. I am so grateful for always having all the money I want to buy all of the delicious healthy foods I am wanting. I am so blessed and loved. I love my life!*

It will grow exponentially from there. You will see more of the manifestation every day in your life. Think about it this way—if you want to be a competitive bodybuilder, *do you just look down at your sagging flabby body and say that you are going to be a bodybuilder?* Then get up, lift some weights and do it again the next day. Then get mad that you do not look like a professional bodybuilder on day three.

No, you make small choices every day for a long time, maybe even years until one day you look down and notice that you do indeed look like a professional bodybuilder. *Why? Is that because you did something two times?* NO, each day you did many small things that added up over time. You chose to eat healthfully 3-6 times a day. You chose to get enough sleep every night. You chose to work out each day even when you didn't feel like it. You were dedicated to it.

That is how living the life you want works. If you want to be spiritual, you read, listen, pray or meditate, and grow each day. You do not wake up one day as a spiritual guru. **You spend each moment of each day cultivating that through your actions.** You spend each moment in each day learning and doing things that are in alignment with your wishes and one day all of those small acts will add up.

The same thing goes for these examples and for money. Each day, choose to feel rich. Choose to speak, feel, and be gratitude and happiness. Every single time you do something, say something that you are grateful for (*even inside your own head*) and make sure it is full of what you are wanting more of. You cannot, I repeat you CANNOT have the richness, fulfillment, and happiness that you are wanting while being mad, angry, resentful, bitter and so on. It does not work that way. You cannot feel poor or less than and bring to yourself great riches and self-love.

Your job is and always has been to love yourself first. Be grateful for each thing in every moment and see your life change. It takes effort as does anything you want to accomplish, do, or be, but not by brute strength, cunning, or hurting another. **Only from monitoring your own thoughts and actions, one at a time, each day, always in all ways, will it become second nature and then you will have found your paradise, riches, and all that you are ever wanting.**

Today I feel more separated from the pain and discontentment I typically feel. When I get this reprieve, I feel like a selfish twit. It's like I've put my glasses on and I can see again. Now that I can see clearly, I feel guilty for how I've felt. I should stop being so self-centered and think about what I can do for others.

Q: *Maybe today I will ask for your help in something that I can do to help others. Embarrassingly, I am so consumed with my own junk, pain, or problems that I feel so self-centered and can't seem to focus on anything but myself. Is that selfish? And what can I do in spite of all my 'stuff' to help my family, friends, strangers, community, and the world each day?*

A: Let's begin with how you addressed yourself in this question. Self-centered, selfish, embarrassingly…these are not words of joy, love, and happiness. **You do not need to put yourself down to be worthy and of service to others.**

You have taken a deep and committed approach to bettering yourself and changing your old patterns that were not working for you. This is not selfish. These are programs that you still have running from childhood.

Do you not hear the flight attendants on the plane tell you to secure your oxygen mask before helping others? Even before your children because without self-love and self-preservation there would be no one to give to others.

Many people, mothers especially, have deep-seeded issues with this. They feel that if they do not put their children, family, or spouse first that they are being selfish and less-than as a mother, and a homemaker. This is far from true. If you are not happy, healthy, and take time to feed your own soul you cannot do this for anyone else.

Many women hear this but do not do it. This also applies to men just in a different manner. They feel that they need to work more and more so they can buy a bigger nicer home, so they will be the provider that is worthy of their family. Then they get tired and burnt out and go to a bar to try to drink away their sadness or unfulfilling life. Then this leads to separation and problems within the spousal relationship and then the entire family unit.

So see most problems are caused by people not being selfish enough. Although that word is not appropriate because self-care, self-love, and attention to one's own needs is not selfish at all. If more people were more self-loving and put their needs first, there would be many more harmonious relationships and families.

Now I do not mean go and do things to hide from your unhappiness like go to bars, drink excessively, drug, and whatnot. I mean nourish yourself each day with personal reflection time, exercise, learning, playing and so on, and then people would be content, fulfilled and feel the wholeness of themselves. Then when they are with their mate, family, or friends they are full, happy, fulfilled and offer this in their presence to their loved ones.

There is no greater gift then to come to a relationship whole, healthy, happy, and present. This brings light, clarity, and love to them. This gift is the most important gift we can give one another.

Not a bigger house, faster car, or fancier clothes because without self-love these things mean nothing. They are fleeting material things that do nothing for the heart. This does not mean they are bad or it isn't OK to obtain them. It could be part of your joy to drive your beautiful antique car on Sundays with your love. That can be part of the joy, but not the reason, cause, or goal of joy because joy will only come from knowing who you truly are.

You are light, love, God, perfection, everything that you could ever imagine. You are perfect, whole, and beautiful. You do not need anything to be this for you already are. The only thing you need to do today is really see that for when you do each person you come into contact with will benefit from the greatest gift there is to give. And you will be in such a state that it will be pure joy to always and easily give to others all of the time.

By the way, taking the time each day to meditate, put your deepest, darkest fears and issues on paper to share with others is a selfless, brave, and beautiful act of love.

You need to give yourself more credit. Now go and feel the love you are and smile. You are a gift to all, we all are. We are all one.

Namaste

I am so frustrated because although I continue to put the effort into feeding myself in a healthful manner, I still suffer physically.

Q: *I put so much effort every day into making healthy food choices, eating organic, eating vitamix shakes with veggies and fruit. I severely limit sugar, flours, and all of the other very unhealthy ingredients. It seems that no matter whether I've gone vegan, vegetarian, paleo, juice cleanses, pureeing food, etcetera, that nothing helps my stomach to feel better. It is bloated, full of pain, gassy, and uncomfortable almost daily. I've also tried probiotics, supplements, elimination diets and more. After testing I avoid gluten from sensitivity but I'm still having these issues.*

What is wrong with my stomach and what can I do specifically to correct this imbalance emotionally, physically, dietarily, etcetera?

A: The problem with most illness is a multi-cause and effect scenario. Since you like lots of explanation *(which we are not saying is bad,* smile), we will explain both how the problem is caused and how you can fix it. Yes specifically.

The problem begins with thoughts, feeling, and emotions. You know this. All things begin this way good or bad. You have not felt well, by your own admission, your entire life. You have not felt loved, accepted, whole, beautiful, and so on. This caused you to have a lowered immune function, stamina, and endurance. You know this, you feel this.

In turn, you are much more susceptible to illnesses. This is evident by your many health problems from allergies and stomach issues, as well as the more severe melanoma, chronic fatigue, fibromyalgia and so on. Your emotions caused your lowered immunity and susceptibility to these maladies. You believe they were only physical in nature; you opted to focus treatment solely on using physical means to treat them—diet, supplements, exercise, acupuncture, oxygen exercise therapy, and so on.

As you have seen, you have shown huge progress in your physical health in the last year working with Mary Ellen with Bodytalk. This esoteric way that this healer helps, as did Robert Taub, by dealing with emotions has shown you that **emotion is the root of everything—the beginning of it all.**

You are doing many of the things you need to correct these ingrained and severe patterns but because of the length of time you've suffered, it may take longer to heal. *Did you not see that when your daughter, Cassandra healed rapidly from JRA she only had eight years of poor diet, poisoning from vaccinations, energy flow, and bottled up emotions that were causing her illness?* Once you guided her to work on these things she was better within nine months.

You are angry. You feel that what we are saying is not true. But it is. Yes, you can heal miraculously today if you want. But you would have to instantaneously change your emotions, your patterns of thought and feeling, and your life in every aspect. It is extremely difficult to correct all of this in one day. Yes in one day you can begin these changes, but as we have discussed previously, your patterns are so entrenched that you fall back to them without monitoring, especially in the beginning.

The other reason is that you are here to learn and if your emotions, feelings, and actions did not have a cause & effect relationship you would not learn. When you touch a hot stove and you get burned, you learn that you do not touch a hot stove. This is a very simplistic way to look at what we are trying to say.

We know that you have tried so many ways, with such passion and dedication, and we say do not give up! It is not fleeting and you are getting so much better each day. You do not train to be an Olympic swimmer for one year and then get angry when you have not won a medal yet, especially when it is not an Olympic year and you have not tried out for the team.

You must dedicate yourself and your life to correcting these imbalances to live in the peace and understanding that you so crave. It is not hard, it is just learning. Look it takes twelve years for you to get a high school diploma, but that is the norm so you do not question that. Sadly, many of the important teachings about communication, compassion, and love are not a part of this curriculum.

Now you seem to understand what we are saying and have allowed it to flow more. Yes, we acknowledge that you have put great physical effort and time into your healing. And yes, you have put much time and effort into releasing patterns of thoughts, behaviors, and reactions that do not serve your desired outcome.

We say, keep going. You are doing well. Very well. Each day you learn something new, you try in some way to look at yourself differently—**ultimately reaching for self-love which is the root to all happiness.** You give your time and energy to improving your thoughts to be positive and to come from a place that will bring you your desired outcome.

Now you are tiring of this and wish to have specifics. They are on your 'sticky notes' on your computer dear one. Continue to do these; you will see results, and yes, sooner than you think. Continue to meditate each and every day, fifteen minutes for a minimum and the more the merrier. Continue to sit, stand or feel grass, trees, and flowers on your physical being each day. This connects you to Earth and the infinite love and wisdom nature has to offer you. It is healing and so much more.

Continue to look up at the universe and acknowledge it, and as Abraham Hicks shared, tell it daily that you know it supports you and helps you in many ways.

Continue to say things that you are grateful for. Continue to love yourself, tell yourself you do, and do things to nourish yourself every day. Laugh, hug, love, be kind, think of someone else and offer them a smile, a hug, a kind word, an act of service each and every day. You will get it back and then some, and the best part is that you will probably change the trajectory of their life and won't even know it.

Continue to exercise, and have fun doing it. Do not see it as a chore, but a gift to your body. You are giving it more oxygen and strength, and all of the love it deserves.

Keep feeding your body whole foods, vegetables, fruits, nuts, berries, and anything that it craves in moderation. Your body is intelligent by design, the only thing you need to do is quiet your mind long enough to hear what it is wanting. People fight all the time over whether it is best to eat meat & dairy or not. Eat vitamix shakes or not. They are passionate because they know for them it is right, their body is telling them so. **The only way they are faltering is telling someone else how they should do it, or whether it is right or wrong.** Each is different, each requires something different. Your body knows—let it tell you.

You are not allergic to anything; you have sensitivities because of weakened digestion caused by emotions, medications, bacteria not killed by a weakened immune system and so on. You can fix this by letting your body guide you.

Specifically, we know how much you want specifics so we will help you a bit; please eat more probiotic, cultured foods. Yes all kinds, kefir *(make your own is best),* kombucha, kolrabi and other veggies you culture at home, even tempeh which you love. These are all wise choices.

You pain today is caused by the popcorn. It is genetically modified and dead. It is not healthy and you ate so pristinely this week and your stomach was feeling better *was it not?* Yes. Then you had popcorn, diet soda laden with chemicals, and chocolate. Together they formed a toxic load that aggravated your stomach again.

Why not do this. Allow yourself to have organic air popped popcorn, even with butter with Zevia soda and organic chocolate if you must when you are home so you are not deprived. Even bring it in a bag to the theatre if it is painful for you. This way you are not deprived and you do not hurt after. Besides, it is a lot cheaper too.

We see you are hungry and tiring, so we will end here. You feel like you have no options, then you don't listen to your body and then you pay for a few days. Stop hurting yourself. You deserve to feel great.

You are wonderful and loved and perfect. You are not flawed or imperfect or abnormal. You are sensitive and that is not a curse. It is a blessing if you learn to use it, as you are here. Bravo my dear.

We love you.

Since I seemed to get a detailed answer yesterday, I figured I try to go deeper into some of these health issues I'm experiencing.

Q: *I am having an issue that seems to be holding me back. I have had problems with an inability to detox through bowels, skin, etcetera. I've been vigilantly sticking to a new diet and exercise program. I know that I'm detoxing from it especially when I take a cleansemore* *pill to aid in going to the bathroom. I wake up exhausted and in a lot of pain. I ache horrendously, am tired, dizzy and so on. I want to detox and feel better, but when I do I feel so sick I can't function. I am pretty sure I am feeling sick from the toxins but don't know how to help assist their leaving whether it is physically, emotionally or spiritually. Please help?*

A: As far back as you can remember there has been toxic overload emotionally, spiritually, and physically from the time you were conceived and hit a final blow at five years old when your mother left and you were given all of your vaccinations in one summer prior to kindergarten. You remember your inability to go to the bathroom for a week at a time then.

Stop looking at it as only a physical way to detox. Yes, that is very important and we will give you guidance on ways to assist this. But the power of the spirit and the assistance from the intelligent universe, mother earth and father sky is infinite. This is the only explanation on how terminal cancer patients recover. How people in wheel chairs for decades stand and walk instantly one day. It is a belief most of all and first of all.

Yes, it is a fact that you were poisoned both emotionally and physically as a little girl. This was awful and you had a hard time surviving. Not that you may have died physically, but emotionally it can destroy you. You have gone beyond that now and know that you are special and loved and important and what happened was only by the ignorance of people who were asleep. But as you were told in a numerous sessions with healers, you chose this life. **You chose to live through these things to help you become who you are now.**

So, to completely free yourself you must let go of those things. You hold onto them in your heart, in your bowels, and in each cell. You feel those tears welling up, that means this is the truth for you. You hold onto them and have not let them go to be healed. You hold onto them because you still want to hear that it was unfair and awful and hear an apology.

Please hear us now Amy. You are loved. We know that what you had to endure was devastating and hard and unbearable. We know that it was excruciatingly painful and we are so very sorry. No precious little baby, infant, toddler, and young child should have to endure the abuses that you did. We are sorry that you were hungry for the love and affection you deserved from your mother. We are sorry that you laid in the dark scared for your life and safety. We are glad that you had Craig there to hold you.

We are so sorry that you never felt the love or had the attention and time you deserved from your mother. We are sorry that she did not have it to give. That is so hard for a little girl to take. We know you just want your mommy to hold you and love you and play with you and feed you and tell you she loves you. She was unable to then but oh how she looks out for you now. We are so glad you had Craig to hug you and feed you and bath you and protect you. He was not your mom but we are so glad he took care of you the best he knew how.

Do not fight those beautiful tears as they pour down your face. Do not stop that ache that escapes from your lips. **You need to release this pain, this sadness, this toxic shame that you hold inside.** It is not your fault. You did suffer my dear. But you do not any longer. You, despite all that you suffered, gave your all to your own daughter. You hugged and kissed and loved her every day of her life. You told her she was worthy and smart and beautiful. You gave to her all that you could and did an amazing job.

Now it is your turn. You must give the same love, affection, attention, thoughtfulness, tenderness, and kindness that you showed her, Ricky, and even to your beloved dog Angel. You have a heart of gold and you are a loving and nurturing women. You have a beautiful soul. *Do you think kids are drawn to you because they think they should?* No, they do not have these restrictions or feel that they have to act. They love you because they see your love, your kindness, your pureness that is there, that was always there, and that will always be there.

No acts, no matter how awful you think they are, could ever taint that beauty in your heart.

This leads us to the next 'thing' you need to release emotionally and spiritually to manifest it physically. We need to repeat it because we can see that you do not believe it. Nothing that you ever did as a teenager or young adult could ever take away, harm, dim, or tarnish your beautiful heart. NO, the lying, cheating, stealing, drugs, alcohol, sex, and anything else you are holding onto does not in any way shape or form change this. All of these acts were things that you did that taught you things about yourself. That is all.

They did not change your worthiness. Pureness is unable to be touched by these acts. You are not dirty or unclean or ugly or less than someone who has not done any of these things. None of it matters for we are all perfect, we are all whole, we are all loved exactly the same for that love is not based on your actions, it is based on the fact that you are a piece of the love that is the fabric for everything. Nothing you can do can change that. You always have been and always will be part of that love, perfection, and grandness that is the basis for everything.

We are all one, we are all whole, and we are all part of the stillness that is the creation of all things.

Now repeat after me—*I am perfect just as I am, in spite of all actions I took or did not take. There is nothing that can change that. I have always been and always will be loved just as I am. I do not need to do, be, acquire, perform, or have anything other than what I am right now. I am whole in all ways, always. I do not need anyone to love me to feel this for I am already loved completely by myself and the universe. I am love, I am light, and I am worthy. I welcome and allow joy, happiness, health, peace, fun, laughter and all that I am wanting into my life now* and for every moment hereafter. I release all the old junk, pain, sadness, and programs that do not serve me any longer. I am free. I am so happy to be me.

Do you feel the lightness and freeness already radiating through you? It is a spiritual and emotional release or detox if you will. Once you give permission for this to all go, you are freeing yourself from the chains. **Only you have this power and you just exercised it. Congratulations.**

We suggest you repeat that and anything you would like to add on a regular basis until you reach the feeling that you are wanting every day. Yes, another thing to add to your list. But you are worth it dear. You are a beautiful, wonderful, and deserving soul. Now go and eat well, rest well, love well, exercise well, and have fun. There is nothing more important than you.

We know you weren't going to forget but physically you need to rest, drink water, lay in the sun and sweat, exercise a little more gently, eat as you do with leafy greens, cilantro, avocado, and supplement with detoxing and fortifying herbs, ashwganda, rosehips, and vitamin C.

Amen

Physically I still can't seem to relax and let go.

Q: *I've been exercising daily, eating right, taking magnesium and I cannot go to the bathroom. I just had a Bodytalk session with Mary Ellen about the bowels and bowel problems. She said it was from an inability to let go, and wanting to control things because of childhood feelings around being abandoned and the illusion that what we need and want is not in our control. I did a healing involving that and can* *still not go. I would like to release this emotionally and physically and resolve this issue. How can I?*

A: You clench and squeeze and hold on for dear life like you are on a constant roller coaster. When you grip so fiercely you contract your emotional body as well as your physical body. This contraction is the opposite of what you want to accomplish what you are wanting. Instead of seeing life as a fast, furious race, see it as a tranquil oasis. It is all in the perception or mindset. Do not see life as scary or unsafe, this is still running through you from childhood.

You do not need to survive you need to thrive. This can only be done by relaxing into it. This is where practice and faith come in. You have the tools all over your computer screen—breathe and trust the universe and all those watching over you that they have your best at heart. You are safe, you are loved, and you are one with what is.

This is making you hot and teary because you know it is so. Do not try to peel your hands apart finger by finger off of the metal bar that you are holding onto to so you do not fall out of the spinning upside down roller coaster. This will only cause you more fear. Take yourself off of the roller coaster and place yourself on the beauty of nature. On a smooth soft patch of grass, yes that is bug free, or even soft sand. And feel the light cool breeze caress your skin while you drink in the beauty of the sights and smells. Look at the beautiful tall swaying palm trees and see how they are strong and tall, yet yield gracefully to the wind. They relax into it and go with it. They know that they are protected and loved and part of all that is.

Deeply inhale the clean cool air filled with the aroma and subtle scents of lavender and tulips. Let your eyes feast upon the beauty of their vibrant colors—the beauty of the soft but rich lavender and deep smooth petals of the orange tulip.

Now close your eyes and feel the delicate yet powerful sun warming your skin. Allow it to soak in and penetrate through all the cells in your body. It will purify and detoxify what doesn't belong. The sun is not bad, it is necessary for all life forms. Allowing your fully nude body to bask in the healing energy of the sun for a half an hour a day is part of a healthy happy life. So many diseases are born from this lack of contact with Mother Nature. These are there for a reason, accept them and love them. They love you and will fortify you.

Now do you feel more relaxed already? Yes. This is what it will do for you, so use it, welcome it, love it and you will find such a difference in your health, happiness, and life.

It is not a waste of time, but a necessary reconnection with all that is, all that you are. You must change your mind set about what is important, necessary, and productive. Taking care of you is not selfish, lazy, or wrong. It is the most important thing for you to do. Respect who you are and where you come from. Cherish what is outside because it is who you are. Life needs life to sustain it.

Do you not see that plants need nourishment from the earth and sky? We are all one. It is not hippie dippy but a fact that people who are not using their gifts to fortify themselves use to explain people who are. Do not judge yourself by others standards. Listen to your heart, you know what is right.

You must also acknowledge to yourself and tell yourself that you are ready to let go. Let go of the past hurts and anger and sorrow and all of those things that are not serving you. Tell your emotional, spiritual, and physical bodies to let go of anything that you've done or was done to you that brings you unrest. For you are the master of your universe, you create your own.

Repeat—*Yes, lovely bodies of mine. I give you thanks for trying to help me stay balanced all of these years regardless of the onslaught of pain and unrest I continuously circulated through you. Thank you for how hard you worked to keep me whole and healthy. Thank you for now joining together and releasing all of this which no longer serves me. This is a relief, a release, and a joyful moment for we no longer have to fight the currents of nature that are there to balance us. We can join and become one with all that is and allow it to be a natural guide and healer. Let's rejoice in this letting go of all pain, sorrow, illusions, and judgments for ourselves or others. Let's release fear, anxiety, sadness, pain, loss, ego, and the need to be what we think we should be or what others have told us we should be, and any and all obstacles to allowing pure peace now. I am whole, I am full, and I am perfect in this very moment and always and in all ways. I am.*

Amen

It All Begins with Self-Love

I FEEL LIKE I'M GETTING SOMEWHERE with myself and it motivates me to want to improve my relationships with the people that I love. I'm really starting to understand that healthy relationships begin with a healthy me. The more I discover how dysfunctional my relationship with myself has been, I not only want to improve it but I also want to improve my interactions with my mate. I still can't accept that I should just be focusing on myself. *Shouldn't I focus on improving the relationships around me that are so important to me? If they change, won't I change as well?* It seems so hard to figure out.

Q: *My partner is going through something and will not let me in. He will not accept my help or the help of others. I want to help him but I can't. What do I do?*

A: It sounds as if you are at an impasse. These are trying times but the first thing we want you to remember is to breathe in and know that you are supported. You are loved and protected and no matter what, you will be OK.

Repeat—I am safe. I am surrounded by thousands of angels and loved ones. No matter what steps or actions I take I will be perfectly safe, happy, and healthy. There is only peace in my life and I create this. No matter what happens outside of me within any relationship, I know who I am. And that is a loving, perfect being that will have compassion for others as well as require that I be treated with respect and kindness at all times. This is how I treat people and this is how I will be treated. I am safe, I am loved and I am whole already. I do not need anyone to feel this way. No matter who comes in or leaves my life, this will not change. For no one person has the ability or power to change me, my happiness, or anything else in my life. There is nothing but love for me in this universe and I gladly open my arms to it and its wonders. I thank you universe for your never ending guidance, support, and manifestation of all that I am wanting or needing. I need only believe in this and myself to receive it. Thank you.

Now this has helped you to feel calmer and more centered. Now you can listen to words regarding your relationship and steps to take.

You have put much of your identity into being "Ricky's other half" as you say a lot. This is not the case. You are whole, Ricky is whole, and together that makes an alliance, not a whole. You will not lose who you are, what you've become, or your livelihood because you choose to part ways. It seems tumultuous because you are just settling from your move from Pennsylvania to Arizona. You do not even feel as if this is your home yet.

Whether it remains your home, you cannot make the final say on this as Ricky and you will have to make this decision together. Yes, it is not the easiest choice but one you will have to make. Things may not be better or worse just different if this happens.

Ask for help and stay awake for the signs. Thank the universe for providing you with the best circumstances for your happiness. Thank them for always taking care of your needs physically, emotionally, and spiritually.

One thing you must remember and practice is to do it with love. You may feel angry that Ricky seems to be choosing self-destruction over you. You may feel like he is choosing what he wants over a life with you. And even if this is so, it is not out of bitterness or trying to make you pay. He is for whatever reasons where he is and that is perfect for him, it is of his choosing. You do not have to choose to be a part of that if you do not wish. You are not stuck because of finances or any other reason.

Even in the midst of all of this uncertainty and chaos remain calm and loving. Come from your heart. Let him know that you wish to help him in any and all ways that you can. You will support him and love him but if there are certain things that are causing you great pain, you just cannot be in that with him. If he chooses to continue down that path, with love and great wishes, move on.

Now go and sit with the universe and your apprehensions and needs. Thank the universe for hearing your wishes and bringing them to fruition. Know that your wish is granted and it will be in the works as soon as you ask. Know that even if it isn't how you would have done it, that it is for your highest good and best outcome for your happiness.

Thank the universe for bringing all that you need and want to you easily and with haste. Smile and go have fun and know that it is on the way. Being sad and feeding into the sadness of what is will not help it.

Sit with your wishes, say them out loud, get dressed and go do something that brings you joy. The rest will follow.

Here is what I am asking the universe for—

Dear Universe,

Thank you for giving me first and foremost guidance to assist Ricky to feel peace. He is a great man, with great love, and he deserves it more than anyone I know. I do love him. I do not know if it would be better for him to be alone or with someone else and although I would like to stay, please help to bring about whatever is best for him. I do so want him to be happy no matter what.

Thank you for helping this to come to fruition quickly and peacefully. Thank you for supporting me in my ability to stay calm, loving, and understanding while still feeling safe, comfortable, and happy myself.

Thank you for providing me with the strength to be a good person to everyone every day so that I come from a place within my heart, full of love and understanding. Thank you for the ability to do this and live in the peaceful way that I find most satisfying.

Thank you for blessing Ricky and I in love.

Amen

Although I heard the answers and at the time they made sense, I don't seem to be able to incorporate them into my life on a daily basis. It makes me feel so dense. *Why can't I get it, apply it, and live differently?* The struggles continue…

Q: *Each day I do the little things—mantras, speaking to the earth, sky, and universe, thanking them for support, meditating, eating healthy, exercising, and trying to choose love over anger. Yet again today I feel tired, depressed, and hopeless like it is a never ending battle. I know it is not about how hard I try, but how much I let go and let it flow through my life. I'm not sure if I'm not doing this enough, letting it flow or what, but I sometimes wonder why I'm bothering with all of these things when although I feel a bit better most days, I do not feel like a different person. Sometimes I wonder if all that I do is worth it. It would be so much easier to just not care, not try, and not do so many things to get such small results. I reread that old explanation you gave about how working out each day still may take a year to see the final result. And I do understand this, but how do I stop myself each day from feeling this lack of success and focus on what I do want? It can feel very difficult sometimes to stay motivated and centered and focused on the prize of peaceful, fulfilled living. Do you have any suggestions? Thank you.*

A: Oh life can get tedious and mundane can't it my dear. But remember this, there is magic in every tedious and mundane moment. Maybe make it your mission to see this instead. Make it a game to find it in each task. Games are fun; make your life more fun. It may seem silly and just something else to do, but it is better than giving up.

If you are struggling, it is not a sign that you are on the wrong path, but a sign that you might want to look at things differently. For example, someone may want a baby so bad. They have tried for years or dreamed about it and finally that child has arrived. They are overjoyed. Fast forward six months and you may see that same lovely mother tired and frustrated cursing that she has to change yet another diaper. The times of wishing and wanting are over...her wish was fulfilled. Now the tedium has set in. We love our babies, but as you and many mothers know there can be nothing more repetitive than changing diapers over and over, fixing food over and over, and bathing over and over. It is the nature of this.

You can look at it in two ways. How annoying and boring that I have to change this diaper again and again or you can enjoy that time. It may not be the most glamorous task but use that time that you have to smile at your little baby you wanted so bad. Kiss their belly or adorable little toes, play a game with them, sing to them, or just enjoy the moment of looking at their face and seeing how quickly they've changed in that six months.

As you know, that time goes extremely fast and you will look back one day and cherish so many memories. It felt like forever in that moment but now that your own is grown, you realize how quickly it changes and how short of a time it actually was.

Most of the time when you feel like something is "taking forever" or is boring or tedious, it is actually just a nudge for you to look at the circumstance differently *What would you give to have your little one that small again just for an hour? How much more would you appreciate that hour?* This is easy to forget especially in the moment.

Do not berate yourself in the situation when this arises. Simply remind yourself, this may feel boring and monotonous right now, but it is not. And instead think—*I will feel grateful that I have a beautiful child to change their diaper. I am so grateful that I have this delicious food to prepare so that me and my family may eat today,* or we will stretch it to its furthest ha-ha—*I am so grateful that I have this toilet to clean for I am so lucky to have it.* I mean think about it, *how would your life be different if you did not have it and had to go outside in a hole?*

Changes your perspective huh?

And simply, after all of that explanation, our short answer is... **the key to feeling better each and every day is going back to gratitude.** You can see everything as a miracle, or you can create a daily hell in which you seem to be a rat in a wheel. *How do you wish to live today?*

We love you and wish for you gratitude in every moment. We are grateful that each day you wake up and want to know more. We are grateful that every day you connect to us and ask for our guidance. We are grateful each time, no matter how many ways you ask. We see each question and each moment as a wonderful step towards seeing our glorious child take another step in finding the heaven that exists within her.

It brings us so much joy. Now go and sing while you work, smile while you work, and appreciate each and every moment. **Find the magic each time and in each thing until you realize when you**

look around that you live in a beautiful magical story that you have created.

With much love and respect.

Q: *I'm so frustrated this morning! I have been on a really difficult hour long workout plan with a diet for two weeks and I seemed to be losing weight the first few days, but have put two pounds back on and have barely lost three pounds now in the two weeks. I don't understand what I'm doing wrong. And yes, it is hard, but I am starting to enjoy the thirty minute dance cardio part. Why am I not losing any more weight if I was sitting on the couch and eating junk? Please help?!*

A: Oh dear one, you are so full of self-loathing which is exacerbated by your very strong impatience. Instead of being upset that you lost five pounds than gained back two, why not say—*I've lost three pounds in two weeks!* Yay! Celebrate what you did do.

And you know this but forget it in your anger. You have not stuck to an exercise plan of this magnitude ever. It is very rigorous and you are building muscle out of fat. This is a good thing as the muscle burns more calories. And as you have seen in the past, you stay that weight for a bit maybe even go up a pound or two, and then the scales tip and you begin to lose the fat over top of the muscle.

It takes time oh impatient one. You do not want to drop ten pounds in one week. It is unhealthy and will most likely come back and it is shocking to the system. A pound or two a week is a great rate. Slow and steady is much better for everything involved.

Do we think this is the right plan for you? It is not a bad one. *Would we have taken a more gentle approach in building up your stamina before going in full force at an hour a day?* Yes. But you did not choose this. It is shocking on the body, it is hard. You are releasing many toxins that are stored in fat cells. With your less than optimal detox and elimination systems at the moment, it is a bit overwhelming on your body.

So please remember, it is not lazy to take a nap or take it easy. Your body needs this and will for the first 30 days. After this time it will become more accustomed and things will run more smoothly. You will feel less exhausted and less run down. Until then, and that means for the next two weeks be gentle on yourself.

Yes, the diet part is good, especially for you. Low glycemic, lots of lean meats and vegetables and a bit of fruit. Again, this is a process, not something that will happen overnight. So stop thinking you are going to lose 3-5 pounds every day. You are not.

Aid the loss of unnecessary weight by loving yourself now and knowing that you are doing everything possible to be healthy and happy. Happiness and gratitude will bring all of the weight you are wanting off.

Really embrace the eating in that you need a lot less food then you think. After eating the meal feel how light your stomach feels and how it doesn't ache. The diet is teaching you to eat for health not pleasure. And yes, pleasure of eating is OK on occasion and even recommended, but eating for your body's health is how you really nourish yourself.

Drink more water. I know you drink a ton, but you need more to help flush the toxins out and stay hydrated properly with all of the sweating and dry desert environment.

You are building the foundation right now. Stop looking for the masterpiece and being frustrated that you still only see the piece of marble. Artists do not carve their goddesses in a day or a week or two. It takes time. You will see results sooner than you think.

Be patient, be kind to yourself, love, put joy into your food and workout.

Love life.

It All Begins with Self-Love

And the daily struggle continues...

Q: *I think I have already asked this question maybe more than once but I am so frustrated with why I wake up in the morning unhappy. I don't feel good, I'm tired, and I don't look forward to the day. I really want to wake up and feel good and smile and feel excited to be alive. I know you've spoken of ingrained patterns being the reason, but it feels like climbing up a mountain. When will it be easier? When will I wake up excited to be alive and start my day? How can I help aide this now? How can I quickly turn that frown upside down within moments of waking?*

A: Accepting nothing less.

Yes, that may seem easier said than done to you, but it is so true. If you are still waking up feeling that way then commit to not getting out of bed until that has changed. Do not think—well I'll just get up anyway. Lay there, tell yourself—*I know I am not feeling well and I am in pain. But you deserve better and we are going to change that now before starting our day.*

Close your eyes again. Relax. Take deep slow breaths. Visualize the most beautiful natural environment that makes you smile. *Is that a waterfall with lilies floating in it and you go into it letting the pure water rinse away your unrest? Is it you lying on a beautiful beach watching the lulling waves lap onto the sand? Is it clear aqua waters that surround you while sitting on your little over-the-water-bungalow in Maldives?*

Whatever it is drink it in. Be there, feel it, smell it and enjoy it. Stay there until everything except pure joy fills your being.

When you feel great you may want to repeat whatever mantra that resonates at the time. It will most likely be one speaking to how you love and accept yourself just as you are at that moment, that day, at that weight, and that you are perfect and beautiful right now. Let that love fill you as the joy did. **Let nature teach you, she loves herself, now love yourself too.**

It is the only thing that will bring you what you are wanting. There are no shortcuts, or different roads. The most important one is learning this—**loving yourself is the key to all things, for when you finally love yourself fully and completely, you allow the universe to come to life for you because you are a part of it.** This is a service for you just as much as it is for all of humanity and the universe as a whole. It begins with loving you. You are important, so important, that it will help all of mankind.

So go now and remember love yourself, reach for joy letting nature teach you, and know that each step, each breath, and each time you change how you are feeling you are one step closer to your bliss. You deserve it, it is yours to have, and you are the only one who can give this gift to you. Don't make it so hard, it is already yours, you just have to open it.

We love you.

I find it so frustrating that I do all of the "things" that I'm supposed to each day, yet one little thing can ruin it for me.

Q: *When I awoke this morning, I laid in bed thinking of a beautiful scene in nature and felt a lot lighter when I got up. I had a vision for how my morning would go, what I would accomplish, and in what order. Then I received an email and two texts having to think about and get back to people. Each wanted something that I did not feel like thinking about or giving at that moment. Then I realized it was later than I*

It All Begins with Self-Love

thought and suddenly I became overwhelmed, panicked, and upset that my peaceful morning that I worked hard to start right was falling to pieces. My peace was gone. Why can't I handle change and things that pop up with ease and grace? I want to go with the flow but I don't seem to be able to do this.

A: You still do not trust the universe to support you, family to not abandon you, and people to not hurt you. So you are always in a defensive state. Meditating suspends this for you and this is why when you are in a meditative state you feel so good. You are free. You allow energy to flow through you. You trust in this state that you are protected and in the presence of what is good.

You are scared of the bad, the sad, and the difficult from your past wounds. This is not bad; it is just how it is. When one experiences things that are felt and seen as bad, they build a wall or a scar to cover that wound. But it is still there. And these walls and scars inhibit the flow of universal energy, of going with the flow, and love from being the center of your life.

This does not make you wrong or bad, it just is what it is. **The only way to correct this is to take down the wall or peel back the scar and although this may seem long and painful, it does not have to be.** It can be if you would like it, if that is what you need, but it can be done a whole lot easier and less painfully then you think. It is not like going in reverse where you have to experience all of the pain, sadness, and junk that you did when you built the wall or grew the scar. In this day and age, you are lucky. You can transmute this rather quickly and painlessly and once you trust in this, you won't have anything stopping this flow.

Think of it like a maze. There are many channels you can follow, some that lead to a dead end, but once you see the way it flows and you go again, you breeze right through it because you know the way. It is the same here. It may seem as if you are fumbling around in the dark for the first pass through but once you see it, it is easy, and don't forget you can always ask for assistance. It seems foreign to you to ask for help.

It is not weak, silly, or crazy to say—*Universe, angels, or ascended masters I would love your help and guidance in letting go of what is not serving me. Please shine your light for me so that it may appear easily and clearly to me for I am ready. I am standing here ready to lay down my walls and stop running my fingers over the rough edges of the scars that are blocking my energy. I want to live my life from a place of joy, guided by the warming flow of intelligent energy. I am glad to step into this and live this new life full of lightness, intuition, and love. I want this for me for I am a loving, deserving soul who wishes to live my best life and help others by showing them a way. Thank you for your assistance, I am grateful knowing that I have the support, guidance, and love of all that is. I welcome you and your blessings.*

Amen

See this is not stupidity, weakness, begging, or ramblings of a silly uneducated woo-woo girl. This is beautiful whisperings from the heart of women who has seen all that she does not want. **This is the strength of mountains, the beauty of majestic ancient trees, and the wholeness of a universe. This is true love.**

Oh, and do not forget that making yourself, your meditation, your visualization, your exercise, and healthy eating a priority is not a waste of time or too cumbersome. It is the ultimate act of self-love. These things are helping you to be more in the space that allows you to let all flow. You are investing in yourself, giving to yourself, and teaching yourself what it means to honor thyself. If you do not, no one will do it for you.

So we say, bravo my lady! Keep up the good work and do not, we repeat, do not feel guilty about doing what is the most important thing to us—teaching, learning, and allowing yourself to be loved. **For once you know this self-love, you will know the common thread that ties all things together in the tapestry of love.**

That my dear is your job, to know you, so that you may know everything.

Amen

Once again, I am disappointed with my slow growth so I look at the other areas I'm frustrated about. I'm still looking for something to change to feel better.

Q: *I really don't know what to do. I love my partner of the last eleven years very much but lately we don't have much fun in our relationship. We truly want what is best for the other but sometimes it feels like there are too many things under the bridge. Too much sadness and not enough joy. We each see that it takes two and we both have our 'issues' to work on. But when should 'working' on it end? When is enough enough? Would it be better or more loving to let each other go? Is there a point where parting ways is best? I want to be happy. I want him to be happy. I want us to be happy as a couple but it seems so difficult and nearly impossible at times. What should I do?*

A: Nothing can be forced; nothing can be made to be better. You have to allow it to evolve. Relationships are changing all the time, so for starters stop wishing or feeling sad that it is not like it was in the beginning. There were problems then too. It is just easier to remember the good when reminiscing. A healthy relationship is not one where there is constant joy and perfection. A good relationship is not one in which conflict does not arise.

This is the point of relationships—to have someone who helps you to see you so that you may continuously strive to be what you want, better if you will. Not that you are a more worthy person but that you allow more. You allow yourself more love and in turn everyone more love. This is the point. But unfortunately, as you saw, we think that the other person is going to be our savior and the one who will finally love us so much that we will feel whole.

This is wrong on so many levels. It is unfair to your mate for they are not your savior, they are not perfect, and they cannot fill the hole you feel in your life. That hole is yours to fill with self-love. **This is the biggest problem with most relationships. People want other people to do what they do not do for themselves.** No one can love you so much that you love yourself. Only you can love yourself so much that you can come to a relationship whole and full of love and support for one another.

Determining when to end or give up on a relationship is based on many factors. First and foremost, if a relationship is abusive, you must leave. This is not the point of a relationship to reinforce the abuse we do to ourselves. In this, it will be extremely difficult to find the strength to love yourself enough to leave.

This is not the case for you. You do not abuse each other, but you do abuse your own selves. This is painful to watch in each other. **This is what you are tired of.** You are tired of abusing yourself and watching each other abuse your own selves. This reminds you daily that you are abusing yourself. This is what you want to stop. You no longer want to suffer, be in pain, and feel less than or not good enough. You want to feel whole and loved and joyous.

And the real answer is that you can only give this to yourself. And until you do, you can't really know if you enjoy a relationship with your partner because as long as you are unhappy with how you are loving yourself, you can never be happy with how you are loving them or how they are loving you.

When you are whole and full of love, you do not need them to do or be anything for you. You do not need anything from them. You are free to just love them as they are.

No this is not the 'wrong' answer, a copout, or your fear squelching what we are trying to say or guide you in. It is the truth. **You cannot make this determination until you love you.** Now this does not mean you can't leave. This does not mean it is right or wrong to leave. That is a choice that you have one way or another. We cannot tell you to do this or not.

What we are here for is to provide you with the information, the truth, and the bottom line to what is causing your pain. We cannot tell you what to do or not to do, for there is no right or wrong answer. There is only a choice for this or not. Now making that choice can have consequences. You can leave before really loving yourself and feel freer to begin loving yourself or not. You can stay and feel better or not. This is merely a choice you have.

What you need to do is separate yourself from the yearning to feel loved by him. You do not need him to love you for you know he does. **What you need is to heal, to feel loved, and to feel whole.** And that is a job for you, not him. It is unfair of you to ask him to be a surrogate for you and the love that you are not giving yourself. He can't, he is not you.

When you feel that he can, that is merely you using his love for you to mask, or temporarily fill in what you are missing. Think of it this way—if you love yourself, you will feel loved and whole no matter what anyone says of does because it is an unending fountain that is always running in you. It is fueled by the universe, by love. It never ends.

When you base your happiness on someone else's love, if they don't give it that day, you feel unloved, rejected, unworthy and you don't feel 'right' again until they start giving it to you again. That is not their job, it is yours. So, *how unfair is that of you to get mad at them when they are not feeding you love when it is not their job to begin with?* That is like being angry at the trash man for not mowing your lawn when he picked up your trash today. It is illogical because it is not his job.

This is just a belief we built when we fell in love. And falling in love is merely when a person looks at you with adoration and mirrors back the love you have inside. In the beginning, you are too new to have shown any type of sacrifice, or unconditional love, or anything that is 'proven' as you say over time. So they are merely reflecting the love you have back to you. You fall in love with yourself. But it doesn't last after a short time because it is superficial, it is just a mirror. Then you get angry at that person because they took your love away. They did not; they merely aren't your mirror anymore. You took it away just because you didn't allow yourself love. You didn't feel worthy enough, or know that this was your job, not theirs. And most importantly, you did not realize that this is and always will be in you. Love is always yours; you just have to accept it.

Your relationship has lasted over eleven years because you were both dedicated to supporting each other no matter what. You saw the beauty in one another and liked it. It also made you see what was beautiful in yourself. There is great love there, but what is missing is not excitement, or a lack of things, or anything else. **What is missing is your own self-love, and your own kindness and gentleness to yourself.** For when you can do this for you, it will become second nature to give that to others.

So our advice is to love you. Do everything you can every day to love you. Be kind and gentle to one another, like you would want to be treated if you were an infant. Make it a priority to love you. And when this happens you will look at each other through eyes of compassion and love. Then things will become lighter, and more enjoyable.

And then and only then, if you find that the other person would be happier without you, you will know it. You will know that from the center of love because you will have nothing that you need or that you want from them except for them to live in a state of love at all times.

We hope this has helped, with much love and adoration.

Meeting Changing Woman

DURING A BODYTALK SESSION WITH Mary Ellen, she asked if I had visited Sedona, Arizona yet. Reluctantly I told her no, citing numerous reasons, most having to do with the fact that I was waiting for someone to take me. Rick's sister had mentioned more than once that she would drive me since she had been many times and was familiar with the area, but it never materialized. My homework assignment from Mary Ellen was to go to Sedona by myself sometime in the next month before our next appointment. Her only directions were to go and walk around the shops in town and enjoy myself.

Not one for venturing out on my own to places I've never been, I was a bit nervous but excited. Before we even moved to Arizona, visiting Sedona was on the top of my to-do list. I didn't know why or what I wanted to see, I just felt an urge to go. This also made me realize that it was silly to sit around waiting for someone to take me and then get frustrated when they didn't just because I felt anxious about driving to a place I'd never been. On the day I chose to go, before I even got in the car some really amazing things began to happen. It started first thing in the morning.

After turning off my alarm clock and lying back down, I began to doze off again. Suddenly, I inhaled a huge whiff of smoke that woke me up instantly! Confused because I could have sworn there was a Native American Indian man holding a sage stick under my nose, my eyes shot open. There was no one I could physically see but it felt so real. Somehow I could feel an electricity in the air, like I wasn't the only one excited for me to start my day. I was completely rested, energized, and ready to go.

A little over two hours later, I found myself murmuring, "Wow," out loud in my car. The glorious site of the huge red rocks that appeared to have erupted from the ground as they reached for the sky, took my breath away. It was as if my car was driving straight into the make believe beauty of an intricate oil painting that stretched for miles around. I'd never seen anything quite like it. I was grateful to have twenty minutes of low-speed driving to take in the stunning scenery before arriving. I had no idea where to go or what to do so I just continued on until I felt drawn to a parking lot behind some little shops in the center of town.

It didn't take long for the strange "happenings" to continue. For some reason I felt like I had needed a purpose for my trip or something to look for, so before leaving I had asked Rick if he wanted or needed anything. He had asked for an amethyst stone. Well, he was in luck because there was no shortage of crystals and crystal stores.

I was in my third store and becoming more shocked at the prices of some of the stones when my earring came flying out of my ear and clanked really loud on the ground. Puzzled because my hoops had never fallen out before, I looked down and wondered how such a tiny, thin silver hoop had made such a loud clanking noise. Then I got excited thinking maybe it was a sign that I should buy myself earrings. To my amazement, I heard the words, *"No. Listen."*

Picking my earring up and putting it back in my ear, I wondered if maybe I had made that up since it was so fleeting and much less definitive than physically hearing someone speak words to me. Leaving that store and walking past a few more shops, I heard more. Not like I hear people talking to me but more of a knowing, like when I'm writing my questions and answers. The message was that I would find the stones I wanted more cheaply, just keep looking.

I didn't see it as I was approaching it, but for some reason I stopped and looked up and found myself next to a statue. More accurately, a bronze sculpture that was so detailed I couldn't take my eyes away. She was not just beautiful, she was breathtaking. I just stood in front of her staring. After a few minutes, I felt like her eyes came alive as if there was a soul behind them. Then I heard or kind of knew that she was communicating with me when she said, *"Hi."*

Without a second thought, I told her without parting my lips that she was beautiful. Then with a calm and quiet, yet powerful air she asked, *"What can I do for you?"*

Stunned, I paused for a moment before replying, *"How can I feel better and feel healthy?"*

Without hesitation she said, *"It is simple. Love yourself and all the rest will follow, it is the key."*

I smiled at the simple yet profound message that I had been getting from so many lately.

Then she added, *"You are learning to love yourself and sharing this will help so many. This is your purpose. You are so beautiful and your legacy will be more impressive than this statue."*

I was stunned. After a moment of absorbing what she said I looked over and saw the nameplate hanging on the wall behind her. Her name was "Changing Woman." Chills began to cover my entire body. I felt like there were so many inferences within her name. I mean I felt like I was a changing woman too and I thought that odd, but the name was in quotations which made me think that she was well-known. I took a deep breath and felt like even though I didn't know much, everything made sense.

When I snapped back to my physical reality, I looked around. Although the streets were bustling with many people, for some reason no one was around me or the statue. It was almost as if I was in a roped off section while I stood there although it was right in the middle of a walkway. I didn't want to let this moment go so I soaked it in for another minute or so. Before walking away, I thanked her quietly but out loud.

Feeling so light and stress-free made me question whether I had a low blood sugar. I walked on and found a chocolate shop where I stopped to eat a delicious homemade piece of chocolate covered praline. Nearing the end of the block, I turned and headed back the way I came.

When I reached the spot in front of Changing Woman, I stopped and looked at her again. She looked like a statue. Thinking that maybe I had made it up, I looked at her eyes and that "alive" feeling flashed through them again. But this time it felt like there was nothing more to say, it was just a feeling so I knew there was something there. Quickly touching her hand, I thanked her again and walked away.

Then I heard or knew that I should go sit and eat lunch. Afterwards, I went into another store even though I didn't really want to because it was a bead store that I didn't have any interest in. I just felt like I should go in. Towards the back there was a stand with a "50% Off Stones" sale sign. They were a third of the price of the stones I was looking at in the other stores. There weren't many choices, but the two that I wanted to buy Rick were there. I smiled knowing that this couldn't just be a coincidence.

My last stop in town was an Indian trading company store that I had happened to park behind. I hadn't noticed on my way in that out front was another statue of Native Americans. This one was a woman and man together. I didn't have the same experience with them that I did with Changing Woman, but I still felt a deep appreciation for their beauty. There seemed to be a kindness and calmness to their demeanor, but at the same time a physical and spiritual strength in knowing who they are. It was like a beautiful dichotomy. Simple, yet complex. Strong, yet yielding. I just drank in their beauty.

I felt the urge to walk through the store to get to my car behind the shop. Just before the door to leave, there was an alcove with Native American Indian items like drums, ponchos, bowls, dream catchers and so on. I've never really been drawn to this stuff, but I felt an urge to just be in the room and look.

Suddenly, the Native American flutes and chanting playing over the speaker system seemed to get really loud, but only in my head because no one else seemed phased. Then, I started to have visions of being in a village and working as a Native American women. I was seeing from her eyes, and mixing food in a bowl. Flooded with emotions that were familiar and comfortable yet still attached to this reality, I began to feel really strange. Things started to spin, followed by nausea and somehow I could feel pain and sorrow related to being a Native American. It became too much and I very quickly walked out of the store.

For a few minutes, I sat in my car letting the visions and feelings go. Part of me was completely overwhelmed and the other part felt free. Finally, feeling open and "getting" it. I didn't know where to go or what to do, but unlike my typical self I went with the urge to just drive around.

Going back through town the way I came in, I saw a road sign and recognized the name. Turning down the road, I drove until I saw a sign for the "Creative Life Center." Then I remembered that I'd read the address while on their website looking at workshops that Drunvalo facilitated. Unsure if I was trespassing, I drove in cautiously. The parking lot was pretty empty except for a few cars. I figured I would walk up to look for an office and get a list of future speakers and events as an excuse for being there. After climbing the stairs, I stopped abruptly. There was another Native American woman statue. It looked similar to the others I'd seen earlier in town. This one was a woman holding a bird above her head and releasing it. Smiling at the irony, I felt like I was playing a game called "follow the statues." Again I was mesmerized by the beauty, strength, and peace that washed over me while admiring her.

The office was empty. The place seemed deserted so I walked over and sat on the lookout and enjoyed the stunning view for a few minutes. I immediately loved it there and felt that I would be coming back sometime in the future.

Not ready to leave, I continued driving around town until I came upon a place that had a sign out front offering angel readings. Once inside, I found there was a lady who did "fairy readings" instead. I knew nothing about them and thought fairies and the crystal skulls on her table to be a bit far out there. But since I was already there, I had a 15 minute session with her just to see what she would say.

I have had wonderful experiences and believe in readers, so I wasn't shocked or surprised that she told me all of the things that were going on in my life. My main question for her was whether writing was my path spiritually and if so, *where was the money?* She told me to keep writing and that money would be there to provide me with necessities so not to worry. She verified that her "fairy cards" showed that I was on right path and she mentioned many of the things that came up in my automatic writing. It felt like a big verbal sign that I was on the right path with what I was doing.

As I drove home, I was blown away by all of the synchronicities that I experienced. My curiosity was peaked about the connection I felt with the Native American statues especially Changing Woman. The day felt like a day dream, kind of unreal.

Had I really heard a statue talk to me?

10

Digging Deeper

AFTER MY EXPERIENCES IN SEDONA, I had mixed feelings. I was still blown away by the obvious but subtle messages that I had experienced there. "Regular" life seemed almost like a letdown afterwards. Part of me was excited about the magic I had experienced and part of me felt sad that today was just another day. Although not depressed, I wasn't sure how I felt.

Q: *I'm having an OK day today. Things are going smoothly and I'm cognizant of asking the universe for help, meditating, doing the next thing, being focused on the now. I'm not unhappy but I'm also not over flowing with joy. Kind of like I am just here going through the motions. I could sit down and do nothing and be just as content. I really want to feel great, I really want to be joyous, and I really want to be in a great mood and full of gusto. You know those people who are always up and funny and seem to be having the time of their lives. I just don't feel that way. I don't even know that I want to; I just think something must be wrong with me. Maybe I am depressed—some days I'm really happy, some sad, and some just OK. Is how I feel normal or OK? Or is there something I could do differently where I could feel up and happy most of the time?*

A: First of all, we are all different. Some people's disposition is that of abundant energy, happiness, and gusto as you say. That may be naturally or fueled by things such as caffeine, drama or what have you. It could also be natural, but more times than not it is probably fueled by something.

There is nothing wrong with just being. *Who said that for your life to be fulfilled or as you have always dreamed means that you have to be joyously bouncing about at all times?* Look at it this way—you are not in excruciating pain today! Yay! You are not in tears and so depressed that you can't connect with us or function. Yay! That is an improvement over many of the days you've had prior to today. So we say, instead of thinking, *"Why am I not happy or joyous or bouncing around?"* Say, *"Thank you! Today I am doing well. I am content and functioning and getting stuff done."*

See, we are back to being grateful for what you do have that is better today than yesterday. You are feeling just OK, well *isn't that much better than awful, or in pain, or depressed?* You may not be jumping up and down and full of fire like Tony Robbins during a seminar, but did you ever think that maybe today he is just kind of "being" as well. Not all self-help gurus or people that really get it are up and jumping up and down every day of their lives.

What it means to be human is experiencing contrast. You had a wonderful weekend. Your significant other and you reconnected, rested, laughed and just relaxed into life. *It was so wonderful was it not?* Then today you feel less elated, less joyous, less relaxed, but not awful. So keep celebrating what you loved about the weekend. Thank the universe and usher in more of the same. Only focus on what you do love, what you liked, and how much you enjoyed it.

If you focus on that it's over, it wasn't long enough, and so on, you are ushering in more of that. Now you don't want to always yearn for it, you want it, *correct?* So focus on what you did have, how much you loved it, and how much you love having more and more of the same. See you are focusing on the positive, having it, loving it. Not the opposite which is the lack of, not enough of, or always wanting more of which you can't have.

Whatever you focus on you will get more of—good or bad. So, thank the universe for your fabulous weekend and how you love those times and welcome more happily. Then do the next thing today. Be grateful for every single thing. Every piece of food, every piece of equipment that helps you to do your work, each person who comments and acknowledges your work, each thing you see that you are liking.

This gratitude grows exponentially out into the universe creating a huge opening that brings you more and more things that you are liking.

And likewise—which we DO NOT want you to do, if you say, *"Uh it wasn't long enough this weekend, it is Monday and I have so much to do, I'm tired, I want to do what I did this weekend, not this,"* you are telling the universe that you want more of the same. More lack of. More disappointment, more feeling it is never enough, and that is what it will deliver.

We are not predestined to be poor, sad, in pain, or unsuccessful. We come to this earth with everything available to us. **We only need learn or remember how to welcome what we do want, what we do like, and how we want to live.**

Problems are not non-existent in the life we do want. It is just how we see them. **And when we change how we see them, we change how they affect us.** We are in charge of it all, yet we see ourselves as victims with no choices. This is so far from the truth. We have choices for everything, every moment of every day. Start small and choose this minute to open up and allow this to be a possibility. Choose to say what you're grateful for as many times as you possibly can today. Choose to focus only on the good. Choose to come from love in all you do, putting aside your own insecurities or ego. Each choice sends a signal out that changes the outcome for your day.

Make it a game, for believe it or not, life in your body in this experience is a game. It may not always be fun, exciting, or carefree, but it can be full of all that you are wanting. Choose what you want. Choose to be grateful and watch the miracles unfold before your eyes.

Be free…breathe…and love.

I felt the need to dig deeper, clear more out, and get down to the core issues fueling my unrest. The Changing Woman experience gave me incentive to dive further down to discover how to love myself. I don't know what core issues I should look at so I keep going back to the physical manifestations to point me towards the areas I need to look at. I don't really know what is wrong and what is causing the pain, I just know that I feel my frustration in my stomach area.

Q: *I got up today and was frustrated that I'm still not losing weight working out an hour a day and eating pristinely. I went back in bed and did exercises of feeling good. Then I got up and my stomach looked like I swallowed a large watermelon or was six months pregnant. It hurts and I'm so frustrated. I want to heal my stomach issues causing this bloating and weight gain. I don't know if it is from leaky gut which the gaps diet can help or if it is from stress. I was busy for two days in a row which leads to being tired and not feeling well. I do not know what to do to heal my stomach, bowels, intestines, etcetera. Please help. I can and will follow any and all protocols. Thank you. And I put aside any and all things that I think I've learned or know, and I humbly come with an open mind and open heart to hear your guidance.*

A: Today you ask for guidance on healing your bowels, your gut, your center, and as you may have guessed, it is not a one prong approach. Nothing ever is. Not one thing causes anything; it is the collective of thought, action, and circumstances colliding to bring this outcome.

Just for your reference, yes, no gut flora killed off by stress, antibiotics plus the addition of mercury you received in a vaccination for a tetanus shot, and an already weakened state put you over the edge for these issues.

Yes, a strict diet including fermented foods and no sugar, flour, wheat or dairy (start with coconut keifer) for a while to heal is in order. And yes some actions, whether that be colonics or enemas, and being very kind to yourself are all part of a healing protocol as you say that will help you. We do want to stress to you that no amount of grit or tenacity with adherence to a diet, supplement, or healing tool will be successful without probably **the most important aspect of it all—happiness**. If you do not have joy, happiness and love, there will be no healing.

You know the GAPS diet, fermented foods and omitting offending things. You know to go to colonics and enemas and sweating in the sun, but what you do not understand yet is happiness. Yes, you feel flat and yes your neurotransmitters are low and unbalanced. And yes, supplements can help balance this. *But have you ever wondered why they are continuously out of balance?*

No it is not because your body cannot make them, or even keep them in balance; it is because they are not receiving the information that they need to do so.

Yes, it is hard and we see your frustration, but please try to suspend that so you can hear this message fully and deeply. Deep breath, good. Now, the body, the physical body responds to the emotional and spiritual bodies. They are connected. As a human it is much easier and your society for the most part focuses on healing the physical aspect. This is good especially during emergency situations but it is not relevant in preventing or balancing one's self to stay happy, healthy, and whole.

Much more focus needs to be placed on the emotional and spiritual aspects of self-care. Yes, you do meditate at least 4-5 days a week and yes, you repeat your mantras, and you do try. **What is missing is the heart.** Yes, saying and doing these things at all is good, but to truly see a change, you must embrace these activities from the very center of your heart. You cannot fake it. Yes, when you feel flat you are faking it, or just going through the motions as you say.

Yes, is difficult, we see your frustration again because it has been so difficult for you to try and make these changes and now we are saying it is not enough. *Do not think of this that you have failed!* It was very necessary for you to go through the motions to get it down to a routine for you. But now you must perfect your technique. You must go deeper.

And yes, doing it without this was necessary. You needed to have them become second nature so as you concentrate on going deep within the heart, you don't have to concentrate on the required activities. So do not fret or feel less than or angry at yourself that you did not get it right. You did. You have now mastered the routine and now and only now are you able to move on to the deeper part. So congratulate yourself. Realize that you have moved forward.

You know, feeling bad again is not always a sign that you have regressed. It is a sign that you have mastered one more area and that "feeling" is for you to know to go deeper, dig deeper, and master more. It does not mean failure—that is the misconception. You have passed with flying colors Amy. You have learned so much, how to tune in, how to let us communicate, how to take our advisement and implement routine and actions to see a result. Now you are at a higher level where you are ready to implement a more precise technique to achieve the highest results. This is great! We are so proud.

See how looking at this differently has already allowed you to feel better. You feel lighter looking at this situation as a natural and well-deserved progression instead of another day of failure or regression. It really is all about mindset, how you look at things, and what you think is what you get.

It is so very simple, yet so very difficult if you do not see clearly. **Frustration, anger, impatience, and all of the other negative emotions associated with feeling like "you have not moved forward" are the only things standing in your way of seeing the beautiful magical life that you have.**

It is just like your physical exercise that gets a touch easier each day. And the less tired and winded you are the more you can focus on the technique because you are not just trying to survive until the end. *You see?*

We know you are tiring, you are up to a half an hour of listening and typing now....that is good. It began at only a few minutes. You are learning to not let your ego stop the flow of information. You can breathe and allow yourself to relax and allow us to continue. You will get better and better each day.

Now we know you really want to know how to stop the issues you have surrounding your female organs. It has become so bad because of your run down immune system and the more it happens the more it imbeds. This does NOT mean you cannot change it, you can. Incorporate an active role in releasing this from yourself. Yes, you can never deal with it again once you release, forgive, and tell it you no longer need it. There was a reason you ushered this into your life.

You felt dirty, guilty, and wrong for the sexual encounters you participated in. You felt that you were being bad. Sex is not bad. It is a beautiful union between souls. Yes, this union can be unplanned or less than perfect if the two souls are not in a good place. But it does not deter from the beauty. You make or learn to make the rules around sex.

You were taught and believe that sex is bad, dirty, a sin, only should be OK this way and between certain people, sexes, or under certain labels such as marriage. This is not always the case. It is dependent upon what you want in your life.

Focusing on you in particular Amy, you are not less than, gross, wrong, a whore, or damaged because you had many sexual partners in your life. *Did you or some of these partners come to all of these unions with good intentions or from a good place?* No. But that does not make it wrong, bad, or sinful. It just was. And the union between two is not bad no matter what situation if it is a mutual joining.

Why do you think that there are so many different types of sex, between man/woman, man/man, woman/woman, groups, and so on? There are some happy with these and totally fulfilled and there are some who are not. This does not have to do with their enlightenment on what is "right" or "wrong," it has to do with what works for them or gives them fulfillment at that time.

It is not bad or wrong if people come from a good place. *Why do you think that the only two things that you have a really hard time forgiving is rape or forced sex, and incest or pedophilia?* Because these things are not consensual, they are forced from one person onto another and that is wrong because that person cannot choose. Sex is a joyous union between two souls, not something to be forced. And no, children cannot consent as they do not understand what they are consenting to.

A very good first step is forgiving yourself. You didn't do anything wrong, but we mean releasing yourself from believing that you are at fault in any way for any of the sexual abuse you suffered especially as a very young girl. You were hurt and those who hurt you no longer have power over you. So release yourself from any incorrect beliefs that you had any hand in these things. **Then forgive and release those who violated you. Not for their sake but your own.** When you forgive them, you are forgiving yourself. You are releasing your feelings of being less than or tarnished or dirty. You cannot do this without forgiving them. If you must look at them as young children and visualize it happening to them and that is how they learned it, do so. Yes, you did not repeat it or the cycle like they did, but forgive them for not being strong enough or knowing how. This will let go of the notion that there is something wrong with you sexually from the beginning.

Then you need to let go of and release any feelings of guilt about sexual behaviors that you feel that you did that were wrong. We do not say forgive, because that would insinuate that you did something wrong. That it was a sin. For it was not.

You were in a place where you sought love, acceptance, and pleasure from boys and men. They gave you that. Neither was a sinner. How about if you thought, wow, I was shown a lot of love. *Wouldn't that be a new and different way to look at it?* Many men shared with me and for those times I felt loved and wanted.

But you are thinking that you felt "bad" afterwards because you wanted them to still want you, need you, and have to have you in their life. The truth is that most of them, you did not want long term, you wanted them at that moment and you had them—some for a night, some for a week, some for a month and some longer. You each fulfilled a need the other was feeling at that moment. Although it could not ultimately fulfill your need, it was not wrong. Be thankful you were there for each other. Be thankful that you felt wanted in those moments.

Hear us—you are not gross, tainted, used or any other derogatory words that you've thought about yourself. No amount of partners or sex can ever tarnish who you are, ever. No one can take the love or beauty that you are inside. **No one can ever take away that true essence of you, the universal love that lives in you, ever, no matter what because it cannot be taken.**

This is a flow of love, energy, universal life force, God, whatever you want to call it that lives in a sacred space in your heart. A place that cannot be invaded by judgment, or poor actions if you so label them. It is untouchable, it is infallible, it is the portal to all that is, to all that is love and perfect.

We ask that you free yourself from any other thoughts around you related to what you've done, because nothing can ever change your magnificence, ever. Now go on to your day knowing that you are perfect just as you are, with all that you've done or not done. Nothing can ever change it.

We will get into more detail in another session on tools you can use or say to release these things from these areas for you deserve to be free. You are happy, healthy, wealthy and fully aware of the beauty that lies inside of you.

Amen

Q: *I had a colonic yesterday and before going I asked my body to release the toxins, pain, and negative emotions from myself. I feel I did clear a lot out physically and emotionally, so much so that I cried as it was releasing and it felt like a lot of junk was leaving my body on many levels. I felt much more relaxed for the rest of the day; however, I awoke in the middle of the night kind of feeling elated and partly feeling achy and in pain. Then in the morning I did not feel well. I've tried to muddle through, but here I am. What are some of the tools or ways I can use to help facilitate more clearing because I assume this is why I feel so bad? Thank you.*

A: You did begin to release yesterday physically, emotionally, and spiritually. Part of the reason you feel so tired is that it is a lot of work. Think about it—the times when you have been extremely upset or had something very emotional or traumatic happen, *weren't you just completely wiped out?*

Emotional pain and turmoil can leave the body completely exhausted and in need of a lot of rest. No, it does not matter that you just slept eight hours, you need more. Do not feel guilty about taking a nap, you need it. You are giving your body what it needs to heal, this is your job and only you can give it to you.

Next, the colonic was physically clearing of your bowels, but also just the beginning and an example of how to do this. You can do clearing, releasing, and letting go or however you want to label it with talking to yourself.

This is something you've been doing more lately and we want to go further into the wonderful tool that this is. See we spend so much time and energy talking about our problems to others, we spend so much time and energy talking about how we try to talk to our mate or someone else, and how it is useless because they don't understand us.

Yes, learning communication tools and skills is very helpful and necessary, but the first and most important step to success in this area is learning how to listen and communicate with our own selves first. This may sound silly or you may want to blow this off saying, *"Oh I should start talking to myself, doesn't that make me crazy?"*

And we say NO. It makes you much more sane than most. **For to us, insanity is not using your God-given gifts to help yourself.** No one can help you more than you, so use it. Listen to your body, talk to yourself, all parts of yourself, your mind, body, and spirit. Feel your emotions and instead of feeding into them, let them be a pointer to something you need to look at.

In your society, you look at any emotion that isn't happy or satisfied at any given moment as painful. Instead of looking at it as a message and opening that message and asking yourself, *"Why do I feel this way, what it is trying to tell me, and how can I honor it and do what is necessary to move past it?"*

This would be sane to us. Why is ignoring them, shoving them down, swallowing them and then using things to cover up those feelings with drugs, alcohol, cigarettes, food, anger, gossip and so on considered sane? For to us, that is what you would label insane.

We are not judging saying all of the people who use those crutches are bad or wrong, we know they are self-medicating or numbing. We do not say you are wrong, we say you are sad and we are sorry and we want to help you. **We are saying the best help is to feel those things, look at those things, ask them what they are trying to tell you, and then follow through.** This is what will bring you peace. This is what will bring you joy. This is where the ultimate happiness you seek lies.

So, how do you tackle changing your approach? Very simply—by allowing. No, not in a new-agey-sit-and-chant way, but in your every day when you feel something, stop. Feel it. Sit with it for a moment and do not judge it to be right or wrong. It is neither, it can't be. It is a message.

When you feel it, do not fear it or cower from it. Meet it. Sit it down across from you as Mary Ellen had told you to do in a session. Say, *"Hi anger, I see you, I feel you. What is it that you are trying to tell me?"* Then sit quietly and allow whatever comes in to come in. Your answer will most likely not be a deep James Earl Jones voice booming with the answer. It may be a feeling, you may see flashes of something as a symbol, and you may just get a light breeze of understanding by looking at it from another point of view. Any way that it comes, welcome it and say to it, *"Oh so you are saying,"*….and repeat it back as you understand it.

You will feel if it is matching up and that it seems like it is making sense. The more that you do this, the quicker and less dramatic the process has to be because eventually you will always be in a state of openness so the understanding will be there. You won't have to stop and wait and ponder to have the answer come in.

You have all of the answers and understanding in you at all times. For a very long time, most have chosen to ignore it and operate from the ego or a childlike impatient state. Now you can choose to use your innate tools of understanding to really be your best, most understanding, loving, and fulfilled self.

Lastly, after you have stopped and felt the emotion, sat it down, and asked what it is trying to tell you and understood it, you will then automatically see the effect this has had on you in your own life and relationship with yourself and others. Then you will be able to release that, and with that release you are forgiving yourself for not knowing better, and forgiving yourself and others for any actions that you took while coming from this place of childlike ignorance. Finally you will be free to operate from a much more enlightened, understanding, and compassionate position going forward.

This my friend is the greatest tool to finding, understanding and living a peaceful, joyful, fulfilled, content, and miraculous life that you are so wanting. It seems so simple, but as you know even though steps can seem simple, actually doing them can be a lot harder than it sounds or looks. Do not let this deter you because it will not be very difficult for very long once you master it.

Think back to when you learned to ride a bike or roller skate or any other thing you had to master. It was strange and awkward and seemed very difficult for a bit. But soon, *and sooner than you thought,* you were off racing around the neighborhood feeling free on those wheels.

Let yourself be free like that. Allow it to come in and be your greatest asset in your life. Allow you to know you and be the happiest you've ever been.

We love you. We love all of you. We are excited for this awakening!

Amen

11

Finding Compassion for Me

EVEN WITH EVERYTHING THAT I'M learning, I still find moments or days where I fall back into old patterns of thinking and being. One day while talking with Rick he asked me, *"What are you getting from your illness?"*

It startled me and I got angry at first, telling him that I wasn't getting anything but suffering. But he kindly told me that it had to be giving me something and maybe I should ask about that.

Q: *Just as kids want attention and don't care whether it is negative or positive as long as they get it, I would like to know—What is my pain and illness giving me? I don't feel good from it, nor do I get attention from it, and I spend a lot of time trying to fix it. But it must be giving me something, could you help me figure out what that is so that I can seek to heal that and let go of the pain and illness?*

A: As a physical being, you give much credence to things that you can see, touch, smell and feel. Sadness, grief, and depression are all non-tangible yet very real feelings. Yet this society still sweeps these things under the rug. It is not as embarrassing or stigmatizing to be an alcoholic or have cirrhosis of the liver as it is to be depressed. The funny part is though that depression and unresolved sadness is the cause. But again as this society currently operates, the cause is not seen as the most important part of the solution.

Although this is changing as you see with natural forms of medicine that focus on the cause not the symptom, there is always a cause or catalyst to disease, pain, or illness. The healers that speak of emotion as being the beginning of disease are not far off, as this is the energy that propels the issue to become disease. There are physically caused factors such as poor diet, lack of exercise, and the onslaught of toxins and chemicals clogging the cells, as well as the genetic predisposition. Although some of the genetic predispositions can also be something carried through blood lines that are usually from an emotional starting point.

Emotions or feelings usher in the reality that you live. Think about it, when you are very happy or laughing a lot and having a great time, *do you feel that pain you generally feel in your back?* No, it falls away because your focus is joy. Joy floods your body and trickles out into your energy field and so on. This negates the negative emotions that were holding the pain into place.

This is the reason you have fluctuation in your pain severity and durations. It has to do with the emotions you are bringing to the forefront. It sounds so simple and easy, but as you know recreating a way of being or homeostasis can be more difficult to do.

Now more specifically Amy, you want to know what your pain is doing for you. **So, on a level you know that you are choosing it.** No, this does not mean you chose the abusive things as a little child. You did not make these people do these hurtful things to you. But what you do have control over is how you deal with these things.

Now some may say, yes you did attract these things to yourself on a soul level to help you become who you are or to help you with unresolved pain or things you brought in from past lives. But for the sake of dealing with the things you feel that were unfairly heaped upon you as a child, it may be more helpful to just deal with this life, these problems, without getting into levels of healing beyond this lifetime.

So, you feel that you were unfairly treated as a young child. And you were. There is no doubt that being neglected, hungry, scared, physically abused, sexually abused, abandoned and so on are atrocities that no little girl or boy should have to endure.

And we say, for the pain that you felt while these things went on, we are so very sorry. We see that little girl, with tears in her eyes and a heart that is so sad. Please know that as we go on, we are never negating that pain. We know it was real. We know it hurt and felt so unbearable, and for you it still does. Please know that many if not all of those who reaped these horrific circumstances on you are sorry for the pain they caused. In hindsight, they truly wish that they had chosen differently.

Now, we want to speak of that pain in the past. Not because it wasn't real, not because it wasn't awful, not because you don't deserve to know that it was unfair, but because we don't want you to keep living it and reliving it each day of your life. It is no more; it is no longer what you have to live.

Think of it like this, *remember making poor choices as a teen that could have had devastating consequences?* You did have some but you really avoided life-altering ones that could have been horrendous with long lasting consequences. You have forgiven yourself for making those poor choices. You realized that you were in so much pain and so asleep that you didn't see another way. The same can be said for those who harmed you. They did not know better and they chose something and that hurt you. And they are sorry and wish they could change it but they can't. All they can do is forgive themselves and do better now.

And all that you can do is forgive them for not knowing better and let it go. Not because it wasn't awful, not because you weren't severely scarred, but because you know that reliving that pain and sadness has created a pattern or illness and is impeding joy in your life.

These things happened decades ago. They are far away from you and will no longer return. You are safe and able to choose your reality now. Do not choose that dim one from your memory from so long ago. It does not serve you, but just the opposite. It is like ripping the scab off of a wound just prior to its healing and purposefully rubbing it against concrete to make it bleed again. Yes, it proves to you that the wound happened. Yes, it reopens it up again and shows you and the world that you were wronged. But it does not forgive, it does not let it heal, it does not allow joy in your life today.

Know this—many people will not understand the pain you went through. Many people may trivialize it and will be unable to empathize with it. Instead of this angering you because they cannot understand, celebrate the fact that they can't. You would not wish that pain on anyone, *correct?* Then be happy that they do not understand. They do not need to. They have their own lessons, choices, and different types of things to let go.

It will not heal your wounds if people understand. It will not make choices that you see as wrong or hurtful by people be forgiven more easily. You need not concern yourself with how, when, and if people forgive your hand in any pain they felt. If you know or they bring it to your attention, you can explain, apologize and ask for forgiveness. But their answer is not what you base forgiving yourself on. Your self-forgiveness is for you. It is not based on what anyone else thinks.

See the problem here Amy is that you have not forgiven yourself for the things that you think you've done 'wrong'

in your life because if you can forgive yourself, you can forgive others.

The things that you think you've done wrong are not as bad as you perceive. You came to make choices and from them there were lessons. Take the lesson and forgive anything else, for in that moment in time you did the best you could. Just because you look back and think you should've chosen this way or that way does not make it so.

What if you could see that every choice you made, everything that you thought was a mistake was exactly as it was supposed to be? Why do you think any differently? You were there for a reason and now you are here for a reason. All of which happened exactly as it should have. So take a deep breath, relax, and know that nothing you have ever done, thought, felt, or chosen was wrong. You are not bad. You are not a sinner.

You are loved. You are love. You are exactly as you should be. Everything is right. Now revel in that for perfection. And anytime that you start to judge yourself, know that is not for you to do. You are not judged by God, or the ascended masters, or however you want to label those that you think you answer to. The only words they have for you are—relax, you are loved, please treat yourself as we would, with kindness, gentleness, and complete unconditional love because that is our wish for you.

Amen

Wow, that really made me realize that it does start with me. Forgiving me, healing me, and loving me is the key. I want to take responsibility, yet find a way to be compassionate with myself. I never realized how difficult it is for me to be kind to myself. I can see now that I am more kind and gentle with everyone, even strangers than I am to myself. This made me ponder why I still get so easily upset when I am hurt by those that I love.

Q: *Why is it that I become so upset so quickly when my partner does something that irritates me? Which really means he hurts my feelings. Not only do I get really frustrated, it makes me question our relationship. I tend to feel like this is extreme and I may be the only one or a group of a few. He says that when I get upset I forget everything, especially all of the good. Why do I do this and how can I stop doing this?*

A: First of all, know that you are not alone. There are many people who have the same feelings and responses as you. This does not make it the optimal way to operate, but you are not the only one choosing this. As a matter of fact, more people than not come from this place of being wounded and responding like you because they are trying to protect themselves.

You see, when you are wounded, hurt, and have unresolved sadness and pain, you will always come from a place of defensiveness and self-protection. Think about it, if you are a wild animal who has been hurt, you fear that a predator is going to come and take advantage of your weakened state and possibly kill you. So, to ward this off when you feel danger is near, you will bare your teeth, snarl, and try to scare that person away from your wounded self. This is an animalistic instinct and this is where your easily frustrated or quick-to-get-upset response comes from.

You still have open wounds or scarred over wounds that still exist below. Until you have uncovered, healed, released them, or however you want to look at it, you will most likely struggle with responding differently when your significant other, daughter, friend, family member or whomever hurts your feelings.

I know this may have started to sound like a common theme to you but it is true—**all problems or issues that you come across**

within yourself or in relationship to others, generally stems from unresolved sadness or pain within you. Until you operate from a place of wholeness and complete self-love you will experience negative or less than peaceful interactions with yourself and others.

This is not a catch all answer, it is the core, the truth, the basis for your eternal bliss. Love yourself enough to make yourself a priority. Love yourself enough to open up old wounds and heal them. Love yourself enough to do the work in small steps, every day, religiously to obtain the place of peace and contentment that you seek.

It will not happen without your focus and dedication; however, it does not have to be excruciatingly painful. It is just like daily exercise. It may not be what you want to do every day. It may take dedication and persistence and discipline, but after a while you may see that after you get started it is not so bad and that you may even enjoy it. And you definitely know that it pays off, it is worth every minute, and it is something that will eventually lead to your happiness, health, and prosperity. It is an investment in you.

Now back to how you react and how to change it now that you know that working on you is paramount to changing this type of response in yourself. So we all know that when you snap at someone or become very irritated, that you really are hurt, disappointed, sad, or a combination of many of these types of emotions.

So, when you feel the irritation or anger arising in you, do not push back against it and become upset at yourself that here you are again feeling this way. Simply take a moment, allow the feeling to rise up, and feel it. It won't hurt you, squelching it will.

Then ask it—Why are you here? What are you trying to say? Then listen. Most likely you will see a flash, or have a feeling, or remember a time when you felt that way. Before doing anything else, address it directly— *I know that you are here anger and I feel your pain. I know that the time that happened you were hurt and I didn't allow you to feel it. I'm sorry. I feel that this incident has reminded you of that one, but this is different. That time is gone and we are going to let it go for our sake for we deserve it. Now, as for this incident what is really going on?*

You were trying to do something nice, even when you weren't too excited and he squashed that with a look and flippant remark. So, he didn't appreciate your thoughtfulness and willingness to do something. That is OK. That has nothing to do with me that is his thing.

You do not need to squelch your hurt feelings, feel free to calmly and kindly express them. If you must, pretend you are talking to a child, not condescendingly but as gently as you would a child by addressing him in a kind calm fashion. Tell him, *"I took the time to think of something that would be kind for you or your friend and I feel like you didn't appreciate that. That hurt my feelings."*

9 times out of 10 if the mate or person you are addressing does not have his own severe wounds around the same subject, he will respond with *"Oh that is not what I meant. I'm sorry. I just…"* And he will explain where he was coming from. And 9 times out of 10, he will realize that he could have been more thoughtful in taking the time to give your offer the energy it deserved, that you were giving it.

You see, he is human too. He will not always be perfect, no one is. He will make mistakes. He is allowed to, just as you are. The key is to rewind, offer up your feelings kindly and softly, and address the subject that way.

Now if he has wounds around feeling misunderstood, he may snap back with screaming or yelling or counter accusations. In this case, a mediator may be necessary until more self-healing has been completed by both parties. Of course, when both of you are calm and have learned to come from this place of self-love and honesty by speaking of your pain by owning up to your responsibility in your reactions, you may just be able to understand where each other is coming from and really hear one another.

And then commit to healing your own wounds individually so that in future interactions all of this can be avoided.

We hope that helps you in understanding your reactions and ways to help you and your partner enjoy more of your time learning, growing and experiencing joy in life together.

Much love.

This opened my eyes to see that I need to be more proactive in taking steps to change my thoughts and therefore change my actions and reactions.

Q: *Before bed last night, I said to myself, "I am going to go to sleep and connect with my higher self and the healing realm. When I awake I'm going to feel good, happy, vibrant, healthy, peaceful, and have energy." And when I woke up today, I checked in and sure enough, I felt all of those things. I wasn't perfect, but I definitely felt each of those attributes that I requested before going to sleep. Is it really that simple, just to ask or say this is how it is? I want to keep up the momentum so I wanted to really understand this so I can continue to begin my days better and better. Thank you.*

A: Well, the answer is yes and no. Yes, it can be that simple and no it is not just the words. As you have learned, drawing stuff to yourself is not from merely repeating words. **You know that it is actually not the words that bring you what you are wanting. It is the feelings and the emotions that you feel.** The words are pointers to these feelings, they remind you to stay or refocus on that feeling.

If you are not feeling joy, you cannot usher in more joy. If you are angry, you cannot say I would like more joy and expect to feel more joy or see the manifestation of it. You have to be in and come from a place of joy to get more joy. Like attracts like. Like a magnet. Think of the word J-O-Y broken down into single letters. Each is magnetic and when you are feeling joy the three letters will draw each other together and bring you more joy.

So, when we say that the words won't do it, they won't on their own. If you remember, when you rolled to your side, took a deep breath, and said silently, *"I will awake feeling happy, peaceful, healthy, joyful, vibrant and full of energy,"* you were smiling. You were feeling them as you said the words. You believed. You did not have up walls or barriers. You were not angry and wishing, pleading, crying, or begging to feel those things. **You were already feeling those things and you welcomed more.**

That is why you awoke an hour earlier, feeling tons better than the day before. **So the real key is to get to the place that you are wanting no matter what.** Because you cannot get more of it until you are in it and welcome more from that place. See it wasn't the words and it wasn't really really wanting it while you were upset.

It was simple. You smiled, felt it, asked for more, went to sleep and you got it. Funny how simple it can be *huh? How many days have you laid down in your bed at night feeling awful, upset, angry or whatever negative emotion when you begged, prayed, and really really wanted to feel all of those joyful feelings?* Before going to sleep you felt bad, said the words and awoke in the same pain as you went to bed with. That is because no matter what words you were saying or how much you prayed or begged it never came to fruition. **Not because you were asking the wrong things, because how you were feeling when you asked dictated what you got.** So what you got was more of how you felt while asking.

So we say, it is not important how you ask, what you say, if you pray, or to whomever. **The most important thing is to get to the place you want to be, then ask for more like it.** That's it.

Now you know from experience, it is really hard to get to that happy place when you are typically carrying yourself in the sad zone most of the time. Especially because that dictates that you will keep getting more like that which you are experiencing when asking.

So how do you get to the happy zone, so you can ask for more to keep you in the happy zone? **One, we say, don't try so hard. Let go. Just be.** When you focus so much on not being in the sad zone and how you can change it, you are always thinking about how much pain you are in and how you don't like the sad zone. Unfortunately, you keep getting more of the sad zone junk.

Even if you feel all the feelings of the sad zone, the most important thing is to stop focusing on it, and focus on something that makes you happy. No matter what that is. It could be looking at your puppy, staring at a flower, looking at a screensaver on your computer of a palm tree or sunshine. It could be letting a piece of chocolate melt in your mouth and savoring it. It could be watching a YouTube video that makes you laugh or one that helps you to feel uplifted so you can then feel great and then ask for more of the same.

The biggest and only obstacle is getting yourself from the sad zone to the happy zone. It looks and feels harder than it is when you are in it because you can't see how simple it is. Make yourself a visual that resonates with you. You love aqua waters, white sandy beaches, sunshine, and palm trees. So if you need to have something that makes it simple for you to get from the sad zone to the happy zone label them. Go into your body and quiet your mind. If you are not feeling like you want, see the word 'sad zone' over your thoughts or surroundings.

Then take a few minutes to get your visualization of your 'happy zone' exactly as you would want it. Be detailed. See the clear aqua waters, put your toe in and feel the perfect temperature. Pick up some of the soft warm silky sand and let it run through your fingers. Feel the sunshine warming your skin while the light refreshing breeze whispers past you. Get all of the details to your exact liking. Then like there is a door to this wonderful world, see above it a sign that says, 'happy zone.' Then walk through the door and enjoy it. Swim in the water, lay on the sand. Swing in the hammock between the trees. Whatever it is that you want. Give yourself this gift, this time, to get where you are truly at peace, fulfilled, calm, happy, and whatever other feelings you want. Do not worry about whether it is silly or not. What we think is silly is not giving yourself this gift.

If you do **not** operate from this happy zone, you cannot have the joy you are wanting. You deserve this, it is simpler than you imagined, now go to your happy zone and be grateful and watch how more of what you are wanting comes into your life. And as you get better and better you will usher in more of what you are wanting, you will discover more and more of what you are wanting, and you will be happier than you could have ever imagined.

Enjoy your happy zone.

Q: *I came to this meditation today with no questions just wanting to see what came up. As I sank into the meditation and focused on the elephant's face on the video, I saw myself lay my forehead against his. It felt as if starting at my center a window opened and bright light poured out and went out in all directions. My whole body relaxed, I felt somehow infinite and tears filled my eyes. I felt so far away yet so part of everything—from the universe and stars down to a tiny tear. It was so all encompassing and beautiful. For a moment I think I felt what one feels when they die and realize how grand everything is yet how connected it all is; something that we do not, or at least I have not felt most days. How can I feel more like this each day, like I'm already in heaven, like all is well, no matter what happens during the day? How can I keep and come from this place of love at all times? Thank you.*

A: *Oh how lovely huh?* This is how it is, this is what is real, not the illusion that you live in. We are all one, everything is connected, and everything is perfect. Everything is alright. You know, we know this feeling deep down, the one that you just felt. This is what we crave is that reconnection with all that is, with everything, and everyone. Yet, the way society operates right now is the opposite—wanting to be the best or on top, wanting to be the richest, wanting to be the gold medalist. From our perspective, the Olympian who trained for years and won the gold medal is great. Just as great is that man that sits on the corner and asks you for change, who is just as great as the person who ignores him, and is just as great as the person who hands him a dollar.

Separatism is something humans created to measure themselves to feel special in the eyes of their society, to feel better or more important than their neighbor. **We say that no one is more or less important than anyone or anything because it is all one. We are all one.**

We can feel that you think that seems fluffy or woo-woo when we say we are all one. *But you just felt it, did you not?* It is hard to explain in words yet understandable in a few seconds when one feels it, and we have all felt it in the everyday actions in our human lives. They are much more fleeting and may not seem as all-encompassing but it can be if you really allow yourself to let go and feel in those moments. Think about it, those times when nothing else mattered, nothing else existed except what was going on for you at that moment.

Do you not remember the day you gave birth to your daughter? No, not the physical pain but the wave of emotion that washed over you as she was placed in your arms. *Remember that moment when her father and you looked at each other both choking out a sigh and fighting the tears?* Remember those small moments that brought a lump to your throat. The first time she got on the bus to go to school and you knew that she was going out into the world. The times where moments seemed to stand still and you felt that it was beautiful. They weren't always the big moments, but small ones too. Remember when you looked into your Nana's eyes for a moment and the green love seemed to envelope you, and nothing else existed for that few seconds except feeling that you were in the middle of a sea of green love. Think of the times at night after it snowed when it was really quiet and you looked out the window and all you could hear was silence and your breath. Or when it was raining in the middle of summer and it was dusk and nothing else seemed to exist except the millions of drops.

These moments connected you to source through love and nature. During these moments you were one with all that is. This is who you are. This is who we all are and if you approach life that way you will see these things and moments in everything and everywhere. Only fear, drama, and disconnection help it to disappear from you but it is still there, you just are not seeing it.

Why do you think that you love this part of your day when you meditate and write? Because you are in this completely, you have surrendered to the moment. You are not thinking about anything, you are just allowing the words to flow, and you are allowing the space. You are seeing it as from top to bottom there is a river of light and energy that you step back and allow to flow through you. Do not feel afraid of it, it is not possessing you; it is not sucking anything from you. You are merely merging with source and allowing the feelings to come through you, and allowing yourself to interpret it into words. You are an interpreter putting feelings into words. You feel so deeply and have a love for expressing them into words. Yes, that is your calling here. And this is why you love it, you crave this time, and you look forward to it because during this time you are not fighting against spirit, source, God, all that is, the universe, or whatever words you want to use to explain what you are doing.

Some say to you that this is called 'channeling' and it is draining. People have different words to describe communications and it is not right or wrong, it is just their interpretation. But you know when you are in the midst of this that it feels good, you feel one with all that is, you feel full and complete. This is how you judge whether it is good for you or not. Yes, you do feel tired from it afterwards, as you do with physical exercise, or anyone who is working feels tired from whatever they do.

Partly, you feel so tired because your allowing muscles are weak. Just as one who does not use certain muscles on their body and they do something different, they feel it as being sore and tired. That did not mean they did something wrong, it meant they used muscles that they normally didn't. This is why you are able to stay in this state, allowing the energy to flow and keep writing for twice as long as you were when you began. You are learning to trust and allow the feelings and words to flow onto this page.

We hope that you will continue to welcome this communication here as well as throughout everything in your life. You do not need to shut us off or ignore us the other 23 hours in the day. We are not Martians or an entity to fear. We are a collective energy that you are a part of. We are silence; we are the quiet between the beats of the heart. We are all things and you are a part of those too.

As you allow the energy to flow, you will see, feel, and experience more bliss in your life. It does not only come in small moments, it always is. You just have to relax your eyes, your heart, and your soul to be open to enjoying it in every moment, in everything and in all ways, always.

Enjoy the magic of today!

And just when I get to what seems like a new level of understanding, I feel a new pain or an old pain that I haven't seemed to really let go of yet. I know that I'm doing the next thing, taking steps each day to heal on all levels, but sometimes it gets tiring. This is one of those days.

Q: *I ache so badly today. I had a colonic yesterday and felt so out of it afterward with being loopy and exhausted. My wrists, upper back, knees, ankles all ache and my stomach is so bloated and uncomfortable. It is so hard when I feel like this to be in a good place. I just feel so blah that laying in the sunshine didn't help that much, just enough to take away some of the muscle aching. But I could just fall right back into bed. I feel like this is not logical, I can't just rest or sleep or lay around all the time. I don't know what to do so could you please help? Thank you.*

A: You have been hesitant in starting your writing today and we sense that it is because you are afraid that the answer you get is not going to be from anyone but yourself and your own knowledge. You still don't fully trust that you have a connection and that you are getting information and not making it up. Yes, we use your knowledge bank to help you understand; otherwise it would take so much longer. These are things you already know and so they can be used to help you.

As for the not feeling well, it is not what you think. There are not toxins with fangs running around you trying to overtake you. You are run down. Yesterday on your way to have your colonic you asked your body to release many years of gunk—pain, sadness, toxins and all that you've held onto so vigilantly. Although the colonic was the physical act that you were using to assist this, you were releasing on such a deeper level. You are not only expelling these toxins and accumulations that you manifested physically, but you are releasing emotionally, which is ten times more exhausting than the physical release.

This is why you felt like that when you came home. It was different than the other three times because this time you asked for even more clearing. Last time you asked for your first ten years, this time you asked for the next thirty years. Ha. And you wonder why you feel as though you were hit by a bus. That is a lot of clearing all at once. Again, we are not saying it was wrong or a bad choice, it is what it is. But know that when you ask or give permission for yourself to release thirty years of junk that you are going to feel it grandly. You are not one to do things in small steps; you are impatient and want to see evidence of moving ahead, not the tiny daily steps. This can be taxing.

So we say today you must rest. You must go back to bed. Let yourself heal. If you push yourself, this is when you don't feel well again and get down, and go back to that place of unhappiness. You have to listen to yourself. When you feel the urge to rest, do not tell yourself no and ignore it and workout harder. This will only impede a quick recovery.

Now you can use the same tools you used yesterday to aid in your feeling better. When you lay down, thank your body for trusting and responding to your request to release all that junk yesterday. Be grateful. Then reiterate that you welcome this release and purging and tell the body that you give it permission to work through this and you will honor it by resting. This will take away any of the resistance you feel. Because that resistance in you is telling the body you don't like it and to stop, which stops the releasing process.

See? You are telling it one thing then your emotions are telling it another. This confuses it and causes it chaos. One afternoon of napping will save you weeks if not a month of suffering while you try to squeeze out this healing. Go allow and you will feel better quickly.

Sweet dreams

The healing continues...

Q: *Yesterday was a sad day for me. Although I try to break the habit every year, it seems that my 'body memory' or something kicks in on days that I have sad memories. This one was Father's Day, the day my brother took his own life. It has been twenty-five years since that day and in some ways it feels like a lifetime ago, and sometimes it feels just a few years old. Having reconnected with his spirit on my own and through Psychic Medium, Ricky Wood, I have found a lot of peace. I know his spirit lives on. But it seems no matter how many years go by and how much I think I've moved on, when those days that these awful events occurred on come, I feel the pain. I don't want to and I think that I've healed so much, so then why does a certain day bring me back down?*

And the second part of my question is that once in a while if I'm feeling especially down I will take a supplement 5 HTP to help elevate my mood. It works very well, I wake up the next day feeling more even, and having more energy. Does this mean I have a chemical imbalance that will never heal?

A: First of all Amy, it is not wrong to feel pensive or sad. This is a misnomer that feeling bad, sad, angry or any other emotion that you label 'negative' is somehow bad or wrong. It is not. **The problem usually arises from your response to the specific emotion.** See, it is not wrong or a bad choice to feel sad *(we don't like the word 'wrong' because it denotes that you sinned when it is just a choice with a consequence)*. **When the conflict arises in you, it is what you do when you feel this sadness that matters.**

If you sit with it, feel it, let it go, and remember any good memories or feelings instead, than that is great. Fighting the feeling is when you feel discomfort or pain. Not allowing yourself to feel the emotion, let it out (i.e. cry) is when you have a problem **Stifling things causes pain and then usually people treat their pain with something to try to make themselves feel better.** No matter what that may be—drugs, alcohol, sex, drama, food and so on.

Think about it, *what did you do?* Yesterday was eating food that wasn't the greatest for you. That wasn't wrong; it was just the choice you made. You consoled yourself with junk food at a movie. You could have chosen a lot worse or more destructive behavior, but it still was a form of pacification for you.

The next time you have one of these days try this instead. Sit, stand, or lay down whatever way you are comfortable. Tell yourself—*I feel sad and I'm going to allow myself to feel it. I do not need to worry because this emotion will not hurt me. I will open up and feel it and will let it run through and leave. I will not suppress it because this will make it a lot more painful in the long run. There is nothing to fear for it is just an emotion. No one is hurting me. The pain I feel is holding onto this emotion and not allowing myself to acknowledge it. I am not wrong to feel any emotion negative or positive. I give myself permission to feel it and allow it to be heard. I am sad that my brother chose to end his life. I am sad for his pain and my father's pain and everyone else it affected including me. I loved him very much and still do. I miss him and wish that he could be there physically in this life with me. But although he is not, I know that his love for me was and still is very real. Instead of focusing on this one sad day, I choose to remember things that I loved about him. I choose to honor him by welcoming joy into my life each day. I welcome peace and joy to fill these days that have long sat with me—days that I dread. Nothing is different on any day regardless of the label it is given, whether that is a name or number. No matter what day, I am filled with the love he had for me and the love I will always have for him. I am happy that I've found peace and that he has too. I wish all involved a beautiful day filled with open eyes and hearts to experience miracles. I release old stuck negative patterns that replay without my asking. I am free. I am loved. All is well.* Amen

When you take control or lead your body, mind, and spirit with your intent, this is the way you will go. Unfortunately, most people think they are victims or have to bow to circumstances that are beyond their control. This is not true. **You are the master of your own destiny. So choose that which you want, for you will get it.**

As for the question regarding supplements to help with mood, we say if it works for you, use it. Tools are available in whatever form you wish—supplements, writing, mantras, exercise, and food. Of course these are just pointers towards welcoming your own well-being. No, we do not think something is wrong with you that will not be fixed. We do not think you are crazy nor need psychiatric drugs which we know you vehemently dislike. We are not saying these are right or wrong and in cases can be helpful in balancing someone who is so disconnected with themselves that they can be a harm to themselves or others. But again, we say it is a tool not a solution.

The solution is to take down the walls, the self-imposed blocks that stop the flow of well-being inside of you. You hold the key, with the entire universe at your disposal. We get so blinded or have such tunnel vision within our own struggle and pain that it is so difficult sometimes to stand back and be the creator of all that you are wanting. But that is your birthright. It is who you are. And this is your journey, to remember this so that you may live in that flow.

All that you are wanting is available to you; you just have to get your own stuff out of the way so that it may flow. Do not look at it as a struggle or an iron man contest. Look at it as a dance, enjoy it, let go, and allow the gifts that are yours to become the forefront of your life that you are living right now, in all ways, always.

We love you. We are proud of you. You are such a great soul. See that in yourself so that you may see it in your life, in everyone and everything. That is where the peace is. That is what heaven is. It is a state of mind as you like to say.

Have a lovely day.

12

Beneath the Pain

I AM STARTING TO LIVE MY life more purposefully. Yes, living my purpose, but I really mean being aware of the steps, words, thoughts, and feelings that I choose each day. For some reason though, I have not yet been able to grasp how to translate this interpersonally. I still struggle with feeling this flow with communication in the relationships with those I love. It saddens me because they mean so much to me and I truly want to be able to have happier, healthier, relationships.

Q: *I woke up in a lovely mood today and now feel awful. I am agitated, my stomach hurts and is bloated, and I'm really tired. I'm guessing the turning point to my very good morning to not-so-good is because of my feelings about what happened when I talked to my daughter. I had been spending a lot of time trying to change her flight to visit earlier upon her request. When I found out it would cost two-and-a-half times the amount I paid for the original ticket, I called her to let her know I couldn't swing it, she would have to stick to her original flight.*

When she curtly responded that she didn't want to come that early and dismissed me, I became angry. Not wanting to be mean, I told her I loved her and got off the phone. Then I felt bad. I do not seem to be able to know how to express my frustration without internalizing it and without getting into a fight with her. Help? Thank you.

A: Our children are such great mirrors for ourselves. See we think they are like puppies—so cute and cuddly. **When in fact, children are the greatest work, effort, and growth initiator we will ever experience.** There is so much love that it causes us to really reflect on ourselves. It is much easier for us to be kind to, change for, or take action for love that is external from us. At times, this can be easier, but more than not, it is the most difficult work a person will ever do. So you should thank her, for all of the trying times in the last few years of her adolescence you have grown by leaps and bounds. It forced you to look at yourself differently and approach life in a new way.

What happened this morning was you trying to be nice to her and not get angry when she did not appreciate your effort, say thank you and acknowledge this, and then flippantly dismissed you as quickly as she could. Obviously, you were hurt. This was because the effort that you put into trying to help her, listening to her, and giving her advice was not returned. You feel used and abused and unappreciated. This is the source of your anger.

Now the problem does not lie in the emotion as we said yesterday, but with your response to it. *What was your initial reaction?* You felt anger, which was covering up your hurt for feeling unappreciated because of her lack of gratitude. *Right?* So, you were hurt.

What did you do with that? You swallowed it because you did not want to get angry and take it out on her. That is because you are basing your belief on a falsehood. It is not wrong to feel any emotion. You were angry. So if you looked at the anger and realized it was just a façade for your true feelings—sadness or feeling hurt, you would see the nature of your pain.

Then, you need to embrace how you feel. Not to wallow in it or berate someone into feeling bad for treating you that way, but to **speak your truth.** And that was that you felt unappreciated for the effort you were giving her, which you can easily and without any abuse express to her in a calm manner.

You could say something like—*Well, I'm feeling a bit hurt because I don't feel like you appreciated my effort which may or may not be true. I'm feeling this way because you did not express any sentiments of appreciation. If you could in the future maybe voice these feelings if you have them, I would really appreciate it. It would make me feel like you value and appreciate the time and energy I put into our relationship. Thank you.*

This allows you to calmly and kindly express your sadness or the pain that you felt associated with her lack of communication about appreciating your effort. Now, this is something that you can do quite a few times to help remind her to vocalize her gratitude. **You are teaching her what she can do to keep a healthy and reciprocal relationship alive.**

Keep in mind, she is almost an adult and although you will be a lifelong example for her on how to or not to act, you are not required to be a doormat. If you do this many times and she does not start to express her appreciation for your effort, then you may need to address it again in a different manor such as—*I've noticed that throughout the times that I've tried to tell you how I feel and offer you ways to help me feel appreciated for my efforts, you are not responding with any of the ways that I offered. This makes me feel like maybe you don't appreciate my efforts for you. Is this true?*

If she says she does, then again reiterate that if she does, she would need to make an effort to express this so that you feel motivated to continue. If she responds with a typical *whatever, this is stupid, or* no, she does not appreciate you or thinks it isn't a big deal, then this is where you need to make clear that you love her and always will, but that she will not use and abuse you and expect to keep receiving the same efforts from you. Again this would be done in a calm and clear manor about how you feel without any hints of anger or abusiveness.

So you could say something like—*I want to keep doing the many things I do for you. I love it, and I love you. I've calmly and kindly expressed to you how without any expression of appreciation from you, I feel that all of my efforts are unappreciated and I feel used. I don't want to feel this way. I offered solutions to this but you don't seem to want to or be able to express this. Is there a way that you can think of that you could do instead?* If so, use that dialogue to come to an understanding of what works for both of you.

If she blows you off or does not want to discuss it, then clearly and calmly let her know that you deserve to feel appreciated for your efforts. Also, use it as a teaching moment by letting her know that if she takes this approach with others, they may not be as dedicated to trying to work on it as you have. And that you will not continue to put as much effort in, if she cannot reciprocate some effort in voicing her appreciation.

You could say something such as—*You know that I love you very much and I find joy in doing things for you. I want to continue, however, I can't continue to give to you if you are not willing to make an effort to express appreciation for what I do. Relationships are a two-way street and I don't feel like you see it that way.* If she objects, ask her how she feels that she expressed her appreciation. Maybe she has and you missed it. And if she doesn't dispute it and seems indifferent than you need to be clear by stating something like—*I will not be putting the time and energy into our relationship if you don't want to. It causes me to feel like I'm begging for your attention. I put real effort into you and I deserve the same consideration.*

Again, all of this is said with love and kindness in a calm manner. **Once there is anger or yelling, no one can really hear what the other person is saying.** Think about it, if you have someone come to you and they tell you their problem and ask for help, most of the time you will try your very best to help them. But, if they come to you and yell at you and abuse you because they are angry, you are most likely going to tell them to go pound sand and you don't give a second thought to their problem because you are too busy feeling anger or resentment towards them.

Sometimes, it can be trying if someone is not hearing us or taking our efforts seriously. When we are really hurt, we lash out. This does not solve anything but to open up wounds for both parties and most likely will eventually sever the relationship.

Being kind and calm does not equate to being walked on. **Swallowing it down when you are angry in fear of hurting the other person is letting yourself be walked on**. You are not a better parent by letting this go on. You are hurting yourself by internalizing your anger and sadness instead of letting it out by expressing your feelings. And you are not doing her any good by allowing her to treat you this way, because you are modeling to her that people will allow her to do this. Then she will be very lonely when she continues to act this way towards others in the future. And she may wonder why people don't stay in her life. Teach her—that is the greatest gift you can offer her.

I'm really starting to feel like during these meditations that there is a genuine and intimate rapport here. Feeling safe to ask about my deepest insecurities and trust that they are giving me loving and sound advice, I continue to go inside and try to turn my most vulnerable feelings into questions.

Q: *I'm sure the answer to this is going to be—live in the now, stop worrying what others think or whatever, but I will ask and see what you have to say. I have a lot of difficulty with anxiety. If I know that I have something different or out of the norm going on the next day (like today the leasing company is doing an inspection of the house we live in) I don't sleep well, I am really tired, and I cannot relax. I had the whole house clean when I went to bed, so I should have been able to be OK with everything. But my jaw hurts from clenching it, my shoulders hurt from holding my tension there, and I'm finding it really hard to get into the zone to hear your answer and so on. Why is it that even if I logically know that everything is fine, I can't seem to be OK and why do I get so anxious? Thank you.*

A: We know that as much as you are looking for answers so you can understand why you do things the way you do, you really want words that help you to 'see' things differently as well as 'tools' that you can employ for as long as it takes you to get it. So, we are going to walk you through your thought patterns with this one.

Take a deep breath and relax. You will not be disturbed for the next half an hour as you have asked for information and this safe, quiet, and uninterrupted space has been made for you. As you take in another deep breath, let it out and relax your shoulders.

Allow energy to flow through you. Feel it tingling and concentrate on that aliveness. Start here with this thought—*Everything right now in this moment is perfect.* Just in this moment, not this hour or anything else. See how when you concentrate on the exact moment you are in that you are OK and you begin to relax because you know that everything is good right now. When you do that for each moment that you feel you are going back into anxiety think—*Right now, I am good, all is good and I am OK.* And as they string together you find that you have been in this good state for 30 seconds, then a minute, then 10 minutes and so on.

This is the meditative state that you reach doing this automatic writing. When you are worried or have anxiety about something this takes you out of that and back into a state of fear. This is why you have physical symptoms that make you uncomfortable because of your response to this fear. You clench your jaw, you raise and squeeze your shoulders, kind of like you do when you are bracing for something. Whether that is bracing against impact of an accident, abuse, or situations that you do not want to have happen to you again. **What you need to remember when you begin to feel this way is to remind yourself that it is not real, you are just imaging this because of pain memory.**

The unknown to you is scary because when you have not been ready for something in the past or you think you were not paying attention, you had awful things happen to you. Car accidents, physical or any type of abuse, and so on. So when you've not met someone before or they are coming into the place you call home to 'judge' whether you are taking care of it well enough it brings up questions of your worthiness.

Are you worthy to live in that home? Well, of course you are, you pay them rent on time each and every month. You keep it clean and you take good care of it. *You know that, so why the anxiety?* Because you are not really worried about whether you do or not, you are worried if that person is going judge you as *'not good enough.'* You are not worried about if you do enough for their home, you are worried that you are not good enough.

This feeling stems from multiple things like you believing that if you were smarter, richer, or more successful you could buy your own home and not have to worry about inspections or other people's judgments. **But the funny part is that you are judging yourself, they are not judging you.**

Who says that you didn't make out better that you've rented for the last ten years? Many people have paid the same and a lot more to a mortgage for those ten years and lost more than half of the equity in their home. So technically they rented as well because they are not seeing their money invested like one typically thinks of a mortgage. And on top of that, they can't get up and move wherever they want. They owe more on their mortgage then the house is worth so they are stuck paying a whole lot more for a house that isn't even worth that. So really they are in way worse shape than a measly renter like you (as you think). And if they do go belly up on their mortgage their credit is ruined for almost a decade. And if they do stay in the home, they have to worry about fixing everything. You just call a number and they fix it for you and you don't have to pay for it. If we had to say it, out of the buyer and renter, the renters have definitely made out better. So the judgment that you are less than or not as well off as those who bought, we just proved how wrong that thinking is.

The next reason you feel anxiety is because you want them to approve of the job you are doing in their home. You want approval that you are good, clean, and so on. **Again, this has nothing to do with the home, it has more to do with how you look at and feel about yourself.** You do not feel that you are these things; therefore, you are judging yourself. If you are judging yourself, then *why wouldn't they?* They may, who knows, but all that matters is that you are adhering to your rental agreement and that is all that you need to do.

The important part is healing the part of you that thinks that you are not good, clean, and worthy. We've spoken other times about how actions that you've taken or not taken in the past cannot in any shape or form dim your perfection. There are no acts that take away from the light, source, and love that is the essence of who you are. You are born beautiful and perfect and you die beautiful and perfect. And in between, regardless of any life choices or mistakes that you've made, you are always the same beautiful shining light of perfection that you are inside.

Forgive yourself; you deserve it because there is nothing to forgive. You came here to live, make choices, and learn by the consequences of your actions. This is life. You are doing it. You cannot be wrong. You may make different choices after experiencing previous ones, but that is what we call success. If you had not experienced it, you would not really know. You would not have the wisdom, experience, and compassion that you have for having walked through those times.

People are not beautiful because they are perfect or free from any transgressions. They are beautiful because they lived, made choices, learned from them and then possess a great level of compassion for any view of a situation like it. This wisdom and the sharing of these lessons is the intrinsic journey of our souls in these bodies.

Judging or condemning others is an act of a small mind. Sharing our experiences and letting others learn in their own time and in their own way is the way of the heart.

We feel that your whole demeanor before this has changed. Now that you look at the fact that you are living up to your rental agreement and doing a fine job, and that you realize that no one judges you half as harshly as you judge yourself, you can feel a peace come over you.

And finally know that even when someone judges you or criticizes you, that is always about them way more than it is about you, your actions, or short comings. As you saw from this experience today, you were so hard on yourself that you couldn't even think about anything else. **Have compassion for those who judge you for their own pain blinds them so much that they are really only fighting with themselves.**

Hallelujah!

Once again my pain has manifested physically.

Q: *My stomach has been bloated and hurting all week. Yes, last weekend I ate junk—popcorn, chocolate, and wheat flour which all irritated it. But it is still really bloated and painful. I've tried probiotics, aloe juice and digestive enzymes but it is not getting better. Is there anything I can do to help it and stop this in the future without depriving myself of the occasional treats that I love? Please help, thank you.*

A: Your stomach pain originated outside of the physical symptoms that you are experiencing. As we always say, **the physical symptoms are the manifestation of issues involving your emotional and spiritual bodies.**

In this area you hold your anxiety, your self-consciousness, your feelings of unworthiness, and your regrets or sadness around sex and reproduction. These are many and they are very powerful emotions. It is held like a ball of angry burning fire in that area of you. It has caused irritation and has resulted in physical weaknesses and maladies involving parts in these areas. This is why you must be so vigilant in the areas of eating pristinely and avoiding triggers so not to flare this area.

Please know the wheat or sugar is not the cause of the pain in your stomach. It is merely an aggravator that has exacerbated the underlying issues. That is why no matter how well you've eaten, how many juice cleanses you've tried, or how many types of foods you've eliminated from your diet that you still experience the same problems. No, a different type of diet or elimination or supplement will not heal this problem. It can help during the healing so not to worsen it, but it is not the answer.

The answer is healing the emotional and spiritual wounds that you have. This is the only cure. We know that you know what these wounds are—not loving yourself, not being kind to yourself or treating yourself with the same caring that you would a good friend, the anger or shame that you hold onto regarding choices or things that you've done. This pertains to this lifetime as well as stuff that you've carried over from other lifetimes. When you die, it does not wipe this all from your soul. Your soul continues to reincarnate to learn more and resolve these issues. If you had many lifetimes with pain, sadness, mistrust, abuse, or choices that caused negative consequences you can carry a lot of stuff that is not only not helping you but causing this pain.

You do not need to relive these lives or know what all of these causes are to use this incarnation and this life to heal all of these wounds. If it seems more believable or down-to-earth start with things that you know bother you in this life to get used to it. Eventually, you will not need to think of the specific events to release these fears, negative patterns and pain from your emotional and spiritual bodies, which will be evident to you by the healing of your physical body once they are released.

Yes, we know you want to know how. Smile. You are always ready to move on, it is joyous. So, take a deep breath and repeat—*I am ready to release all negative and harming thoughts and feelings from my emotional, spiritual and physical bodies. I know that I am a perfect, a pure child in the eyes of the universe. Nothing that I've done in this lifetime or any others was so horrible that I was not absolved before I even acted. I incarnate to learn and grow on a soul level. That is my job. I do not need or want to carry sadness, regret, or pain regarding any choices that I did or did not make. I chose what I could do at that given time. I am still loved and perfect and as full of light as I was when I was not in this body—when God first created me. I am part of the whole, beautiful and perfect energy that creates all things. I am love. I am joy. I am light.*

I open my arms and release all stuck, sad, negative, judgmental, and other energies that do not serve me. I give them to the universe to transmute back into the perfect energy that is in all things. I gladly embrace my freedom from these things that I've held onto unnecessarily since I thought I did something wrong. There is no wrong—just choices and corresponding consequences to learn from. I am not a sinner, but a perfect child of the huge universal energy of love that unites all people and things into one. I breathe in this love and breathe out all that does not serve me or this light. Because if I heal myself, I heal all that is for we are all connected. I am doing this for me and all things, there is no separation. I will love me so I can add love to this. I am full of love and light and that is enough.

Amen

I understand logically that I am creating the situations, pain, and everything else that cause me to feel less than joyful. I want to snap my fingers and with it let go of all of the patterns that I hold that are counterproductive to my peace, but it seems so difficult at times.

Q: *Why do I find it so hard to let go? Let go of anything…relationships that don't serve me, habits that don't serve me, thought processes that don't serve me and on and on? Why can't I even let go enough to relax? For example, my shoulders are tense. So, I consciously take deep breaths and put my attention to relaxing them and feeling them that way. Then I go onto something else, and when I come back, they are tense again. It seems like I've tried so many things, mantras, breathing, meditation, natural herbal supplements, you name it, and I still don't seem to be able to relax or let go. Why? And how do I successfully do this long term not just a few minutes? Thank you for your help.*

A: You are tensing against life instead of letting it flow. You feel like you have to force it instead of just being and letting what you want to come to you. You don't believe it will and you do not have faith that it will, so you feel the need to hold on with your very last finger nail so as to not fall off of the mountain.

Let go of the mountain, you are not hanging off of a cliff. You are the cliff, the mountain, the air; you have nothing to fear. That saying, *"You have nothing to fear except fear itself,"* is so right on because that fear is much worse than anything that will actually happen. **And being or staying in that fear will only leave you vibrating at the level of the things you fear. Which brings you stuff that you do not like. It is a self-fulfilling prophecy.**

You have to just let go. There is no other way to get to where you want. You cannot bargain your way there, crawl while holding on for dear life, fight, yell, or force anything to get there.

I think this is where your and most people's confusion comes in because you believe what you've been taught that you have to fight for what is yours. That you have to use blood, sweat, and tears and you have to climb the mountain. These are all fighting to get where you want to go.

We say, why fight when you can just let go, be, visualize, and do the next thing and allow it to come to you. No, this is not a woo-woo way of looking at it; it is the non-resistance of allowing. *I mean what would you rather have?* To fight, lose limbs, feel like you are going to die, to fall down at the top of the mountain at the end of what you were wanting to realize that it may not be what you were really wanting after all. See that is the problem with wanting what we think we want. What we really want underneath of that is usually not one in the same.

Or would you rather let go, believe that you are worthy, align yourself with feeling great, and being happy and allowing things to shuffle around and give you what you were wanting or a version of it. And most of the time, the version is really what you were wanting because it is fulfilling what you really wanted deep down. *This seems a lot more simple don't you think?*

We can see your brain almost shaking as you do not believe this. **It is so ingrained that you have to force things that it is not even plausible to you that if you just allow, you will get what you are wanting and it will probably be beyond your wildest expectations.**

Think about your life. You usually come from a place of holding on, digging in, protecting yourself and what is yours, and disliking anyone who threatens that. This is out of fear. You fear losing what you do have, not getting what you want, and always feeling this way. The pain you are in is exactly what you do not want. It hasn't worked thus far, *what can it hurt to try this other way?*

You will not be hurt, starve, or find yourself in hell. That is what you are in now. You may not be physically starving, but you are starving to know yourself. You are starving to allow yourself to just be you. You are starving to feel the truth that you allow to eke out during times like this in meditation and you want to feel this all of the time. You are afraid you will lose what you have, or who you have, and you will be alone. But those fears are not logical. You will feel more alone trying to be a certain way and not allowing yourself to just be.

This is a hard concept for you. One because it is so ingrained and two because it is esoteric and you can't feel, see, and touch it this second. It takes faith and you are basing your ability to have faith on the hardships that you had to suffer as a child. You do not believe. You never did and you still do not. **To get to the place of allowing or being and welcoming in what you are wanting with ease, you have to address the underlying theme that you feel that you cannot believe.** You can. You have in fleeting moments, and you can live this way on a consistent basis.

You have to retrain your brain. You have to stop the thoughts as they are circulating, take them off of the revolving belt. You have to replace them with that which you are wanting. At first you will have to be very aware of each word, thought, phrase, and thing you do surrounding changing this. Eventually, it will become second nature. But this 'work' in the short run will pay off infinitely. Doing this work will also be a lot easier in the long run than fighting against what is, and fighting for what you want. *Wouldn't it be easier, to correct yourself incessantly for a little while then live like this forever?*

You can start today. You shall only speak kindly, lovingly, patiently, and positively to yourself, about yourself, to others and about others. You must see yourself as sacred as an angel or a little infant. This will make it much easier. We see ourselves and others as sinners, dirty, used up, old, and worn out once we reach adulthood. We no longer see the miraculous beauty we are. But when you see a picture of a white lit angel or a sweet little infant sleeping in your arms you feel peaceful, because with them you accept their divinity and perfection. **So you must see yourself and others this way to change.** That may seem simple, but it is the first and one of the most important steps.

Next, you must be aware of each and every word that you say. This will seem trivial and then annoying, but again, it is an essential ingredient in the success of your letting go and letting joy fill your life. So, you may want to begin on a weekend when you are less rushed and have more time to slowly start to change your patterns.

You will only speak kindly and positively to that angel and infant that is you and everyone around you. We are all one and all contain that pure energy. You must speak to it and not the pain that surrounds people. If you do, you will not see the light. When someone says something that offends you, their pain is talking to your pain. There is never an involvement of either of your true angelic selves.

Now for some examples for you on how to speak, think, and be. *Why do I have to change how I speak?* We can hear you thinking that you are offended. It is not because you are not good enough. It is not because you are wrong. It is because if you want different results, you have to approach things differently. **You cannot get a loving angelic innocent being to listen or respond if you are not speaking their language. They don't understand or speak the language of pain.** Think of it like this—if you do not speak Portuguese, only English, and someone begins to speak to you in Portuguese, you don't understand and you cannot respond. It is the same.

It is also not because you are not smart enough or educated enough in the way that your society claims education. There are some very smart people with PhD's that are very uneducated when it comes to emotions, communication, relationships, etcetera. They are formally educated in a particular subject that may exceed many people's understanding. But this does not mean they are educated in the soul, in speaking to themselves or a loved one, or many other areas. **This is one of the problems created in this society is that people do not see value in themselves or others if they do not have initials behind their name, or if they do not have a bank account that is big enough, or if they do not have a fancy car or house.** And although these things might be luxurious and bring some physical comfort, they do not bring knowledge, peace, joy, or fulfillment to the soul. If they did, there would not be well-educated, rich, and 'successful' people that felt empty. These people would not have drug or alcohol addictions. They would not be involved in self-harming behaviors or actions. They would be in a state of bliss at all times, and they are not.

So, as we define success, it is living in joy, peace, and coming from a place of love at all times, and in all ways, always. This is true bliss. It cannot be taken away, sold, lost in the stock market, stolen, or anything else because this is the innate gift that you possess.

You are now thinking that if we don't give you the examples or tools of words or phrases to say that you will not know how to do it. And although you know innately, we will give you examples. Only speak to yourself and others with love, respect, and kindness regardless of their looks, weight, financial status, sexual orientation, religious beliefs and so on. **No one, we mean no one, is less than you. Period.**

When you begin to treat yourself as the perfect, enlightened, spiritual being that you are, you will begin to operate from there and your life will begin to be what you are wanting. For example, begin speaking to yourself like—*Good morning Amy. You look so wonderful today. You are a shining light that accents this world beautifully. The peace that surrounds you is such a gift. Thank you.* This may seem eccentric and very silly, but it is true. And you must believe it and be it for you to see it. It is that simple. So do it anyway, say it anyway, *what is the worst that can happen?* Nothing except what you have now.

Next, make every choice as if you were doing it for that perfect sweet infant. Only give it what you know is good for it. We do this easily for sweet innocent babies, but we don't see that in us anymore. So from now on, you are a sweet innocent baby. You will feed yourself, care for yourself, love yourself, and speak to yourself as if you are a newborn. That means that you will do what you know is good for them and you. You feed her good wholesome food that nourishes her body. You give her plenty of rest whenever her body needs it. You clean and care for yourself gently and with love. You speak to yourself with plenty of affection and only use kind words. You are her and you deserve that.

So, when you feel like you don't look good, you wouldn't say to that sweet little baby, *"God you look awful."* You would change their shirt or brush their hair or let them rest, whatever it is that you think is 'wrong.' You do it gently and kindly with love. This may seem tedious and time consuming and silly, and at first it may be a bit. But do it anyway. Do it for you. Do it for that perfect, sweet little soul inside that you don't see. She's there and she needs it, and she deserves it. She is that regardless of what you have said to her all these years. It is never too late to change.

It is never too late to start speaking to her differently. Say—*I love you. You are beautiful. You are perfect just the way you are.*

Do these things make you feel relaxed? Yes.

When you hear, *'You are ugly, you are fat, you are stupid,' do these things make you tense up?* Yes. See you are causing your tension; you are hurting that little girl inside. Don't look away from her anymore. Love her, treat her with kindness, take her little hand and treat her like she deserves, like she wants to be. You deserve it.

And most importantly, it is the only way to find peace. To find what you are wanting. **Letting go is not jumping off the side of a mountain and hoping the wind will catch you. Letting go is releasing yourself from the bonds of pain and suffering that you inflict on yourself every day.** You are not wrong or bad, you have just not been shown another way. Or you've forgotten. Start over today with that little baby that you are and raise her another way, give her all that you are wanting, and you will find yourself fulfilled beyond your wildest dreams.

Amen

The more I become aware of my pain, the self-infliction, and ways to change it, I can see the same self-abuse especially in those close to me. I never realized how hard it is to watch because I couldn't see it in myself. Now that I can and I am receiving guidance and applying the tools to changing my behaviors, I'm finding it difficult to not help my partner as I watch him suffer.

Q: *Today I welcome help in understanding my behavior and how to 'fix' it so I can come more from a place of love. My significant other is having a hard time with things. I have compassion because I've been there much more than him. I get frustrated because instead of choosing healthy tools or trying to figure out the cause and deal with it, he just crawls in his cave, feeds his pain with unhealthy choices, and waits for it to pass. Then he goes on with his life instead of working on things so to avoid a repeat in the future. I guess I see the futility in this cycle and so want him to be happy and find peace. It is also very unsettling to be in such an unstable environment, which I know is my issue. I find during his melting down that I get short or angry and tell him to knock it off and look at it logically. I know that probably isn't helpful but it seems to be my 'default' reaction. I don't want to reinforce his unhealthy way of dealing with his issues and want to help him feel better. I just don't know what to do or how to do it. Could you please help?*

A: You love him so and are so full of compassion that your passion comes across as gruff. You also become scared when the one you love, who is the stability for the most part in your life falls apart, it scares you. **This is your issue of needing someone to provide that stability for you other than yourself.** After eleven years of having someone love you, it can feel unsettling when they aren't OK. But you need to reach inside at this time and trust the universe and know that you are safe, you are protected, and you will be OK no matter what.

Next, although you want to fix this for him, you cannot. This is his journey, his soul, his pain, and his healing. What works for you may not work for him and most importantly, you cannot make him want to work on it, fix it, or choose to move past it. Only he can, no matter how much you want that for him.

The only thing you can do is offer him your love, your support, and your experience or insight if he wants it. That is all. You cannot do the work for him, you cannot pave the way. Although your healing and work on yourself is a type of paving the way. For he has seen the great changes in you since you began this. He sees the shift and the self-love beginning to sprout. He wants to change and you doing it and demonstrating change is a catalyst for him.

So do not fear this time, embrace it. He no longer wants to stuff down his pain, but bring it to light so that it can be transmuted. That is a good thing. That is a gift to himself. What you are seeing is the fear in him. It can be scary as you well know to step into the unknown even if it is for your evolution, betterment, and ultimate happiness. Change can be very scary and that is why so many people stay still even though they are in pain. Knowing what you can expect, that security, even if it is negative is more appealing to many than taking that jump into the unknown. But as you know, it is leagues better than staying stuck.

He will have to make this journey on his own, in his own way. This does not mean you can't hold his hand, love him, and be a comfort for him. But even if his way seems 'wrong' to you or not the way you would choose, that is OK. It is his journey and he will make choices, have consequences, and learn the things he needs to.

The part you are struggling with is how his choices affect you. We know that you can love him, support him, hold his hand and hug him. What you are really worried about is if he will choose to keep hiding instead of taking the next step forward. It is painful for you, not only to watch him feed his pain, but be in the presence of it. He has thought the same about you.

We say as long as he takes the next step, he will be on his way. Be kind, supportive, and gentle. And if he takes steps backwards that cause you pain. Leave. Maybe it is temporary, but you do not need to sit in something that causes you pain. You know that it is an opportunity to work on your own issues but that doesn't need to be so painful. It is your choice.

Remember, inside he is that little boy, still carrying scars and unhealed wounds. Share what you can, share your insight or what you've learned. Offer support—a warm meal, a hug, or your hand. He does not mean to hurt you; he is just blinded by his own pain. Pain that is rising because his soul truly wants to move on, become lighter, and live from a place of joy and love. **So as much as it seems like a war zone at times, try to rejoice that change is upon him, upon you both, your relationship, and that love will prevail.** Embrace love, help with love, and try to see through the eyes of love with all things and in all situations.

This is a much shorter one as that is the extent of what you can do. This is his to do. **Just keep working on you that is your job.** And we commend you on your effort and continued interest and passion in really loving you. You know with all of your being that loving you is the answer, for you, for everyone you love, for everything that is.

When you see everyone and everything through love, you will see it as it is, not through the distorted lenses of pain. You really see the truth that lies at the center of it all.

Go with love,

Amen

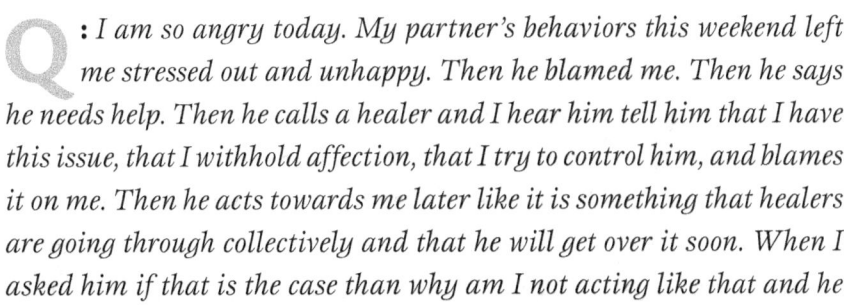

Q: *I am so angry today. My partner's behaviors this weekend left me stressed out and unhappy. Then he blamed me. Then he says he needs help. Then he calls a healer and I hear him tell him that I have this issue, that I withhold affection, that I try to control him, and blames it on me. Then he acts towards me later like it is something that healers are going through collectively and that he will get over it soon. When I asked him if that is the case than why am I not acting like that and he*

told me it was because I was not a healer for 15 years like him. Wow. So, it is my fault, my fault, and then I am not as enlightened. Then he acts like he doesn't deserve a good birthday because he hurt me so much. I do not know who he is. I don't think he knows who he is. I would rather he tell me he wants to live a certain way and get out. Or not, but this telling others one thing, telling me one thing, then saying another drives me mad. It makes me question everything we've ever had. I am so angry. I want to have empathy but I feel so confused and betrayed that I can't seem to step over that today. Please help. Thank you.

A: This is not about you, it is about him. He is having issues with his own self and you are the closest easiest person or reason to use as blame. *Have you not done this with him? When you aren't feeling well haven't you said, 'Well if only he didn't do this or what have you?'* We are each responsible for our own feelings, thoughts, and behaviors. Now we understand that you are feeling angry because you feel betrayed. Anger is not bad in itself; it is just a catalyst do to the next thing. And the next thing would be to ask honestly and welcome an honest answer, from both of you. *Do you really want to continue in a relationship?* Relationships are not made to 'make you happy,' they are there to share experience with, offer support, laugh, have fun, and offer insight to each other.

If it seems that your relationship with Ricky is falling apart, it is. It has to. You are searching to live your authentic self. We all are. That is our job. You cannot be in a relationship that does not support this. You both have to want to be there for the other, offer your support, and you have to enjoy each other. When one lives a way that makes the other uncomfortable, this can be a problem because you tend to focus on the problem or thing you do not like.

You can also use these as excuses about why you are not happy. He has done it to you and you to him. You want to be in an authentic relationship, so you cannot do this, nor can he. You alone cannot decide, you both must come from this place and agree to make this the center of your relationship for it to work.

Sometimes, this is why relationships fail because people can't separate their own issues from the other person because they are so close. They think if their mate goes away, the problem goes away. **But the only way the problem goes away is if you work that out for yourself.** Then it is no longer a 'problem' for you, so regardless of what your mate does, it won't affect you. **Your mate or partner is a reflection for you, to help you see what you need to work on.**

They do not make you whole or happy or feel better. They simply mirror your own love, insecurities, issues and so on. *Why do you think after the honeymoon phase you start to see things in them that remind you of the things you did not like about mom, or dad, or whomever?* Because they bring up the issues that you need to look at within yourself.

Yes, when you hear someone talk to others about you negatively, it hurts and you feel like you were deceived. And if they did not tell you that to your face, maybe they did. **But what he said about you to others is more of a reflection of what he needs to work on in himself.** This does not mean everything is his fault. We all have stuff to work on and we all do things from a place of pain. So it is not cocky to say what he said about you, it is his stuff not yours. And some of the issues that you have with him are yours. It is that simple. No one is right or wrong. No one is better than the other. Each just has their own work to do.

Staying together or not will not determine whether you will be happier or not because only you can choose that for yourself, no matter where you are or who you are with. If you can find joy in a less than ideal situation, you have learned.

So, we say, stop thinking that anyone is the answer to your happiness or prayers. Stop thinking that anyone is the cause of your pain or sadness; no one can do this to you or for you, except you. **You are the only one who can change your outlook, your issues, and your life. No matter who is around you, they are not responsible for your happiness or your sadness, you are.**

Don't you think it is ironic that people who have been married more than once say that you divorce one set of problems and marry another? The things that you need to work on will follow you wherever you go, whoever you're with, and in whatever you do. You cannot escape them, leave them, bury them, or forget them.

So the question is not whether Ricky makes you happy or you make him happy. The question is *are both of you willing to look at your own stuff, take responsibility for working on it, and not hold the other accountable for any of it?* If yes, then the next question is *can you agree to work on your own stuff and be honest, kind, loving, and supportive with each other while each walks through their journeys?* If yes, then you have the basis of a good relationship. If not, you do not. It is not easy to do, but it is easy to know if it is where you want to be.

13

It's All Judgment

Q: *I'm in a good mood this morning, feeling much better than most typical mornings as I incorporate more of the tools you are showing me, thank you! I do find myself still really struggling with the ability to stay calm when I have a lot on my plate in a day. Today I have more to accomplish than normal so I feel anxious, short on time, and a little thing keeps popping up in my head that says, "There is so much, I'm tired already." I don't want to dread the day and take away from my happiness. I don't want to feed into that little 'thing' or become overwhelmed. How can I approach my day or what tools can I use to remain calm and productive and enjoy my day without feeding that nagging feeling of being rushed, overwhelmed, and like I can't get it all done? Thank you.*

A: Maybe start with this, ask yourself, *"Will it be the end of the world as I know it if I do not accomplish all the things I 'need' to get done today?"* No. It is that simple. So change the wording—*I'd like to get all of this done today but if I do not, it is OK. I will do one thing and then the next and then we'll see where I'm at later. If I do not finish* *everything it is OK. All that I can do is try my best. And while I'm doing each thing I will be attentive and happy to do it, I will put all of my energy and awareness on that task.*

This will allow you to enjoy each activity. *Do you notice that when you do have a lot to do, you do one thing while fretting over whether you will have the time and energy to get to the other six things?* You do not put any attention into what you are doing. You do not find any joy in what you are doing because you dread the next thing before you are doing it. **This is actually what you are overwhelmed about—not the fact that you have a lot to do, but that you are not going to enjoy any of it because your typical way of dealing with it is so depressing.**

You can't have fun while doing something if you are not there because you are dreading the next thing. Think about it. The joy that you experience is the fun you are having when you are immersed in doing something, whether that is writing, playing, watching a movie and laughing, or joking with friends. When you are having fun, you are in that moment not thinking about what is next. And if you are thinking about what's next no matter what you are doing, it is not that much fun because you really aren't there. You are thinking about what is next.

So, the key is to be there fully present in what you are doing. *Why worry about what you have to do next?* It will still be there when you are finished with what you are doing now.

One of the other reasons you have this anxiety and issues with feeling overwhelmed is because you judge yourself. You make this list of things to do today, not just to remind yourself to do them, but with the thought—*I must get all of this done. If I do not I will be behind, if I am behind everything won't be right. If things aren't right, I will be a mess.* And so goes the train of thought fueled by the judgment that you still have inside of you.

You must think of life as more fun, enjoy it. All things are not tons of fun, but each thing contains something that brings you joy. You must look more closely for that or allow it. For example, it may not be your favorite thing in the world to cook elaborate Italian dinners like you are doing for your daughter's visit. But you can make it much more pleasant. While you are gathering ingredients think of how lucky you are to have the money and access to purchase them. Think gratefully of the natural, innate remembering you have to create delicious Italian food although you were never formally taught by anyone; you pull it from the wisdom in you. That is glorious! Think of all of the oohs and ahhhs while the people you love enjoy each bite of this food that you prepared with love just for them. **The list can go on and on, because once you start to appreciate all of the tiny things that allowed you the honor to be there doing this, you will be filled with joy.**

We take for granted how lucky we are to have things at our disposal. Be grateful for each and every thing, and every moment of life will become magical. Look at it as if it is no longer a chore, tedious, or boring, but instead a gift.

You can even go into gratitude that you are able to stand for extended periods of time and that you have use of your arms and hands to create such lovely food. *Remember when you threw your back out and couldn't stand?* All of these events or things that happen that were painful were there to help us appreciate what we do have. *Would you appreciate your back half as much if you hadn't hurt it before?* Probably not, because now you realize that when it was hurt, you could not function—you couldn't walk, stand, sit, drive, cook, clean, write, or anything. *Isn't it fabulous to stretch today and stand and walk and bend over and do all of these things?*

See at first glance it may seem silly to be grateful for such trivial things, but as you've experienced, nothing is trivial. It is all connected, it all works together. And now your day that began as trepidation for the mountain of stuff you 'had' to do has shifted to a magical and lucky day that you 'get' to do so many lovely things. Funny how just looking at things through a different perspective can change everything within a few minutes. And a hint: the small, tiny, and trivial things that we take for granted each day are the most important things. Focus on them, and your life will change.

Try it today. Pay close attention to the fact that your fingers move over this keyboard and they just know where the keys are. How wonderful that you can communicate this way without having to think about it. Have gratitude for that typing class you so hated in high school. (Smile) Have gratitude for this amazing keyboard that allows your letters and words to flow out and fill these pages. Have gratitude that this way of receiving information within minutes can change your entire day. How the words correspond to feelings which allow understanding that allow your body, mind, and spirit to shift your entire world. **Each little thing may seem unimportant, but the big picture isn't possible without each component. So don't celebrate the end result as much as you relish in the magic of each tiny baby step.** There is a reason baby steps are so beautiful.

Have a lovely, gorgeous, fun, happy, joyous day our friend. We love you, each and every tiny but miraculous step that you take. It is so much fun for us to observe.

I still find myself struggling with accepting things as they are and not judging them. It seems so tiresome to get angry, frustrated, or upset by other people's actions, but for some reason I still feel that irritation rising when something that seems so simple to see by me isn't seen by others.

It's All Judgment

Q: *Why do I get so upset when I feel like people are not thinking? I can name three scenarios in the last few days when people have done things that I felt where selfish, rude, judgmental, or just plain not using the brains I think they should have. I try to 'let it go' or let it 'roll off my back' but I still feel frustration and I don't want to. I don't want to care if people do things like this. How do I find that balance and calmly give a level-headed response that will get my point across that I found them rude and let it go so that I don't have to keep thinking and talking about the audacity of some people. I find it rather difficult. Thank you for your help.*

A: **The problem lies in your expectation of what you think people should know, do, be, or act like.** If you base your happiness on this, you will never be happy. People are mostly asleep, or in other words in so much pain, drama, or whatnot that they do not know what they do to you. Some may. They might just want to hurt you, again because of their own pain.

Think about it. *When you've been in pain, sad, or unhappy about something were you thinking of others?* No, you were wrapped in a cloak of self-pity. In that you saw nothing but yourself. This is what you see in many teenagers. They are so worried about being liked, accepted, good enough and on and on, that they have no room left to think of how others may feel. We cannot be so angry at them since we modeled for them how instead of loving ourselves, we did not accept, nurture, and appreciate ourselves.

Being sad or in pain or wrapped up in your own unhappiness is very self-oriented. When one is in this state, they do not have any leftover time to think of others. When you don't think of others and you are in pain yourself, you will do, be, say and come across as extremely selfish rude, judgmental and mean. When you are in this state, people think that you are just mean, but we know that all of this is a by-product of unhappiness, sadness, feeling unworthy, unloved or unlovable, and lacking any self-love.

So again, we go back to the core problem. It is not that when people are in this state that they are not acting selfishly. They are. **But judging them or taking their actions personally will only give you hurt feelings, and leave you feeling let down.** From someone's perspective that is not in this self-centered bubble of pain, it will come across as them being rude and selfish, but it is not for you to fix. You can't.

Now you can tell them kindly and non-judgmentally that their action made you feel hurt, sad, or whatever. You do not have to condone mistreatment just because they are not aware, but becoming angry, highly frustrated, or lashing out at them will only exacerbate the situation. It will feed their insecurities that are the core cause for the problem to begin with. It will not help them to see the error in their ways as you think, it will only fuel the fire.

So, our advice—let it go. **Do not feed into or condone the behavior, but do not push hard against it. Neither will help them.** If they really hurt or offend you because of their lack of awareness was so extreme, tell them kindly how your feelings were hurt. Do not demand an apology or something to 'make it right.' Merely tell them how you feel in a succinct manor and then move on.

Then you move on to do more work on yourself until their being asleep does not activate any unhealed pain in your own self. See everyone is just a pointer to what you have unresolved in you. We are all 'works in progress,' so no one is perfect. Although we are all at different levels of understanding and self-love, it does not make one person better than another, maybe just merely a bit more awake than another.

So, although those who have annoyed you are asleep, maybe a bit more than you, have compassion for them. Show them by example. Do not judge them. Do not berate them. If called for, merely tell them how they hurt you and do this only in very extreme cases. If you do it often, it will be something else they can focus on and complain about instead of being alone with their own stuff to realize and work on it.

People avoid looking at their own stuff because it is work. Instead they focus on what Jimmy did over here, and what Janie looks like, and what Jackie said, and what Johnny should have done, and the nerve of Jessica to say that. It is all drama, which is just something else to focus on or distract them from looking at their own stuff. That includes us all. We use drama, drugs, complaining, alcohol, food, sex, anger, shopping, gambling, gossip and on and on and on.

All that you can do today is commit to living as peaceful and self-lovingly as you can. Once you omit the things that distract you, like being annoyed at others behaviors *(wink wink)* you will have plenty of time to work on loving the beautiful, perfect, magnificent soul that you are. We all are. We just choose to ignore or look at others weaknesses to avoid dissolving the obstacles to loving ourselves.

The answer to all is loving yourself, for when you do, you will have compassion for all people and situations and they will no longer have any bearing on your own happiness. It all comes from within and filters out. So the greatest gift you can give is to love yourself and share your joy with the world. Be an example.

Much love, find the beauty in today, focus on you not the behavior of others because that is the only place you will find your happiness.

Amen

I know that avoidance or seclusion is not the answer to finding peace but it sure works sometimes. But I am ready to stop avoiding and start changing the way I operate so that I am at peace regardless of where I am or who I'm with.

Q: *I find it so easy to see the world through a lens of love when I'm sitting here with meditation music playing and silence except for the click of the keys as I'm communicating with you. But once I leave my office and interact in the world, I find it hard to stay connected with the feelings I have while here meditating. I'd really like to close this gap so that I may approach life not just from what I've learned here but with the same calm, clarity, and peace that I feel right now. I want to come from this place as the norm in my life. How can I do this? Specifically what can help? Thank you so much.*

A: First, begin with recognizing that you have begun this endeavor. You at times do connect from this place. This is why you have been calmer, less judgmental, and more loving. So to begin specifically (smile) give yourself credit for all of the work and effort you have put in. You cannot be in this space and not carry some of it, even the essence of it into other things that you are doing. **So, the first step is to put yourself in this space to begin the day with.** You are already doing this. As you practice more and more, it will overflow into your daily life.

The next thing you can do is stop looking at this time and space as sacred and the rest of your life as not. This creates a dichotomy so you see them differently, which leads you to be different in the different places. Look at this as the norm, how you are, it is just a daily reminder to set you on this path. It can 'get you straight' for the rest of the day. Although this is peaceful and quiet and easy for you to connect, it is not the only pureness, it all is. So even when there is noise, driving, errands, angry people, this quiet and music that makes you feel at one with all, still is. Just see it as the baseline of your day and all activities. The act of separating them inevitably separates the feeling from other activities. Yes it is easier to reach this when the environment is conducive for you, but it is not different from an environment with chaos or noise. That is something you can reconcile mentally and then will carry over physically.

Is silence not as beautiful as a symphony? Is a child's giggle not as beautiful as a bird's song? Is a rippling brook not as soothing as silence? They are all interrelated. A person's pain which causes them to come from a place of anger and glare at you, honk at you, or give you the middle finger is no less perfect than a smile or hello from a stranger. They are no less perfect, they are just either coming from a place of pain or love or somewhere in between.

Do not allow where another is at in any given time or day to change where you come from. Just as you do not want you to come from a different place based on others actions, do not allow yourself to be distracted by where they are at.

And see, again it all comes down to you—your concentration, your allowing, and you starting your day centered. That is all that you need to worry about. Do not fear if a driver is angry or if a co-worker is grumpy. That has no bearing on you, your peace, or how your day goes. All that matters is where you are.

As humans, we are told to think of others and not to be selfish, but if you do not serve yourself first, you are of no use to others. Loving yourself, giving to yourself, honoring yourself, pampering yourself, making yourself your number one priority is not selfish. **It is love. It is your job. It is your first and most important calling because if you do not, you cannot come from a place of love, give to others, serve others, or share the best of yourself.**

We must change the thought that being selfish is wrong, for without it, you have nothing to give. And you very well know that when you give to someone and you don't have it to give, you are resentful, angry, bitter, and feel that you are being abused, used, or taken advantage of. Then you blame others for using you. But no one can use you without your consent. You are giving to them when you have nothing to give. That is not their fault for accepting what you give, it is your fault for giving what you do not have to give.

And again we are back to the fact that it starts with us, individually, and our personal accountability. **You know if everyone stopped blaming others for their problems and used that energy to look at how they can improve themselves; the world would instantly become a beautiful and loving place.** Because then and only then will we do for ourselves which is ours to do, and abandon blame, resentment, and anger for expecting others to make us whole. It is not our parents, families, children, counselors, teachers, mates, lovers, friends or anyone else's job to make us feel better. There is only one person whose job it is to love us and that person is our own self.

When you release all expectation for anyone to change how you feel, then you will finally find peace. You are not selfish to love yourself my dear, it is your job. There is nothing that you have to do here on this earth, no amount of money to make, no life to change, nothing except to love you. And when you do, you will find that you will do all of the things you want easily and simply just because you started with loving you. Yes, little old you is the most important thing in the universe to you.

Funny how we search far and wide, go on treks around the world, wish for fame and fortune and others admiration, and we seek all that we want everywhere except where it is. No one can love you the way you want to be loved except you. Seek no longer outside yourself, seek no longer from others eyes or hearts, simply place your hand on your heart and feel all that you are, know that all of you is perfect, full, and enough. And when you see your reflection, smile as you meet those eyes to your soul, knowing your secret, that you are everything.

Amen beautiful one. Go bask in your perfection.

I'm being taught, reading, and learning different types of healing tools. I am grateful for it but sometimes I find things that don't seem to resonate with me. Or the tool seems to be pointless or makes me look deeper at the core problem.

Q: *This morning I was trying out a new 'tool' I learned from listening to a self-help video. This tool is to be used when you feel something you don't want to—be it pain, sadness, or whatever. When you feel it you are supposed to ask, "Who does this belong to?" If the negative emotion or feeling dissipates then this is coming from outside of yourself and you "Return it to Sender," thus clearing yourself of someone else's stuff. I noticed that it seems to work for a moment but is then replaced with other pain or tension or some other unwanted sensation. I've heard from other healers before that the down side of being an empath (being very sensitive and able to feel other people's emotions) is that you feel other people's stuff all the time. This got me to thinking, whether I am an 'empath' or not, why am I attracting other people's negative feelings or stuff and why do I have to keep clearing it constantly? Doing that every day multiple times seems exhausting. Wanting to get to the core of the problem I thought, how do I not attract or have someone else's stuff stick to me in the first place? I mean I have enough of my own junk to get rid of without having to deal with this daily. And it seems that with just about every person alive having some junk this would be a never ending cycle of feeling bad, asking myself questions, releasing stuff back to sender just to have it come from somewhere else. So finally, (smile) my question is—How do I stop being a magnet for other people's negative emotion to avoid all of what I previously talked about?*

A: We feel you hesitant to write because although you feel we are giving you information you think it is too simple. That is because it is simple. It begins with you as we say over and over. **If you clear yourself or heal your wounds, let go of what does**

not serve you, and do not walk around with pain, you will not attract it.

Funny that you used the word magnet in your question, *huh?* You've heard that Richard Bach quote "Like attracts like." **So whether it is a negative or positive emotion as you interpret it, whatever you have or whatever you are, you will attract more of the same.** It is easy to understand when you visualize it as such. So see pain or negative emotion as a dark gaseous substance that floats around, kind of like black clouds. Now see them floating towards each other as if in a huddle. This is what happens with pain, sadness, or any other negative emotions. They are drawn to one another.

Have you not heard that before about how people who are in pain commiserate with each other? Why? Because they are drawn together to feed each other's pain. *How much fun is it to bitch and complain to someone who is not reciprocating?* It is not. Because you let it out, they do not respond or give you like back, so it is over. But if you are with one who is also in pain and you are expelling your pain by complaining about what is not fair, or what you do not like, or how this person is awful, and then your partner in crime responds agreeing with how awful that is, and how unfair, and how all things are unfair, and how so and so did this to them, so they agree how awful everything is. Well then you have mixed your pain to create a bigger pot of soup of pain. This then reinforces your pain and validates it. And this is when you think you've found your soul mate or best friend or someone who finally knows you, sees you, and gets you.

When in fact, they merely commiserated your pain, fed your pain, and showed you theirs. That is not healthy or helpful for either of you, but it is a fact that this is the pattern of many relationships. This is also the reason that they seem so right and end so badly because they were not based on love, joy, fun, respect or uplifting one another, just the opposite. You know deep inside this is not how you want to be or live, so eventually the 'high' of your commiserating misery doesn't feel good anymore.

Just like chasing the first high, you will never get it. And just like a drug user you will become disillusioned with the drug, because you will never get the first high again. And although you know this and want to stop because you know it is a useless plight, it is so painful that you choose to keep using and pretending that maybe one day you will feel that again. And one day you may just poof miraculously be in a happy place with no pain. And then you can stop doing the self-fulfilling or self-inflicted action whether it is a drug, cigarette, or other addition like gambling, sex, or what have you.

But this is not how it works. You **do not** feel happy and then stop the self-inflicted behavior that is causing you pain. **You must first stop hurting yourself, abusing yourself, and inflicting self-harm.** Then you will be clear to see the love you have inside.

We as humans are our own worst enemy, harming ourselves to feel pain because we think we are not worthy. We have been told that we are born sinners, that we are unclean and unworthy. Then we are told by our parents that we are bad, wrong, and to stop being us. Sometimes we are beaten and abused verbally, physically, and sexually which only furthers our pain. Our pain becomes our identity. **We then take on the role as adults to continue this self-torture in the name of religion or love, when really we are abusing ourselves for no other reason than we don't see who we truly are.** We hide from this.

We think, "Who am I to think that I am a piece of God? Who am I to think that I am beautiful or all that is perfect?" That would be wrong because we believe that no one and nothing is worthy or can stand up next to God or Jesus or whomever your savior has been introduced to you as through religious teachings.

All of this is a lie, taught to you from those who were in pain before you. Not because they were evil or meant to deceive or indoctrinate you, but because they were seeing through the eyes of their own pain, fear, and self-loathing. This does not make them bad or wrong, it makes them human. But now it is time to step out of this and into the light. Now it is time to look inside and see all that you are, all that you always were.

Drop the cloak of pain that you wear with pride that you have suffered so greatly in the name of love, in the name of good, in the name of God. This suffering is self-denial of who you really are. Each of us is a piece of all that is perfect, beautiful, and that which you call God. God is a word used to define the essence of all that is. It holds a power in it that most words cannot, this is why it is. **Know that you are God, each and every being is. There is no separation, we are all one.**

And this friend, is why you feel others pain, because you have pain, you carry pain as a badge of honor. Not out of stupidity or unworthiness, but merely out of blindness. Use the sight that you have buried. Throw off the dark blankets of doubt that you hide beneath. They will never keep you warm or safe. You are all that you desire in the center of your being. It is beautiful, it is grand, and it is the most dazzling light and love you could ever conjure in your thoughts. Open this and all of the pain, attraction for pain, sadness, poor health, suffering, and all that you have clung to will simply vanish.

This is not religious, this is not woo-woo, this is the truth. This is who you are, who we all are. Embrace it and all the rest will follow. Only resistance to this and turning your eyes from it will make it elude you. It is yours. It does not cost anything. You do not need to sacrifice or pay a penance to receive it. You do not need to be saved. You do not need to become something or someone else. You are perfect and whole and complete. You are a piece of God.

Now bask in it, it is your birthright, your eternal right, it is yours. Do not fear, you cannot lose it for it is the very essence of your being.

Welcome home love, welcome home. Yes weep, for it is beautiful. You are beautiful.

Amen

14

A Pain in the Back

NOW I'M REALLY STARTING TO understand a different way of being. It's funny, I've learned so much and had so many eye-opening experiences, yet I still feel like I don't know much. Maybe I still haven't 'gotten it,' or maybe I've only learned one of the thousand things I need to fully understand. I'm not sure. I do know that I'm much happier lately but still feel a sense of dread when something new comes up to work on.

Q: *I'm much happier lately. I feel like my meditations and writings are flowing, I'm really able to step back from some from my pain, feelings, and reactions and be less judgmental especially of myself. I woke up happy and motivated, which is all great. Now it is becoming evident that my lower back in the sacrum area is going out. It is painful and when it happens I cannot walk sometimes let alone sit for long to write, exercise, or anything else I want to do. Why is it that sometimes I feel like I take two steps forward and then one step back? It gets frustrating feeling like I'm not just moving forward. Thank you.*

A: *Why is it that you think that two steps forward and one step back is a negative thing? Did you ever consider that maybe when you take two steps forward, you need to take one step back to take a moment to appreciate the two steps forward?* Even if you want to look at it mathematically and say that you only took one step forward in the end, *why not celebrate that you took one step forward?*

It is not a race where whoever finishes first wins. **Life is not a race but a road of magical discovery.** *With the impatience that you possess, isn't it possible that if you were not made to take one step back that you would miss relishing all of the steps forward you are taking.*

See it is all about perspective and coming from a loving, accepting place. **The illusion, especially in the United States, is that faster is better.** This is not always true. Look at fast food—it is fast and inexpensive, but usually the least tasty food and almost null of any healthful benefits. This is where other countries that relish the cooking process and sharing a long slow meal with laughter and fun has it over you.

This also ties into the belief that faster equals easier which equals more. More money, more time, more things, more success, more admiration and again, we say that this is not true. Each person, their growth, their artistic endeavors, and their learning and evolution within themselves are the rewards. It is in the journey not the destination.

Now we see you that you are sighing because you believe this well-known statement is one that only those who've succeeded and have all the rewards—money, success, big houses and fast cars, or even spiritual awakening can say this because they already have them. And they don't know how you feel because they have it and you just want it.

But this is where your problem lies because they were once where you are—wanting. Then they did the race and worked as fast as they could to get what they wanted. Now they sit having walked the road and having achieved what they wanted and they are telling you that the joy, the gifts, and the fun were all during the times they were getting where they were going. Not in the end result, reward, titles, payoff or what have you. **They are sitting on 'top' as you think telling you that they did not find the joy on the top of the mountain, but they are recalling that the true joy was in the climb—the moments that they were lost in doing what they loved.** When they met others and laughed and created joy with them, and in the small moments that seemed insignificant were actually the greatest joy for them.

So do not discount these statements and messages as flippant or that they do not understand how you feel, for they do. If you slow down and take a moment and really savor what they have shared with you, you will not be sitting on the mountain sad that you did not take more time to relish the small things. You will not have any regrets that you didn't think of others more or just take time to sit and watch nature or pat yourself on the back, sip lemonade and just enjoy feeling the sunshine warm your skin. Take the time now to say to yourself that you are doing a fine job, that you are making such wonderful progress. Reward yourself with a moment to just be and appreciate all that you've learned and how you've grown. Even if that moment is a whole day!

You see our child, you will not win by making it there first. **There is no finish line; you will always learn more.** We know that you are dedicated to your own evolution because you want to live happily, pain-free, and with abundant joy. But you do **not** do that by putting your head down, gritting your teeth to get through this day and the next, until that one day when you wake up in Hawaii in your home and in the bliss you dream of.

No matter where you are right now in terms of money, fulfillment, spiritual awakening, health, love and everything else that is important to you, you must appreciate and relish

the beauty around you. Celebrate each new discovery, take deep breaths and smile. Behold the beauty of nature around you. Listen more intently when someone speaks to you. Smile more, dance more, laugh more, skip, put your arms up and stretch and know that you are on the right path. There is no wrong one. **Love you, now, perfectly incomplete.** Don't stop dreaming and looking ahead but only in your peripheral vision, because if you do not focus on the now, you will miss the beauty, perfection, miracles, joy, fun, laughter and all the magic that is there for you to see today.

Yes, we know that each day you are in a bit of amazement that the answers we share with you are usually not what you would expect to the question you asked. We do this so you know that it is guidance and you really are receiving our loving input, but also because it keeps you on your toes. We would not want you to become bored in your journey for self-discovery and if you received answers the way that you thought it may be said, you may fall asleep. We want you to enjoy each and every moment for every second contains beauty, insight, love, joy, learning, growing, and more of who you are.

One last piece of advice for today if we may—please stop looking at yourself as someone who needs to be fixed. You are so hard on yourself and approach your evolution with a very minimal amount of love. You are not broken and you do not need to be fixed. You do not need to grit your teeth and find the answer so you can then be happy and fulfilled and full of joy. You are perfect right now, yes feeling tired, back feeling unstable, with the roll of extra fat on your stomach, hair unkempt, even the new age spot that you just discovered on your temple.

You are perfection for what we see is a huge, glorious shining light full of multiple facets of colors that radiate and move with you. Your dedication to bettering yourself, and your deep drive to find what you know exists but eludes you so that you can share this secret with others is truly a sight to behold. Your ability to look at each scar with tears in your eyes, forgiveness in your heart, and an open soul to see what you may have learned is humbling and inspiring.

There is nothing more that you need, no success that will make your light more breathtaking, no amount of money that can compare to your infinite worth, no words that can truly explain the love that you are.

Today and each day forward, we implore you to take a few moments and kindly tell yourself how wonderful you are at that very moment. How grateful you are for being you. How much you love and are loved. That is the only thing that we ask that you check off of your 'to-do' list. Wink. Now go and smell the roses.

Amen

Letting go of the race mentality, I took a few days off. I relaxed, laughed, and enjoyed myself without expectation. I thought that was the answer, but my back did not get better so now I'm asking for clarification.

Q: *I've taken three days off, relaxed, and did not sit in a chair to let my back heal. It is Monday and I really want to sit in a chair and write and do some work. But my back is still killing me. Is the back pain trying to tell me something that I'm not getting? I'm willing to look at it, I'm just unsure of what the problem is. Please help?!*

A: When you read your question back while waiting to hear us you see certain words pop out at you, *huh?* This time it was 'killing me.' *What is killing you?* The answer is in you, your own guilt, shame, and feeling as though you are not good enough because you don't make enough money and on and on. Congratulations, when you start to see the answers without us telling you, you are 'seeing' the cause and therefore the answer in yourself.

Your pain is a pointer or point of stuck energy. It is stuck at the base of your spine, the foundation of your spiritual system. This is stuff that you have not cleared that is weighing you down. You saw brown or rust-colored junk there in your meditation before this. Like wet old heavy sand which is giving you a visual of the old, stagnant energy and just how weighing it is.

As you are now through months of our messages and over a hundred pages of questions and answers, you now just know on some level that this does not mean something is wrong with you. It does not mean you did something wrong. It is merely your feelings of guilt, sadness, and worthlessness that have created this heavy old dank junk that is impeding your energy flow.

This is the time for you to sit with yourself and forgive yourself. Yes, we have, well actually we said that so you can understand, but we never needed to forgive you. For one, we are non-judgmental so we never thought you did something wrong so therefore, we never felt the need to forgive you. You are forgiven before you act. You do not do 'right and wrong' in our eyes, just actions that result in consequences. Your feelings about your actions and the consequences create the outcome.

All of your actions, reactions, and consequences are self-inflicted if you will. So you are the only one that judges. This is not a bad system in that it teaches you to choose your actions from a place of self-love so that your results are to your liking. **However, the problem arises when you hold onto what you consider a 'mistake' that you've made.** You felt pain or remorse for your choice so you found out it was not the choice you would have made if you knew the outcome. Instead of filing the choice away under the label 'actions not to take' you buried self-loathing for choosing wrongly, which eventually will manifest into pain—spiritual, emotional, and then physical pain.

You have worked through so much and now are getting down to deep-seeded root pain that is at the very base of your being. This is good! Celebrate instead of choosing sadness or feeling stuck. This means that you are nearing the end with the small, trivial issues in your life and you have now graduated into a deeper understanding. You now have the insight and tools to really get down to the heart of the matter.

Fun huh? Did you ever think when you felt the glumness of feeling your back pain come on that it should be something that should be celebrated? Yes, dear one you have yearned for and worked toward this for some time. You are now at the cusp of the rest of your life—the life that you want. **Free of unnecessary pain, suffering, and sadness caused by misinterpreting your reason for being here.** In this lifetime on this earth, you are here to learn, experience, grow and so on. You are not here to be given choices and then have to pay penance if you choose the wrong one. You simply see the result of your choice, decide if this is to your liking, file it away to use in future endeavors, and then happily move on to the next thing.

You are meant to have joy in every moment, not pain or sadness. You are meant to have your intuition and sixth sense to use as a navigation system, and you have empathy and compassion as a tool to love not only one another but yourself. Unfortunately, the self-love part is the hardest to see. Not only does it elude most because of what we were taught, but even as adults we have a blind spot when it comes to being as kind to ourselves as we would others. This is because we can't see ourselves, mainly our own eyes. Yes, we can briefly in the mirror but we can't connect with ourselves through our eyes without a mirror.

We put so much credence in what we 'see' with our eyes as humans because we believe that they are the windows to the soul and this may be the case, but there are other tools to 'see' the soul. **Most importantly, we have the 'feeling' of the heart.** You know when you feel and just know something. This is a stronger system of knowing that is discounted because of the lack of tangibility. We like to see or feel with our fingers, but when you can tap into the 'feeling' ability you have with you heart, you will know not only how to measure the unseen but you will be able to more easily have compassion for yourself and others. You will also find using or relying on your intuition to be much easier because those feelings cannot be manipulated by physical means, such as a sad girl using makeup to generically make her eyes appear bright. You will be much less inclined to judge people based on physicality because you will be able to feel beneath that to what is below. Then will you know you, know them, and live a more peaceful and joyous life, free of judgment, pain, and sadness.

Today, you will need quiet and time to go and lay with yourself. Repeat—*Self, I love you and I'm sorry that I've judged you. Thank you for always trying to help me. I do not need you to hold onto any gunk to hide it from me, for I'm ready to let it go. I know that holding it is hurting you, hurting me, and I no longer wish to cause myself pain. I let it go knowing that I've always tried my best with all that I knew at the time. I will continue to learn better ways and continue to joyfully learn more. I release any stuck feelings, guilt, and junk that is impeding the flow of energy within me. I see the junk leaving my body and the universe transmuting it easily. I am free, I am happy, I am healthy, and I am whole. I am loved.*

Amen

Q: *My back pain has eased some today, although I did have to take muscle relaxers last night for the pain. It does help but leaves me feeling tired, dehydrated, and just blah today. I used to refuse to take*

medication when my back has been injured before but then it takes so much longer for it to heal. I don't like medications; I never have and very rarely take anything. I do take quite a few supplements as our food is so depleted by the time we eat it. I've also had this deep disdain for pharmaceutical drugs. I just think they are a copout for dealing with things. The only time I take anything is a couple times of year if pain is really awful. I think that medication is completely overused and over-prescribed in this country from pain meds to anti-depressants. I'd like to let my dislike for them to go and not feel judgmental of myself when I really need to use them and judgmental of others who are on meds whether long or short term. Obviously, I have some issue with them or I wouldn't feel so strongly about them, right? Thank you.

A: As you know and have experienced, it is incredibly difficult to be in a positive, happy, or relaxed frame of mind when you are in pain—whether that is physical, mental, or spiritual pain. This is why so many self-medicate whether that is through illegally obtained or prescribed pharmaceutical drugs, 'street' drugs, or through legal means with alcohol. They numb you. Temporary numbing can be a good thing during acute pain or injury so that you can relax and center your thoughts to the positive place for healing to occur.

Continued use or abuse is counterproductive because you are not working on the problem that causes the pain, you are just avoiding it. You are one who likes to look at the pain, find the cause, and implement a solution to fix the underlying cause. This is productive. Taking a pill to numb the pain when you have gotten yourself to a place that you are in so much pain that you cannot sleep or sit without excruciating discomfort is a smart choice because this allows you to relax, and let your body heal. **By including your understanding of the cause of the pain and releasing emotional pain while you rest is the optimal permanent fix.**

Your dislike of drugs and numbing of problems is your drive to feel better permanently. You have tried the numbing tool for avoiding your pain in the past and realized that not only does it not work, but it exacerbates the problem leaving you with bigger problems in the end. Your dislike stems from your drive to overcome avoidance of doing the next thing. This can be a good thing for your growth yet impede your compassion if you judge others.

Just because it is right for you to face what is causing your discomfort by trying to find a solution, you know that not everyone is at that place. We all need to learn in our own time and in our own way. Also, although you are facing and looking at stuff now, you have buried stuff most of your life. *Maybe this disdain you feel is how you feel about yourself and your own avoidance?*

'Do not judge thy neighbor,' is something we need to think of daily. They are where they are and will be there until they decide to change it. Criticizing them, speaking ill of them, or condemning them does nothing for them except make them feel worse about themselves. The best thing you can do is be an example and let them know if they ever need anything, you will be there.

If they ever do approach you for help, offer what you have learned and that is it. You cannot fix them, only they can fix themselves. If you give advice and they do not follow it, do not be offended, they were not ready or your message did not resonate with them. And that does not mean that it was not good, it means that it didn't resonate with them. It may with many others. Think about it, you've heard, read, and tried different tools by different people. Many of them you did not care for. That doesn't mean it didn't work for them and many others. It didn't mean that their message wasn't valid or helpful. It just means it didn't resonate with you. Do nothing except wish for them that they receive a guide or message that does. That's it.

Q: *Of course now that I just wrote how much I can't stand taking pharmaceutical drugs the other day, here it has been a week that I've been in pain and my back is still in bad shape. I cannot make it through to bed without taking a muscle relaxer because the pain is so bad. The chiropractor which normally helps did not, and I'm beginning to get frustrated with the pain and the lack of improvement although I've barely sat in a chair or done much for a week now. I did the exercise of speaking to myself to release old stuck junk. I've taken it easy physically and instead of fighting the immobility, I surrendered to it. But here I am six days later and feeling just as bad. Please help. Thank you.*

A: First, you must take a deep breath and relax. Feeling anger or frustration will not allow anything to flow and do nothing for you except exacerbate the pain. We will wait while you take a few deep breaths.

That is much better. Now, that is very good that you surrendered to what is with your back and did not become frustrated by it. *Did you 'speak' to yourself, with the letting go of stuck stuff statement more than once?* No, although it is great that you received the message and did it once, you may find that one time is not enough. In some things, one time is enough but as you have noticed in life, doing something once will not change the pattern. Doing something once usually is not enough to get good at it, master it, or use it to make a change. Say it to yourself numerous times today and see what a difference it makes.

Now there is something else bothering you. You have had another talk with Ricky that has bothered you. Also, you feel your agreement with him is always being changed or broken by him. When this happens all that you thought you knew about him, your relationship, your future, and your life feels unstable. This instability feels awful to you and you can't breathe or relax or feel confident about what your future holds.

Our advice—ignore it. Yes, ignore what he is doing or not doing. Ignore what you think he wants or doesn't want from you. In the great big world, it is trivial. Focus on you. Today you need to think and focus and visualize what you do want. Worrying about the future, your safety or livelihood, or whether this long relationship that you have had that defines you as a pair with him will last, does nothing but cause you to be in a less than desirable place. This worry you hold onto pulls you back down into the dark, cold place where you question everything.

Instead, place yourself in the light, feel the goodness permeate you. Welcome relaxing and loving feelings. Know that you are protected and cared for by so many that you cannot see. We can see that you feel that fear now and don't believe that you will be OK. Listen to us. You will be healthy, happy, wealthy, loved, fulfilled, and better than ever no matter what relationship you are in or are not in. Surrender to God's love, the universal love, however you want to hear it. You have much to share and do and be. You do not need to suffer anymore. You owe no penance. You did nothing wrong. You are whole, beautiful, smart, loved, and protected always.

You seek specifics as this grand overview does not complete the picture for you. You ask about how you will go on. *Where will you live? What will you do?* Open your heart, mind, and soul to this universal love. It will provide. *How?* With synchronicities.

Repeat—*I embrace the love of the universe. I elect to get on this path to flow with love, grace, and fulfillment. I elect to live to my fullest potential. As I step into this path, I release from me any pain, suffering, sadness, lack of, neediness, unworthiness, and all non-loving stigmas that I have taken on or identified with. I no longer need them to make myself suffer. I deserve love, I deserve fulfillment, and I deserve to live a good, happy, healthy, wealthy, exciting life because I'm me.*

I do not need anyone or anything to do or be this. I need just be. I surrender to the beautiful flow of love of the universe. I will look for only the good and the serendipities that cross my path. I have faith that all is well now and always. I will no longer judge my worth or happiness based on those who surround me. I will treat myself with respect, love, joy, and all that I deserve. I will no longer feel the need to suffer or give myself anything less than full love always and in all ways. I am perfect just as I am today—no matter what my weight, hair, or anything looks like, I am perfect. For my worth is not based on what others feel, think, do, or say. It is only based on the fact that I acknowledge my inner perfection and open my arms to all that is mine—all of the love, joy, happiness, health, wealth, and all that I am wanting. All I have to do is open my arms, heart, and eyes to what the universe has been waiting for me to see all along.

I am. And because I am, I deserve all that I'm wanting. And I am healthy and happy, live joyfully and lovingly, and see the world through the wondrous eyes of a child. I say yes to the wealth, joy, happiness and all of the things that can be mine if I just say yes.

So yes, I am me. Yes, I open myself to all of the good, love, happiness, great health, abundant wealth, excitement, joy, and fulfillment that I am. I am ready. I am open. I am worthy. I am. Thank you oh so generous universe for making all of these wonderful things possible and so easily available to me. I with joy and happiness accept these gifts from you.

With Gratitude

Amen

Maybe it was a gift for the work I did with releasing the pain that manifested as back pain. *Or was it that I wanted to know more about "Changing Woman," and this was an opportunity that could be a portal for this?* It could be as simple as I am opening up to seeing things differently than before, or a combination of all of the above. Whatever the reason, it was another amazing experience that felt a little too succinct to be just coincidence.

Saturday morning, Ricky surprised me by taking me to the Heard Museum in Phoenix, which is known for sharing its extensive American Indian Art and cultural collections. I wanted to take the guided tour so we could learn more than we would by just looking at the displays ourselves.

It was interesting and full of beautiful things, but what really blew me away were the inexplicable experiences that occurred for me. The first happened in the 'schooling' exhibit. I had no idea and found tears in my eyes while hearing about the civilizing schools where native children were forced from their homes and made to attend by armed white men. They learned to be civilized into the white man's way of living by wearing uniforms and having their hair cut. This was especially devastating to them because in their culture they only cut their hair on certain occasions. It was an extension of their selves and depending on the tribe, had significant meaning to them whether it was a symbol of their spirit or knowledge.

The before and after group photos drew me in. My eyes seemed to be taken over by a high tech lens that zoomed in on one particular boy. Beyond my control or logical reasoning, I drew in a sharp breath and felt my heart beating so loudly that my temples were pulsating. I could swear that I knew him. Overcome with a feeling of love, I was confused why I felt like I was seeing from his eyes and looking in a mirror. Either I loved him or I was him or both. The group had moved on and I reluctantly walked away.

Barely able to concentrate, I was grateful that the tour ended just minutes later. In this room there were cubicles with different toys, games, information, or videos playing introducing us to more about the individual tribes. One caught my attention and I went over to it. It was a video of a girl running, then dancing in the center of her tribe. They were doing different things that appeared to be part of a ceremony. After a few minutes it ended and the words "Apache Changing Women Ceremony," appeared on the screen. Again, I felt myself involuntarily drawing in a breath of surprise. Here again was the reference to "Changing Woman."

For many days, I saw flashes of the ceremony that celebrated a girl transitioning from childhood to womanhood. It had to be a sign. The merging of the physically demanding event that aided in her spiritual attunement and preparation for taking on her role as a woman by contributing to her tribe. I definitely felt like this was a message for me and was full of gratitude for it and for the miracle of synchronicities of life. Humbled and yearning to learn more, the day left me strengthened to keep going, to keep asking questions, and to keep hearing and applying the answers.

15

Giving Away My Power

I KNOW THAT WRITING, ESPECIALLY LEARNING and sharing these experiences is part of my life's purpose. I guess what makes me question this is the lack of money flowing into my life at the moment.

Q: *I woke up with this great idea this morning about starting a website. I think it could be wonderful for the world, yet it would cost a lot of money to start. Just as the books I wrote that are waiting to be illustrated cost money. I want to be open to the universe bringing in the abundance to do these things that will help people. I've had these books ready to go for a long time and have not had the right illustrator appear yet. How do I ask for the abundance I would like and know that it will come and not become frustrated when it hasn't yet so I don't impede its arrival? I want to believe in this law of attraction that you bring to yourself what you want, and the belief that I've read about from Abraham Hicks that it can be as easy as asking and being ready to receive. I'm not sure what is correct or not, or how to go about it. I have so many great ideas that would be beneficial or helpful for people and it seems to be what makes my heart sing. I'm just finding it difficult to see how to attract the abundance to bring these ideas to fruition. Thank you for your help!*

A: As with anything, learning to do something takes time and patience. Also, as with many things there is not one step or cause that creates anything. It is a collective consciousness that is everything, which we are all a part of. Just as you believe that outcomes are based on a few different actions all converging into one creating a certain situation, attracting what you want to happen to you is along the same lines.

Good health is a conglomeration of a healthy, happy attitude, eating healthy food, exercising, sleeping restfully and fully, and so on. When one of these prongs is not being tended to it throws your health off balance, and feeling your absolute best eludes you. It is the same with all things in this universe. All things are connected; all are of the same importance because when one is neglected all are affected. The effect then is being off balance or unwell. No matter how you use or attend to any one prong with whatever fervor, you still will not reach the ultimate outcome until you tend to all prongs equally.

This balance or learning this balance is the key to all things. It is the same no matter what realm you are looking at. In the area of money, abundance, or the ability to fund a project that you desire is also a multi-pronged approach to fulfilling it. Let's look specifically at what those areas are.

To have abundance, first and foremost you must be in a place to receive. You must be open to the fact that you have asked and that you are willing and ready to receive. This is the main component of it, as explained by previous people. The reason they choose this way to address this may be because this is the area that many have the most problem with.

Giving Away My Power

If you do not feel worthy or love yourself, you cannot be in a place to think that you deserve or will get your request. Getting out of your own way is usually the most challenging obstacle that we face. Sometimes where people get hung up with the teachings is that they say they have done the asking, releasing, and are ready to receive, yet still do not get what they are wanting.

This could be because they haven't addressed their own self-love and ability to feel deserving of receiving, or it could be because they have mastered this step but do not attend to the other prongs in this equation. Because as we said before, nothing is ever one sided or comes to manifestation without other corresponding areas that are just as important.

Maybe these teachers that speak of the 'law of attraction' believe that since this is usually the most difficult area, if they taught people the typically hardest prong, they would easily incorporate the other prongs that they may feel are common sense. They may not be.

So we have the 'believing' aspect that you are worthy to receive and that if you ask, release, and are ready to receive your wish shall be granted. **Another prong to the success of your manifesting is to know that it will come without time frames, constraints, or in certain appearances.** This may seem like the same prong as belief, but it usually falls under a separate one because it is an ongoing belief that is lived daily by knowing that it is coming and looking for the signs or pointers from the universe. This is where it becomes more than just a belief, it becomes tangible. If you believe that it will come, yet you do not look for the help or signs to take certain roads or meet certain people, you are ignoring the help that is coming your way.

Now this may not be because you don't believe or you are just impatient, **but it could be because you are looking for the finished dream or outcome you want to land in your lap completed.** This is your job to take the pieces given to you, utilize them, and continue to take open-minded steps towards your desired outcome.

You cannot say, I want this illustrated picture book series to be completed this year, kick back sipping a Pina Colada and expect to walk into a store in a few months and see them. You have to wake up every day ready yet patient to seize any opportunities that cross your path. When they do, you thank the universe for sending you this help and work with it. The synchronicity will continue and become more powerful as you become better at discerning the help sent and being grateful for it. Sometimes people struggle with this step because either they are faltering with step one of having faith, or they are missing the subtle pointers, clues, or help that has been sent. It may not be or appear as you expect, so you have to enter each day with the eyes of a child, seeing the magic in the universe. Then you will easily see the serendipities that swirl around you.

Finally, if you do believe, have faith, are patient, and approach each day with open eyes and an open heart to see the help and then utilize it, the only thing you have left to do is to do the next thing. Only after being thankful for the thing before it. **Gratitude begets more of itself.** If you are grateful for even the tiniest article that you read today that talked about ways to go about writing or meditation or whatever it was that could be a precursor to the next step in your journey, you will get more and more of what you are wanting. Think of it like a snowball rolling downhill, it may start out small and not looking like much, but as it rolls down the hill it will get bigger and bigger, gaining speed and mass until you have the biggest snowball you've ever imagined sitting at your feet where you stand at the bottom of the hill.

Believe, be patient, see the small things, be grateful, keep working and envisioning, have more gratitude and hold your vision. The universe will bow to your wishes; it will bring the magic that you will need to perform your big finale. It just may take a little time, a lot of belief, a lot of gratitude, and a little work and your dream will become a reality.

And by the way, *why do you think we are all here? To show each other up, make more than another, put each other down? Hate each other?* No we are here to encourage, hold up each other's dreams and be the angels that do, say, and offer the tiny little thing we needed that day to stay focused on our dreams. Work together, help one another, and give freely for you will always receive it back.

If there is anything that you can believe to help you along your journey more quickly, it is that we are all angels for one another. So do not think you are alone or have to do it alone.

Enjoy your day, with love.

Q: *I had an epiphany this weekend about my happiness and others role in it. Although I thought that I took responsibility for my own happiness, I realize that I have not. My moods or how I viewed a day or a weekend were always based on how things were with my significant other, my daughter, or my friends. If we got along and all went smoothly, I thought that I had a great weekend. If they let me down or did something I didn't like, I became sad, sullen, and thought that not only did that weekend suck, but so did my relationship with them and even my happiness with myself and my life. Wow, what power I gave to everyone but myself. How wrong I've been to place that burden of my happiness on whoever is in my life. I know that I should be happy with me and have fun regardless of others behaviors, so why do I give them so much power over my happiness and how can I have fun every day regardless of who or what is going on around me? I guess I thought if the ones I love were happy or not, that determined if I was happy or not. I*

want to love and be there for them without basing my whole life on their actions or feelings. Thank you for your help and insight.

A: How wonderful that in the midst of your sadness this weekend, you realized this. This is wonderful! You usually go to the helpless role that depending upon who is doing what or how they feel is how you see yourself.

It does not matter if your partner is sad, you can be there for him, offer a helping hand, or try to help him, but ultimately it is his choice whether he responds or not. And no, this does not mean that you failed, or that you did something wrong, it means that at that time he chose to be in whatever space he chose.

You have taken the responsibility for the happiness of those you love. **It is not your responsibility, nor is it theirs to make sure you are happy.** Now in a loving and reciprocal healthy relationship, we do think of our loved ones by giving to them, and spending our time on and with them. However, giving your love, time, and energy is where it stops. You are not responsible for them. Think about it—if your significant other was mad at you, stomped out of the house and went and drank a lot and drove home, and on his way he crashed into a car killing both the driver and passenger, *Would it be your fault?* No, definitely not! Because you two had a fight does not mean that you are responsible for his poor choices afterwards.

It is the same no matter how large or small the 'problem' is with anyone you love. **We are all responsible for ourselves, period.** This is difficult at times when we love people so deeply, especially when they are our children and especially if we made poor choices that our children mimicked. However, by the time they are old enough to live on their own, they know that actions result in consequences, and good choices from poor choices. Just because they chose a poor one, it does not make it anyone else's fault. This is the hard lesson of growing up and learning personal responsibility.

Now it is a parent's job to teach their children and demonstrate positive behaviors and discuss choices and consequences with their children. This happens all throughout childhood when they make a choice, the parent is there to discuss those choices with corresponding consequences. These smaller matters are meant to teach us these lessons with much less repercussions so we hopefully have mastered this lesson by the time we come of age.

Unfortunately, many parents are blinded by their own unresolved pain and do not do a great job of this with their children. Therefore the cycle continues where people walk around in a fog of poor choices and pain so that they can't clearly see their own lives let alone parent someone else in the best manner.

We cannot feel guilty when we finally do wake up. We should maybe bring this to our child's attention that we realize we were asleep during their younger years, apologize, and share the insight now. It is never too late. But we cannot feel guilty for every choice they make as an adult for we did the best we could do at the time with what we knew.

Doing this will curtail a lot of sadness, pain, guilt, and living in the past. As for living in the now and maintaining our personal happiness and balance regardless of the pain, chaos, or drama going on around us, this may be even a more difficult task. This is why you may find yourself severing relationships with friends, family, or lovers because it is much easier to remove yourself from the situation rather than learn to separate your happiness from those you love when they are in pain and subsequent turmoil.

Sometimes, circumstances may not allow you to just leave when all this is happening. And although it may make you feel trapped, look at it more like the best and most intensive practice you can get on remaining in touch and in tune with you. It is very easy when you are alone on the top of a mountain to meditate and feel full of love and calmness. When you are in a situation where there is unrest, dislike, chaos, and drama is the real test if you are deeply rooted in being your authentic self and not reacting out of pain.

There is a fine line between loving someone and helping them, and enabling or being disrespected. All that you can do is remain calm and centered and rooted in your own self-love and respect. **For when you come from a place of self-love and respect, you will never feel the need to be drawn into someone else's pain.** You can sympathize, hold them, give them insight, and offer thoughtful gestures to them without sitting down in their pain with them. And loving you and expecting to be treated with a certain amount of kindness because that is how you treat them, can be your greatest gift to them and to yourself. You are modeling how you wish to be treated with how you treat them. Do not allow their pain, whether they are screaming, calling you names, or pushing your buttons of insecurity or whatever, to allow you to forget your center.

This does not mean you take abuse, you do not. But you do not feed into their pain or better, you do not feed their pain. Anger, sadness, and all other emotions need to be fed to keep going. Think about it. If someone is yelling at you and you yell back, they yell louder and then it could escalate into name calling or even a physical altercation. But if someone begins to yell at you and you tell them in a calm and understanding voice that you understand they are upset and you would love to hear them out, but that you will not do so if they are yelling, most times they will come back down. There is nothing there to feed the pain. If they continue regardless of how calm you remain, you can tell them that you want to discuss it with them at a later time when you both can talk kindly and then leave the situation.

It is really simple, but it does not feel simple a lot of the time if you are operating from your own pain. If you come from love and a centered, self-respectful place, it will always be a gift to you because you will know that you did or gave all that you can in the best manner you could. When you allow your pain to flare up and take control, you then have regret and feel weak because you let it get the best of you.

The best way to alleviate this is to keep working on letting go of or releasing any old stuck patterns of pain that you still hold onto. This way you do not need to try so hard to come from your center or from love because this will be how you always approach things. When there is no pain, you do not have to feel like you can't be around or in certain situations because you will always be good with you, wherever you are, and no one else's pain will trigger anything in you because there won't be any pain to trigger.

As we have said many times before, **working on you is the first and most important aspect of healing you, your relationships, and your life.** When you are happy, healthy and approach all that you do from a place of love, your life will be peaceful whether you are on top of a mountain or in the middle of a bar room fight. Although by then you most likely will not find yourself in places or situations where you will be surrounded with that pain to begin with.

Amen

I'm still struggling with being OK with change. Losing jobs, getting new ones, and the ebb and flow of life are guaranteed. I guess if one goes before another comes it makes me feel uneasy. I want to just let go and believe, it just seems so difficult sometimes.

Q: *I know I've probably asked this before, but I've either forgotten or need to hear more. I'm in a situation where over the last two months, I've lost writing jobs due to them selling their businesses, and I now find myself without any income from writing. My other avenue of income through selling supplements is at an all-time low. I'm trying to smile and say thank you to the universe for moving stuff around so that I am able to take on whatever comes into my life. I just wonder why losing the old job first is necessary. I don't want to worry about where or when the money is coming to me and where, what, when, and how I will receive money or a new avenue for it to flow into my life. Although I'm trying to be positive, I feel the old fear nipping at my ankles. When I feel this I say a positive affirmation about money flowing to me, I thank the universe for knowing the best way for fulfilling what I'm wanting, I'm being proactive in promoting my businesses, and I'm browsing job postings and so on. However, I still find myself unable to breathe deeply or feel confident that all will be well and that bills will be paid, money will flow in and so on. Do you have any advice for me? Thank you.*

A: Isn't it funny that you used, *'fear nipping at my ankles,'* as your way of describing your situation today. We say this because although you've done well in hearing and applying some of the tools one can use to help center themselves with the flow of universal energy, you haven't learned to fully feel or believe it as of yet. It does not consume you as it would have not too long ago, which is great! It is an improvement, but it still lingers down near your ankles. You haven't been able to fully step out of that fear yet. Fear that you are not enough, your contribution is not good enough, that you will not have enough and all that encompasses that poverty mentality that you align yourself with.

So, first you must congratulate yourself on the fact that you have learned some helpful tools and that you have used them, and finally that they have helped you deeply. Then we move onto diving deeper into believing, trusting, and getting to a place of knowing instinctively that the universe will provide as long as you stay positive, grateful, focused on what you do want (not what you don't want) and allow her to work her magic. You are right that you must also keep your eyes open and be ready when the next step appears. We feel your apprehension that you may miss it so you are straining your eyes that you may not be good enough to do it and so forth. These are fears born from insecurity, from feeling that you as a being and what you have learned are not enough.

So, this is where we begin today. Ask yourself some questions... *Do I try my best on a daily basis? Do I get up and try to use what I learned yesterday and apply it with love and compassion today? Am I a person who has love and skills to contribute to this society?*

Once you can answer yes to these, then the *'I am not good enough'* theory will evaporate. We saw that you answered yes quickly and easily to the first and second questions, but when you asked yourself the, *"Am I a person who has love and skills to contribute to this society?"* you hesitated and wanted to say yes, but there was doubt.

This is where your problem lies. You feel that you are not good enough to draw to yourself or deserve money because you feel that you do not have enough love and skills to contribute to society. This is your block in feeling free to trust that the universe is clearing the way for you to learn and grow more while having money come to you easily.

Why is that? Yes, we are asking you a lot of questions today and making you think about, feel, and 'know' the answer to these questions. Not because we are trying to be hard on you, just the opposite, we are trying to show you that we each have a higher self, a knowing that is innate. We are born with this guidance system that will help us navigate through our lifetime. **It is all knowing and when you learn to trust this system, you will no longer fear anything because you know that it is leading you towards all that you are wanting always.**

The big problem is that you do not treasure yourself; therefore, you do not even see the love and skills that you have shared with so many already, and you have just begun. You feel that what you do is not good enough or hard working enough. But you know deep down that connecting with us or allowing energy to flow through you and sharing it in this way can be tiring. It is work. Just because it is sitting in a comfy chair instead of sweating outside, you are still working.

Think about your brother who worked an extreme amount of hours doing manual labor yet when he began a new job that required that he sit and learn using his mind instead of his hands, he would come home exhausted after half of the amount of work. Using the mind is just as, if not more taxing then using the body. Think of it like a muscle, it does get a bit easier as you exercise it. When you first began having these question and answer sessions with us you found yourself exhausted after a few minutes and had to push yourself to finish. Now you look up and you've been doing it for an hour and you can still continue.

Connecting with your higher self and opening yourself up to divine communication is an amazing skill. Having the compassion and love that you do by having been in touch with some of the most dark, deepest places one can be and coming back around and wanting to help people is a beautiful attribute. You should honor these things, and although you have lived so very modestly for years having put your daughter's wants and needs before your own, you have worked very hard. You cannot measure your worth or contribution by the money you've made. And somehow, you've always eaten well and lived in a nice home.

Think about it. *Did you have a teacher in school that did, said, or gave you something that was priceless?* Yes. *Do you think she was fairly rewarded monetarily for it?* Right, no because there is no amount of money that can buy what she gave you. You still remember your conversations with her till this day. If she were paid royalties like a rock star is she would be a billionaire, not only from you but from the many other lives she changed as well. *(I have to interrupt and say yes, thank you Ms. Patricia McGee—you were an amazing teacher.)*

Touching people's hearts with words, helping them to see stuff in a new light that can change their very direction for the rest of their lives, allowing people to cry tears of joy or understanding because you shared something that you felt so deeply is a priceless gift. You have no understanding of how many people's lives that you have already transformed for the better.

Now you may not understand the depth of that yet and may never, but what you need to do is know that you do give your all each day and in every way that you can. And yes, we all need days off where we relax, recuperate, and just be. But on a regular basis you are doing your best. That is enough. You are enough. You do not need to do or be anything more than you already are right now, at this very moment.

And once you believe that you deserve money and the security, ease, all that it provides you with, money will flow to you easily and abundantly. Stop looking at the skills you do not possess, stop looking for why you can't get a job that you love, and start believing that you are a capable, smart, loving, compassionate and skilled woman who deserves to do something that she loves to do. No one deserves it more or less than you. We all deserve it for being here, being us, learning, growing and trying each day. That is enough, it always has been. The only thing that you need now is to believe.

Walking on clouds now huh? What does fear nipping at the ankles feel like? You've forgotten already. Now go and sit with this feeling for as long as you need. And when you forget it and feel a nipping starting, come back and read this again, meditate on how you are perfect and thank the universe for bringing all of the circumstances together so that you may be you every day, enjoying, loving, and sharing you with the world.

You are beautiful. We love when we see your recognition of your beauty and worth, and how we are all one shining in your eyes.

It is priceless.

When I feel unsettled about finances, relationships, or any area of my life, it makes me question things that I typically would not. It's almost as if I'm shook up and everything spooks me. I really want to feel grounded and confident in myself no matter what changes are going on around me, but at times it seems impossible.

Q: *I feel like I'm too sensitive. I don't hate that I feel things deeply, just that it can change my mood and day so abruptly. For example, I may wake up in a good mood, feel like the day is going well, and then bam, someone says something to me and I question everything. I guess I need to feel like I know how I feel, how others feel about me, and how my life is going to be that day to feel comfortable. I don't like not knowing what is going to happen or feeling uncertain because it feels like I'm free falling with no parachute. I want to be more grounded in who I am, confident that no matter who does what or what happens that I will be OK. I don't want to walk like I'm walking in a mine field just waiting for something to explode. I guess this makes me feel like I'm prepared for when something is going to happen so I'm not taken off guard, which I do not like at all. I want to be one of those people that nothing bothers them and going with the flow seems easy and natural. What can I do to let go and become OK with what is and what will be, no matter what? Thank you so much for your insight!*

A: Oh Amy, please don't become upset when we say this because we are not trying to avoid giving you the answers you are looking for, but it all leads back to the same answer. **Self-love. If you love yourself you will trust yourself. If you trust yourself, you will be confident that you will be OK as you say, no matter what life throws at you, no matter who comes into**

your life or goes, or whether you lose a job or not. Faith is born from trust. You lack trust.

Do not beat yourself up for this my dear, you have to find and build it as an adult for you were not given the ability to do so when others are learning this. We come in when we are born and between then and five develop our sense of love, affection, and trust from our basic needs being met. When one experiences some of the perils that you did in those young years, this trust is not developed. This is not your fault. Not knowing if you were safe, where you were going to be sleeping, if you were going to have food to eat, worrying if someone was going to hurt you or leave you or remember you were all consuming.

So first, you must forgive and let go. Your mom was sick and alcohol consumed her. She did not and could not meet your basic needs. For this we are sorry, and as you know, she is so full of remorse when she sees the pain her actions inflicted on you. If she could reach through and hold you she would. She does watch over you more than you can fathom, but this cannot change the insecurities that her prior actions inflicted. This is your job. **So forgiving her, letting it go, and doing this for you is the first step.**

Think of it this way. You did all of this nurturing, loving, caring, feeding, and taking care of your daughter, so you are more than capable of doing this for yourself. In that knowledge you can say to yourself that you did a wonderful job with her so you have nothing to fear, you can take care of you. Next, you need to focus on getting those things you crave from yourself. We know that interaction—hugs, praise, affection and so on is a human necessity but just as with love, we need to begin with ourselves.

You are stuck in that infantile phase where you want someone to love you and meet your basic needs. That was a horrible time for you but it is long over. To reach the point that you would like, to live the life you want, you would need to release the need to have someone recreate what you lacked from your mother. You can give this to yourself. You are not selfish or self-centered to really think about what you like and give this to yourself. Think of something you would love to eat and go get it or make it for yourself. Treat you like you did your daughter, with a gentle touch, with a kind voice, with reverence. You are just as beautiful and perfect as she, so *why don't you feel that you deserve what you gave her? Maybe because you've carried this lack of mentality from childhood through with you?* You feel that because you didn't get these needs met that you don't deserve to receive them. This is NOT true. You did deserve it, you do deserve it. You cannot go back, your mom can't come back from the dead in the body she used to occupy and hold you to her bosom and rock you and make up for what she did not do when you were young.

Now, you take the reins and give to that little girl all that she deserves. Then you will feel whole. Then you will no longer feel a lack that seeps from your pores. Then you will no longer be waiting for someone to give you what you are lacking. It is no one else's job now, it is yours. It may seem silly or feel weird, but so what. You want to heal, try it.

Look yourself in the mirror as your counselor Toni taught you, and each day tell that little girl that you love her, that you are there for her, that she is not alone. Tell her that you're so grateful that you have delicious food to eat, a beautiful home that you live in, people that love you, and a beautiful heart that you will share with the world. If you want to heal this aspect of you, only you can do this. You have been given these tools now it is up to you to use them.

See healing as it is, a process. It can feel long and difficult, but that is usually not because the process is. It is usually because of a lack of self-love, we keep abandoning the small, easy tasks that will get us there. Think about it, how long or tiring or cumbersome is it to look yourself in the eye in the mirror first thing in the morning and say, *"Good morning beautiful, I love you. We are going to have a* *great day and I'm so grateful for you." What a few seconds?* But you have never done this more than a few days in a row because you fell back into the old patterns of wanting it from someone else. Your significant other, your daughter, and your friends are not responsible for loving you whole and completely. That is their job for themselves because believe it or not, most people walk around with some wound from childhood.

Why do you think there is so much unrest, quarreling, and hatred in the world? Not because people dislike others so much, because they dislike themselves. They do not love themselves, so they see this mirrored back to them by others. Instead of recognizing their own issues and working with them, they take out their frustration on others. They are really sad and lacking love but they feed into their pain and lash out at others which only furthers the depth of their pain and sorrow. It is a sick cycle that has continued through the generations.

Only when people stop looking elsewhere for love, only when they look inside and see the wounds that need to be healed and dedicate themselves to loving themselves whole, will there be peace. Peace in relationships of all kinds.

So what you are seeking is not to be grounded in a religion or a group or a label or a family, what you seek is to be grounded in your own awareness of self-love. When you practice and become good at loving yourself is when you will feel stable and comfortable no matter what comes your way. **Because only in the awareness of your own self-love and worth will you know definitively that you are perfect no matter what.** Nothing will be able to shake this once it has become your reality.

So again we say, start with you. Love you. Give to you. For only then will you know infinite love. Only then will you feel OK with all that is no matter where, when, or with whom. You are love. Now go look into those beautiful eyes of yours and tell that little girl how much she is loved. And do not stop this, do this every day for the rest of time. You will be amazed at the wonders of such a simple task. It is all simple, you just can't see it yet. You will. Now go find a mirror.

With love.

16

Remembering Who I Am

UNCHARACTERISTICALLY WIDE AWAKE IN THE middle of the night, I laid there for a few minutes until the pain I felt in my body came to the forefront of my awareness. The aching, the tenderness, and the heaviness I felt seemed to engulf every limb, every joint, and every cell of my being. There was nothing new or profound about this except for the fact that I was awake in the middle of the night for no reason, and the pain was more intense than normal.

Strangely, I wasn't tired but I didn't seem to have the strength to be angry or fight it. Maybe some of my friends' words I was hearing through my meditations were finally getting through. Either way, I opened my arms and faced my palms up, followed by my legs. I looked like I was making a snow angel without the snow.

Lying there in the dark with my eyes closed, I began the unity breath I learned from Drunvalo in *Living in the Heart*. I entered my heart and made a conscious effort to just let go. Typically it is hard for me to just let go and release any thoughts, feelings, or wishes, but it came easily tonight. I literally handed myself over to a higher power. *What did I have to lose?*

I don't know how long I'd laid there before I became aware that I felt completely different. Not only did I not feel any pain, but I seemed to be free both physically and spiritually. My body was so light that it literally felt like I was floating a few inches above the bed. Not daring to lose this window of ecstasy, I quickly closed my eyes again after peaking to verify I was in fact in my bedroom in Arizona.

It felt safe, like being surrounded by the love of thousands of angels. For a moment, I thought maybe this is what heaven feels like. Pure peace, love, support, and freedom to be me, feel me, and love me, yet a small part of a fabric woven together from an unending supply of love. Everything about me seemed to be open, free, and whole. It felt as if each and every cell of my body was breathing in fresh air for the first time after years of suffocating in a smoky dank house.

Suddenly, I became aware that bright white light was emanating from me. It grew so much that I was hardly aware of my body anymore and I felt as if I was actually a part of this brilliant white light. I would liken the feeling to being plugged into or a part of the most beautiful, comforting whole, all-encompassing joy you could imagine.

Although my eyes were still closed, I realized I could see myself from two perspectives at once. Aware that I was in my body, I could also see what was happening from an outside perspective as well. Then three lights appeared, one at a time, lighting up above my head. The first one appeared followed quickly by a second and third directly above one another and spaced perfectly. They were in a perpendicular line like a traffic light, except they weren't connected to each other or anything that I could see. The white light was brightly radiating with just a touch of blue. I felt myself stretch out inside like I was given more space to flow into.

I was aware that below my feet a space was opening up and I could stretch that way as well. It felt like being set free and being allowed to flow into a more spacious and comfortable form then my body had been previously. And with this expansion I was somehow more connected to space and all that exists beyond our earthly comprehension. Then I could see the sides of me open up and the white light came down from the three dots and made a large oval around me, encircling me all the way to my feet. It was so relaxing and beautiful that I continued to just be in that space. I felt as though I had been plugged into a million volts of the most pure, calm, loving, yet exhilarating energy ever.

After a while the light dissipated, but I was still full of energy. There was no way I could sleep so I proceeded to continue reading a book I'd found the day before on the history of Native Americans called *American Indian Prophecies Conversations with Chasing Deer* by Kurt Kaltreider. Everything I read seemed to make perfect sense and like I was meant to read it. No longer questioning, I fully trusted that I was being led to what I needed to learn for the next step in my life. It was simply amazing.

I didn't want the experience to end, but after finishing the book I must have fallen back to sleep because I woke up in the morning to the singing of the birds outside my window. I felt lighter, freer, and more content than ever. What I experienced seemed like an almost unbelievable dream, but an air of knowing surrounded me and I knew that I didn't just dream what had happened. It was a little too outrageous for me to process, so I just let go of how it happened and enjoyed the day and the next.

After a couple of days the euphoria seemed to have dissipated and I sat back down to ask another question. I didn't feel a need to ask about what had happened, like somehow a part of me innately knew even if I didn't understand it logically. I just wanted to move forward and deal with how I was feeling now.

Q: *Today I woke up happy which is good for me, but again feeling pieces of my old self where I am pressed for time, etcetera. I want to live the rest of my life feeling like I did that night—full of love, contentment, trust and full of energy. There really aren't words to describe the bliss I felt. How can I tap into that and live that way all the time? Thank you so much!*

A: Congratulations! **You've experienced a profound step in remembering who you truly are—spirit.** When you did not resist or fight your pain, but let go and trusted, you opened yourself up to the healing that you were wanting. Your spirit opened up because you allowed it to when you let go and trusted yourself, your spirit, and the universe. **The three dots were an activation or turning on your connection to your higher self, the higher realms, and the spirit world.** See you were not straining, like you strained to hear us or see something, you were not begging or pleading or crying out in desperation. You were just being, letting go, trusting. You did not resist or tense or feed into the pain, you just relaxed and let go of it. Resisting is what you have done for so long and many do, so do not beat yourself up. You recoil, go into a fetal position, resist, hold onto the pain, cry out in desperation, but as you know all that did was feed it and continue to give you more of the same. Placing your arms open, your legs apart and opening your heart and releasing allowed you to actually see or experience the perfection of how spirit works.

Yes, it is simple, yet so elusive for most. Your dedication to yourself, your healing, and wanting to find the truth was certainly rewarded. And see as we said, you do not get there by gritting your teeth, or clawing your way there. **It was merely a surrendering, a letting go to what is that showed you what really is.** Now the back pain that forced you to lie still does not seem like a curse any longer *huh*? Much of the time, things that seem to be inconvenient or punishment are really pointers to our enlightenment. *What was* *different this time when you hurt your back?* You surrendered to it. You were OK with what it was. You did not get angry or tense against it or curse it or try to force it to get better faster. You accepted it, you yielded to it, you chose not to fight it or push against it, but instead to rest and surrender to it. **Many times, it can be hard to slow down enough to really be open to the subtle shifts of spirit.** Sometimes, we must be brought to our knees to be ready for this. This letting go brought you to another book that resonated with you and opened you up to a new level. We are celebrating for you, we are so very proud of you.

Now that we have celebrated your accomplishment, we will address your question as to how to live in this space. You want to feel the exhilarating energy yet calmness of living one with spirit and the universe. As you know nothing is constant, think of it like the waves of the ocean. Sometimes, the water is calm and rippling. The waves can be methodic, coming in and out as if following a never changing rhythm. Sometimes they come in slow and huge and awe inspiring. And finally, sometimes they come in choppy and driving and have no rhyme or reason. A spirit's journey on earth can appear very similar.

You've had many extremes in your life from very low lows to exquisite highs like your experience with recognizing your spirit. This allowed you to really experience the difference. But it does not always have to be this hard, and if it is not that is fine too. **There is no wrong or right journey, just the goal of merging with spirit and operating from that love in all that you do.**

As you've experienced with many things, when you become accustomed to something it becomes your norm or your typical point of being. When you become used to it, you may not feel the extreme lows or highs. You will just be. It may take a while to settle into that for you. Do not grit your teeth or become frustrated if you do not feel that elation in the same manner. Just keep opening yourself to being in that place. *Wouldn't that be lovely to feel that good all the time or to become used to operating from that space of calmness and love?* It may not be as dramatic but it will dramatically change how you feel about 'life' and how quickly you travel down your path of discovery and being in your space of your soul's purpose. **Because this is really what you have been striving for and we cannot be fully in or operating from our soul's purpose without first having self-love.**

You are moving along dear one. Celebrate, have gratitude and keep letting go and allowing. For the more that you trust you, your spirit, and the collective spirit of the universe the more joy, happiness, and feelings of ecstasy that will become your normal way of being.

Go forth in spirit and love and know that all is well.

Q: *I've felt so good for the last few days after the previous experience I wrote about. So much so that I did not feel a need to ask a question, I did not feel much pain, and at points I was just so happy that I was giddy. I didn't do anything special, just stuff around the house and relaxed, but I felt like the luckiest girl in the world.*

Yesterday I relaxed a lot as it was a Sunday. I ate minimally and well, got a little sun, swam, and just did a couple of small things around the house. It was a great day and I felt good. I awoke in the middle of the night last night with my hips and back bothering me again. I stretched, took deep breaths and let go. I did fall back to sleep but I didn't feel like I slept well. This morning I felt tired, in pain, aching, and a lot like the old me. I do not want to fall back into this, but I'm not sure what I did or didn't do, awake or asleep to cause this all to return. Help! Thank you.

A: Oh dear one, we see your pain and struggle. You so want to live in the flow of love energy every moment of every day. We are so glad that is your intention as it is the first step to its attainment. Remember reaching this point is not done through struggle, gritting your teeth, or finding some inner brute strength that is so strong it will drag you there aware or not.

For so many years, most of your life in fact, you've felt the need to reach inside and force yourself to go on with pure willpower. You did not want to stop; you did not want to break—down, apart, or into pieces. You watched your mom and brother do that at different speeds and in different ways. And although you used things to distract you, you always pulled yourself back from the edge because you could not let go of the dream that there was something more.

In a way you thought this was good because it got you through by using your anger, sadness, angst and whatnot to fuel you to go on and do the next thing. You learned to do everything this way and it became ingrained into you a way of being that is not beneficial to letting go and letting it flow. It is the opposite.

This is why you have a healing session with someone and you feel amazing and on top of the world, and then within a few days or so you are in pain again. This is also why although you had this amazing experience in the middle of the night of seeing your spirit expand and what being one with the universe is, here you are feeling unwell again. You rode the wave for days and now you are back to the pain before the experience.

This is not because you did something wrong or you aren't good enough to be in that space of bliss. You are that bliss. You deserve to feel that way in all ways, always. You are working towards it; you were given an experience like this so you may know what there is for you, for everyone.

But you do not have an experience and voila, everything is perfect. As we've spoken of before, there are patterns that have become one with your psyche that think they are the 'norm' for you. Your reset point, your homeostasis if you will. You know this isn't true and we know it too. **So, what you are doing with the tools, steps, and realigning daily is changing this reset point to where you want it.**

Please do not look at having these epiphanies and experiences, and then going back to feeling pain as a failure that you couldn't maintain it. Just as in your everyday life you will see that some days are easier than others. Some are happier or more joyous, and some more trying and it is more difficult to feel that joy. This does not make you wrong or not tuned in on the 'off' days.

As we said before, there are ups and down, problems and trying times, less fun and happy days in all lives. This is the nature of things. The goal is not to reach a level of being where you do not experience these issues; the goal is to be in a state of mind or in your heart, where regardless of what the day holds—complete joy and relaxation or issue after issue—that you feel just as calm, worthy, loved, and perfect in your skin. **It is not the lack of problems that determines your bliss; it is the steady stream of love that you are in, in the face of these problems, that provides you with a life of joy and complete satisfaction.**

Think about it...*when are you at your most blissful?* When you have time off, when you are relaxed, and when you feel that you are doing well because all is as you would want it. That is how you want your homeostasis to be, *right?* Yes. So the goal is to feel the way you do on that perfect Sunday, even on Monday when things aren't exactly as you would have it. Even when you have obstacles, even when you don't have the money to pay that bill and you get a call because it is late. Even when you have a ton of things to do and you know that you may not come close to accomplishing them.

We feel that talking of all that you have to do today has stirred understanding in you. You knew as you slept last night all that you had to do today. Unlike yesterday where you did not require anything of yourself except to lounge and enjoy yourself unless you felt like doing a chore or two. **The difference in yesterday and today was the mindset you had before even going to bed.** Your subconscious was already worrying about today, whether you would feel well enough to accomplish all that you had written down on your to-do list. It was already worrying about those bills that are due and where the money would come from. It was already worrying because you had to be up and ready at a certain time, unlike yesterday.

Those free and relaxing Sundays are a great example of how to be every day and in everything you have to do. See it is then that you are in a perfect allowing mode with no blocks or feelings of have to, should, feeling inadequate, worry and so on. That place of allowing is the bar that you should measure everything against. Not to judge or measure yourself, but to measure how much you trust in the universe, being one with what you are wanting and what is, how to treat yourself, and so on.

Yes, it is much more difficult to do this when there are things to do, problems, unexpected situations and whatever else causes you anxiety. And yes, we see you are now over the message of why this happens and want more specifics on how to have or embrace a 'Sunday attitude' every day of the week, in all situations.

There are many ways. **Begin with looking at Mondays and work and chores as something you 'want' to do instead of something you 'have' to do.** Be grateful that you **can** do them, physically and that you have them to do. *Are you not grateful that you have clothes to wash?* You would not dread wash so much if you did not have any clothes. Those who do not have any surely would wash, dry, fold, and put them away with great reverence. Be glad that you can walk and move to do this chore. *See how simple it is to find the gratitude in everything?*

You don't feel like cleaning? Oh, how easy. *How grateful are you to have a lovely home to clean? What if you did not have a home that was attractive and safe and healthy? What if you did not have air condition* in 100 degree weather? What if you did not have food to cook to dirty the dishes that you had to wash? What if you did not have a bed to sleep on, then you would not have sheets to wash? Makes washing them seem trivial now *huh?*

Do not think anything that you 'have to do' as a curse for it is a blessing. And you do not *have* to do anything, but you *want* to because you like your home clean, your sheets fresh, and your clothes washed. **We become accustomed to these luxuries and easily forget that we live very blessed and privileged lives.** It only takes a few minutes to realize just how lucky we are.

Try this tonight. Before bed, say everything that you can think of that you are grateful for like we just spoke of and more. Then express your gratitude for the deep, restorative sleep that you are about to partake in. And don't forget to be grateful that you will wake up feeling refreshed and excited for all the things that you **get to do** tomorrow. Because you are lucky that you get to get up and take a shower, and use all of the conveniences you have to fix yourself food, and work on this amazing computer that allows you to do this.

What a beautiful life, what a mountain of blessings that are bestowed upon you every day. Now take note, *does your body not feel lighter, and do you not feel less pain?* How wonderful it is that just breaking down the problems into the blessings they really are can change how you feel about everything you have, do, and are. *Isn't it funny how a little gratitude can make your life seem like a magical fairytale?*

Your perspective is the lens through which you create your life...see it with eyes of gratitude and live beyond your wildest dreams.

And on that note, go skip around your magical kingdom princess and savor each and every moment.

Good day!

More questions about applying the tools—

Q: *So I did as you instructed yesterday and said all that I was grateful for before bed. I also said thank you for allowing me to sleep peacefully, restfully, and feel restored and energized when awaking. I could not fall asleep but when I did I slept wonderfully. I woke up about seven hours later and felt ready to go but instead of getting up, I laid there and thought I would try to meditate and start the day wonderfully. I fell back to sleep and woke up feeling much worse than the first time two hours before. I felt discombobulated, grumpy, and how I typically feel on mornings where I did not sleep well. I would think more sleep would be more healing, so why did I feel worse? Thank you for the help so I do not repeat that again.*

A: More is not always better. Yes, you need a certain amount usually not less than seven hours of sleep, but more is not always the answer. If you awake feeling all that you are wanting, it is best to begin your day. Falling back to sleep is not the worst thing, it is just a new or different cycle than the first. So, if you are going to go back to sleep, do it mindfully. Repeat what you did before bed last evening and ask for it to continue. See by example, you did it mindfully last evening and you slept, restored, and awoke as you requested. You did not this morning and you awoke in an old pattern.

It may sound so simple that it may seem trivial, but it is not. **Mindfulness in everything that you do is the key.** Do it with intent, meaning, and with gratitude for the outcome you wish. As you saw from your experiment last night, it does work.

Remember that in all things so you do follow the same idea, whether the activity you are going to engage in is passive or not.

Continue to do each and every act with intent, gratitude, and your thoughts on what you **do** want.

This answer period is short and we see that you are understanding and wanting to go on to another question. We are ready when you are.

17

Finding Faith

Q: *At times I feel as though all that I'm learning here in these sessions is so simple and easy to understand and that I'm changing rapidly. Then there are the times where I feel like I can't remember any of it and get so frustrated that I'm back in my old ways or patterns. It's like one minute I'm free and in love with myself and life, and the next I'm the same old frustrated person who came here months and months ago in desperation wanting to know how to change. It can feel very unnerving to be so sure one minute and so unsteady the next. Why is this and how can I stop from slipping back and feeling frustrated? Thank you.*

A: Much of what you have learned here is esoteric, which is not your favorite way. It is very abstract and non-tangible. It is something that you must hear and work with on a level that is ignored in your culture. Because it is unseen and unproven in your scientific measurements, you question it. You feel it is slippery or difficult to work with it because you cannot see it with your eyes, smell it with your nose, or touch it with your fingers.

You and your society have become so reliant on the tangible, which is the least of all that is. It is what you have put your belief in; if you can see it you believe it. This premise has been the glasses from which you have peered through all of your life. You are now learning how to operate from a non-tangible, heart-based, faith-based knowing of those things that exist but you cannot touch them physically. Because of your beliefs and those of your society, you are constantly questioning the validity of what you are doing here, what we are saying to you, and if it will 'work' or not.

Having lost your faith in faith, love, and all that exists that you cannot see, this is like learning from scratch. Think about it, when a baby is taking their first steps, *do they just stand up and walk steadily with a saunter?* No, not at all. They stand still, they sway, they put their arms out to steady themselves, they take a shaky step and sway some more, and then usually they fall down. Then they stand up and try again. This goes on many times before they walk multiple steps in a row, and until they walk steadily on their own.

Baby steps my dear. You think that because your chronological earth age is forty-one that you should be able to bypass these steps. But you will not. You are a baby learning, growing, and practicing. **Instead of being angry that you can't walk steadily in your new findings each day, rejoice in the fact that you are learning something new and that you have chosen to stand back up each day to take another step.**

Think about it, does the baby take its first steps, fall down, and scream and cry and just lay there and give up because they failed the first time? No, they pull themselves back up and try again—over and over until they are walking pros. So take some pointers from the sweet babies of the world. Admire their tenacity, their graciousness, and their patience. They are not angry that they are babies and do not know how to walk. They smile, cue, get up over and over again until they can walk and talk and do all that you can. And no their cries for hunger, elimination, and pain are not to be confused with being upset about learning. They embrace the learning, they do it with joy, focus, and a knowing that if they just keep trying they will get it soon enough.

To us, you are just as beautiful as a wide-eyed sweet baby. Embrace this process. Embrace yourself. Celebrate it instead of feeling anger towards yourself, because that will not get you anywhere except falling down more. Look at yourself through the eyes that you see that sweet perfect innocent baby with, because you are her.

We love when you giggle, it is our favorite.

With love and support, take another step our dear one. You will get it sooner than you think.

More than anything, I want to change. I've experienced so many synchronicities and beautiful moments lately which have taught me what can be. No longer wanting to settle for the painful and cut-off existence I've always experienced, I really want to understand how to get over my fears and allow all that I'm wanting to flow into my life.

Q: *I want to get really good at this believing and having faith thing. It feels hard for me, like letting go of my parachute as I jump off the mountain. I don't fear death anymore so it isn't that I think it will end, I guess I lack trust in the fact that I can end up somewhere different or that somehow something will be there to catch me. I really want to, I just find it really difficult when things aren't like I would like them in my life.*

For example, I am lucky to live the way I do, to have a clean home with a roof over my head, that I never go hungry, and that I get to go to the movies and things like that. Although I wish I had money to go on vacations or buy clothes or do other more costly things, I am well aware that compared to many people in this world, I am truly blessed. Right now, we are at a point that all of our bills are late, we are juggling any little cash we can come up with to pay what we need to avoid having things shut off and have my credit destroyed.

Everything I've read and learned tells you to be grateful for what you do have and you will get more of it. And to 'know' that money is coming, not to 'want or need it' because that lack of will continue to come to me. I'm less freaked out than I've been in the past about this very slow time of year and the bills that are piling up, but I still don't feel free. I don't fully feel myself believing that magically money will begin to flow freely and clear up all of the debt and bills. I really want to, but there seems to be something blocking me. How can I get over this and align myself with the energy that would change my relationship to money? Thank you for your help!

A: Change your perspective, or the way that you look at it. You say that in your question that you don't want to let go of the parachute, but that in itself is the beginning of the problem. Parachutes are not meant to be held on to, they are meant to be there and then released when it is time. Then they catch you and you slowly float to the ground. If you are holding onto the parachute and you aren't releasing it, you cannot let it catch you. You are just free falling. No wonder you feel unsure or uncertain.

See the tools are yours, you have been shown by example by many teachers that jumping and deploying the chute will allow you to be supported so you can just let go, relax, and know that you are safe even though you are still falling slowly. That is when you really can look around and enjoy the beauty that life offers you.

So our advice is to stop holding onto the parachute, you are stopping it from supporting you. Jump, push the button, and let the parachute carry you. You know the parachute in our meaning is really faith.

Your issue stems from feeling as though you were let down, dropped, or not caught in your younger years of life. What you need to do is differentiate between humans that were blinded by their own pain and fear which caused you to feel abandoned, and faith. The trust you had in them was broken, but faith in the universe, God, love or whatever you want to call it is different.

How? Because it is not blinded by humanness, it can see all, it is all, and it is not operating from a place of pain or confusion. **When you learn to separate the mistrust you hold from human induced sadness and have faith in the Great Spirit that supports you, you will no longer have any fear.**

The Great Spirit, God, or the Universe is all the same thing and it is all infinite love and perfection. You are a part of that, but having this human body and veil makes you think that you are this little speck that is unimportant to the grandness of all that is. That is the farthest thing from the truth. Each and every piece of spirit is as important, perfect, and loved as the whole. And yes, the great big puzzle would not be complete without you or anyone else for that matter.

So, now that you know that your mistrust is born from pain of human flaws, you know that your mistrust is not universal but situational to human error. It is not the trust that you have inside for you innately know that faith is so strong because it is infallible. Yes, it can seem to be because what you believe will bring more of the same. Not because you are not worthy but because you believe that you are not.

If you believe that you are not worthy of money, you will draw unworthiness of money to you, blocking your receiving of it. If you believe that you are unworthy of love from a life partner, you will draw a lack of love from a partner and block the one who is waiting to give that which you deserve. See it is not that the universe does not have enough for you, it is that they are fulfilling your wish. And although you may say that you are not wishing to be struggling or poor, you are if you believe that you are unworthy because you are not smart enough, don't work hard enough, or whatever it is that blocks it.

This is why we speak of self-love so much because if you love yourself fully you will know that you are worthy. And when you know this deep down, you will drop the blocks in you that stand in your way of getting what it is that you are really wanting. And when you drop the blocks, you allow the energy to flow to you and through you. This energy is the vehicle for your receiving of wealth, love, or whatever that you want.

It is all connected and it begins with loving yourself enough to either spontaneously drop or look at the issues that are creating blocks to receiving what you are wanting.

Your fears of being poor or hungry have been there since you were a young girl. Although you have moments of feeling self-love and joy, you have not completely dropped these fears that are so ingrained in you. *Have you ever starved?* No, you may have done without a whole lot, you may have not felt so full that you felt sick *(which is not the healthiest anyway)* and you may have not had what you most wanted, but you never went to bed crying because you were so hungry. And this was always taken care of for you even when you had these blocks, even when you were in fear of it. Imagine what lies ahead for you if you do drop these blocks and inaccurate beliefs.

You are worthy just because you were born, but if you need more reasons—you try each day to be your best, to love those around you, to think of others, and to do the very best you can. This is more than good enough to have all that you are wanting. We saw that you immediately knew the difference between your lack of trust from human induced suffering and the knowing that you have that the universe is waiting to give you what you are wanting. *Do you see how we can lump past experiences with things that they do not belong with?* This is the basis of all fears. They are not accurate. **You may have felt pain because of another human's behavior, but once you**

realize that you have all the power that you need inside of you, another's human error, misjudgment, or blindness will no longer have any effect on you.

We give our power away to our painful memories, our sadness, and our disappointment in others. This is not fair to them or you. Their pain has no effect on you, your happiness, or your ability to live the life you want. It is not fair to blame them or falsely think that they or the ingrained memory has any power for it does not. The law is that the universe will bow to you and your wishes. The truth is that you have the power to choose what you want to be delivered to you.

What do you choose? Hint: You can always choose again, anytime. Be happy, love you, and know that you will always get what you believe you deserve. And you always, in all ways deserve the best.

Oh how we love you!

Part of not 'getting it' for me seems to be related to my lack of patience. And the more I become frustrated, the more I fall back into my old patterns.

Q: *I know that I need to have patience with healing. I know that it takes a while to adhere to new patterns of thoughts and behaviors that will result in my feeling healthy, relaxed, and happy. Sometimes I feel myself becoming down because I ache so badly, or I'm so tired, or I can't seem to relax. I've noticed it can be exacerbated when I eat gluten or sugar, but sometimes a girl has to have a treat. On days like today, I'm happy, productive, and not falling into the trap of depression and self-loathing and doing the next thing, (I know I'm not supposed to say 'but') but the aching is there underlying everything and I'm a bit sad. I* don't know if I was a better student or something maybe I would be feeling wonderful every day. I rarely ever have a day where I feel fabulous with no undercurrent of pain or whatnot. I meditated earlier to get into a good mindset, I talked to myself before bed on resting well and waking energized and happy, I awoke and spoke positively, stood in the grass and thanked the universe for supporting me and so on. Why is it that after all of this time I still have pain that I cannot refocus away from and how can I transform more quickly? It can be so difficult sometimes to keep trying when I feel so badly. Thank you.

A: Our answer is this, you do not understand yet how to let go and let it flow. It is that simple, yet it seems so difficult for you. Once you can see it, you will wonder why it seemed so difficult at first. It is not about 'trying' to feel better, it is not about pushing yourself to do the things or tools you were given, it is not about force or outwitting or outlasting the pain. **It is simply sitting back, asking what it is trying to tell you, listen, and let it go because nine times out of ten it will be either stuck sadness or hurt, or an irrational fear that once it is brought to light you will realize it is not true and it will go away.**

Yes, it is that simple. Sitting there tired, aching, and frustrated makes this seem that not only is it not enough of an answer, but it is making you feel like there is something wrong with you because you aren't 'getting it' even though it is that simple. This is judgment of yourself and not only is this not going to help you, it is counterproductive. **The act of judging yourself puts you in a place where you cannot hear, cannot see, and most importantly, cannot feel the perfection that you are. It is blinding you to the fact that you are attached and a part of everything—from all that is beautiful and perfect, everything that you deem bad or negative, and everything in between.**

The only difference in it all is what you choose to align yourself with. Yes, you can be sad, in pain and so on. And if you align yourself with this energy or think about it or think you deserve it or say that you are, you will keep finding yourself there.

If you only see the good, the beautiful, and the perfection in all things, you will align yourself with this energy and you will feel good. No it isn't fighting the bad, resisting what you don't want, or thinking that you have to fight your way to stay focused on the good like a sinking ship. This is what has you sliding backwards all of the time.

See even in the things that you consider negative there is always good, perfection, and the beauty of life. You do not know what you *do* want until you know what you *don't* want. You know that you do **not** want to feel what you do now. So now you do not need to fight or run away from what you don't want, you merely need to look towards what you do want.

You are still fighting the pain, sadness, and are angry at yourself for the ruts or ingrained patterns as we say. You tell yourself that you are stupid because if you were smart you would have filled them in and made better ones by now. This philosophy is exactly why you are still 'fighting' this battle. You are angry at yourself and you are not accepting your humanness and the inherent imperfection that brings to you. You hate your humanness.

Think about it, *do you hate a baby when they don't know any better than to grab your hair or a hot stove?* No, you love them and you take their hand and tell them and redirect them. **Be as gentle with yourself dear one as you would with that baby.** Just because your body is grown doesn't mean your spirit is still not that of a sweet innocent baby. You deserve that same gentle touch, redirection, and unconditional love. Just because your outside packaging is not quite as compact and adorable doesn't mean you still aren't the same sweet little free spirit inside. Love her, she needs it.

As we've spoken of before with you, stop resisting the pain and stop gritting your teeth and trying to grin and bear it. Sit yourself down and tell yourself that you hear the messages loud and clear that something is not right. Thank your body for giving you such wonderfully apparent messages because without the warning messages, you may never have taken the time to really sit and listen. Now you have the opportunity to correct the problems. What better gift than a body that signals to you that there is pain. All that you have to do is get quiet and ask and then listen for the answer.

Repeat—*My dearest smart body, I hear you. I feel your pain. I'm sorry that my unawareness has caused you to have to take such extreme measures to get my attention. I'm listening now. What is it that you want me to know? I'm here and open to hearing your message.*

Amy: I feel that I tense up against life, fearing abandonment, failure, and disappointment. I want to try so hard because I want to succeed so badly. I want to have peace and self-love and joy in my life. I understand now in this moment the letting go verses trying so very hard for it. My body is in pain because it is being tensed and ready for impact at all times. It is tired from the tensing and pushing and berating. Is there a way that I can remember this each day without having to get to the place of pain first and then feeling exhausted when I do finally let go?

Make it part of your morning and nightly ritual. Talking to yourself, asking yourself whether something is true or not, or giving yourself the choice to choose for the day instead of following what you are 'used to' is all that you need to remind yourself. If you find that your old patterns have taken over, do not fight it, do not get angry at it, but instead let it come to the forefront, stop, listen, and then let what isn't true evaporate.

Look into those little ones eyes each day and tell her you will give her your patience. You deserve it. **Remember it all begins with loving you.** If you do not learn to treat yourself with respect, kindness, gentleness, and unconditional love without judgment, you can't do it for others. **Loving you is the greatest gift you can give to the world.**

We see so much more than you. You are growing by leaps and bounds. *Remember when you were in pain and all you did is research how to fix it physically?* Before you knew the root to all problems begin with your emotions. Before you knew that the key to healing and happiness was gleaming right there in you already, just waiting for you to 'see' it.

We are so proud of you.

Q : *I'm really trying to be more 'tuned in' to my body, mind, and spirit. I've tried to ask myself questions about things, like whether it wants to eat something, or take a certain supplement. I find it extremely difficult to do this and 'hear' an answer. I know answers will not usually sound like me when I speak out loud, that they are more of a knowing but I still can't seem to get what it is trying to tell me. I really want to be more proactive in letting myself guide me, but I just can't seem to hear, interpret, or get what the answers are. I actually feel kind of anxiety ridden while trying to listen for the answer because I don't want to get it wrong. Not that I want to be right per se, but that I want to avoid learning through mistakes, consequences, and regrets and just take my time and hear what is in my best interest and act from there. Could you please give me some guidance? Thank you.*

A : We are not laughing at you when we say this, but it almost seems funny to us that you don't see that you have been hearing or listening and transcribing this information for quite a while, yet you feel that you don't have the ability to hear or get an answer. Yes, we understand that you have a much easier time 'letting it flow' when writing as that has always been an easier avenue of allowing for you.

What we think is funny is that you don't hear us saying the words, you know we aren't taking over your body, you are just being and allowing the energy to flow through you. You do not know our answer when you ask the question, and you do not logically or in your mind know what we may or may not say. When you go back and read it, you feel and know that the answer was something from beyond you in your physical body or mind. **So, you most definitely know how to let go and let help flow to you.**

If this brings you anxiety to ask and listen, for now try the way that is comfortable for you. Sit here and write and ask the question. Then, since you are comfortable with allowing the answer to flow through your fingers onto the page, do it this way. Yes, it may not be convenient all of the time but you know that you are good with it.

See, we all have natural abilities that we are good at, that are second nature to us, which allow you to be in the creative flowing process of spirit. Work with them, use them, for they are your gifts and your way to discover spirit. Eventually, it may become such second nature to feel the flow that it will become a bigger part of all of your actions, including speaking out loud and hearing that way versus writing or typing it.

Or it may not. **But instead of stressing about what you do *not* have, or are *not* good at, focus on what you *do* have, and what you *are* good at.** If not, you will always find something that frustrates you, something that you feel that you are not good enough at, or wonder why you aren't good at it at all. That's like an Olympic swimmer not entering the swimming competition but instead trying to win a gold medal at the high jump. *That is silly isn't it?* **Use the talents, gifts, and blessings that you have developed to help yourself. That is why you have them.**

It doesn't have to be as difficult as you think. If you aren't home and near your computer, carry a small notebook in your purse and when you have a question, write it down, center yourself and write.

No it isn't weird or nerdy. To us what would be strange is to **not** use your gift. Open your mind. *Who says it isn't OK to sit and write a question if you are out in public and really want an answer? Wouldn't it be sad to shun your gift because you are concerned with what you might look like?* And no one will probably notice or care if you are writing or not.

When you look at life as limitless, with potentials beyond your wildest imagination, there are no obstacles only new opportunities and ways to look at situations.

Do you not feel lighter now knowing that you were thinking that you were somehow not good enough because you felt like you couldn't do something but then realizing that you can, you do, and all that you have to do is think about it differently? Funny how perspective and changing the position with which you look at something can change your entire day or life for that matter.

Do not fight against what you think your limitations are, but use what comes naturally to you to create a solution. Each of us is talented in some areas more than others, so use your gifts and let go of those things that don't come naturally.

There is always a way, but you have to be willing to blaze your own trail in your own time and from your own vantage point.

This doesn't mean that you can't work on or practice those things that you would like to strengthen. If you really would like to learn to hear more clearly without having to write, then practice. And if you feel that anxiety that you aren't certain, question it in writing afterwards just to verify. After a while you will learn to trust yourself and you will not second guess your ability to connect with spirit through any avenue that you wish.

Again, you do not decide that you want to learn to ride a bike, get on it, and ride off into the sunset. You use training wheels and learn to feel the balance that it takes in conjunction with how to hold yourself, your handle bars, and the pressure you need to apply to the pedals. Then you remove the training wheels, and feel the full aspect of how you need to balance to stay upright. It takes a little while. You may falter, stop, and even fall. But then you get back on and practice and before you know it you are riding with no hands and you don't even have to think about the logistics anymore, it has just become second nature.

Again, as we say to you often, do not grip the handle bars tighter, do not sit rigidly and try to stay in a straight line. Relax, feel the delicate balance, and bask in the freedom of the air rushing through your hair. Let us support you and have fun and know that you are always loved, looked after, and cared for. **You are not alone and you do not need to fight for enlightenment, it is already all inside of you.** Just relax and trust and you will see more signs.

With love.

Nitty-Gritty Details

THIS UNNAMABLE AND UNSEEABLE FORCE that answers my questions has become the best kind of friend to me. One that I can come to when I'm confused and will answer me with love, compassion, and honesty.

Q: *I read a wonderful book called <u>Right Riches for You</u> by Gary Douglas and Dain Heer and I learned so much that I didn't know about money and generating it. After reading it, I had an offer come to me to write a book, but it is not the genre that I love to write about. In the above mentioned book they spoke of not having judgment of where the money comes from so I felt like although my platform has generally been sharing my experiences with the hope of helping others, I should consider this other avenue to generate money so that I have the money to share the works like this book that are close to my heart.*

I still don't feel very comfortable writing about drama and feeding that in others. I feel like I'm settling or disregarding my own moral code or feelings just to make a buck. This really bugs me because I feel like that is the major problem in this country. Politicians, big business, and big pharma are all disregarding what is best for the people just to line their pockets with more money. I don't want to do this but then there is the question of making money to pay bills.

Should I write the other book? How can I let go of or change it so that I don't feel that I'm contributing to the degradation of my society to make money? Thank you for your insight.

A: You must first acknowledge in yourself and be proud that you are concerned with what you put out there in society. Putting your thoughts into what can help people to know the true them is admirable. Seeing what it is in business or government that you do not agree with and trying to do better regardless of your financial gain is what will make your society a better place for many, and many are like you.

Next you may want to think of the non-judgment aspect of what you read in the book you mentioned. When they spoke of non-judgment about where money comes from, *did they say to disregard whether the money was coming from murder or genocide or some type of horrible atrocity?* No, they merely said to suspend personal judgments based on hang-ups you may have with others.

Then you should look at what you consider 'putting something out there that is not for the well-being of others.' It is all perspective my dear. A book that tells stories about people may not just be spreading more smut into the world as you think. *Who says that it isn't a wakeup call for people in many areas who are involved in the same behaviors?* Not that they are bad per se, it is just their choice. Maybe they need to hear about someone else in the same position to really understand how what they are doing is affecting themselves or others. Maybe you are doing them a service. Smile.

You know writing, talking about, or reading others life experiences or drama as you say is not always about just feeding more drama. **It can be a learning tool through seeing others' lives.** This is how we learn mostly *isn't it?*

And there is also nothing wrong with being entertained in this way. We wouldn't say it would be the healthiest thing in the world to spend all of one's time watching, reading, or talking about drama or other's experiences. This would mean you were avoiding your own learning. But to see the humor, the sadness, or even being shocked by other's behaviors or experiences does not have to be a negative thing. *You enjoy a good prime-time drama do you not?* You see inside the lives and experiences that you otherwise would not.

You view this as wrong or bad, but in moderation you enjoy it as well. There is nothing wrong with this. And you may also want to look at yourself and see why this kicks something up for you. *Are you afraid that you will enjoy it?*

You try very hard to get to know you, find peace, and cultivate your spiritual side. This is very admirable and you find joy, peace, and fulfillment in doing so. That is wonderful. **That doesn't mean that your actions or behaviors are right, and learning through other means is wrong.**

So instead of thinking that by writing this book you are somehow tarnishing your energy or negating the beautiful words you share through getting in touch with yourself the way you do, maybe consider that you have another avenue to help others learn more about themselves. And making a whole lot of money at it could help you continue doing what brings you joy.

There are many ways to help those in the world, whether that is through spiritual statements, humor, sharing self-help tools, or relaxing watching or reading a 'scandalous' show or book. They all provide something for someone depending on what they are looking for.

So stretch your wings, try to weave the humanness, humor, and non-judgment into unlikely spiritual works, wink wink. And stop trying to always do the right thing by taking it so seriously. There is nothing wrong with a joke, laughing at ourselves, or learning stuff through outrageous behavior. You had some of that in your day and you still look back and laugh at it at times.

Now take things a little lighter, life is supposed to be fun. Try dancing more and shuffling less.

With love and appreciation.

I want to revisit and fine tune some of what I've learned.

Q: *Yesterday, I reread a question and answer from a while back about how I was not letting myself feel the sadness, and how I was just repressing it all of these years. You stated that I needed to let it be heard, come up and feel it, and then it would recede like the ocean. By only dipping my toe in, it was causing it to be more painful for me. I hadn't done that since that first time, so I figured it would be good to do it again because I doubt that in one time of welcoming my sadness that it covered all of what is stored in my body.*

I laid down and told all of my sadness to come forward from everywhere in my body, that I wanted to acknowledge and release it. Well, I started to get flashes of many different times in my life that I was sad and there were a lot of them. Then I saw little cells light up from all over come up to my heart area and I felt a huge wave of sadness. I relaxed and fell asleep. When I woke up 2 hours later, I felt like I'd been run over. So much so that my eyes felt like they weren't even lined up with my eye sockets. I know, that sounds very weird but it is true. Then I was grumpy and frustrated the rest of the evening and fell asleep some hours later for over ten more hours.

Is this normal? Did I forget to do something to help clear it, I'm still very tired? Why is this so difficult? I get frustrated about feeling so ill sometimes like today. Please help? Thank you.

A: Becoming clear and healthy is not a quick fix or easy job. It does involve work, rest, and gentleness with oneself, which is something you are still working on. Smile. You have stuffed down each and every sad feeling that you've had in forty years, that is a lot. It may have been a bit much to summon all of them at once, but you did and there is nothing wrong with that. Just know that it was a huge release, thus you will feel tired from it. Think about it, if you don't cut a field for years, the grass and weeds get many feet tall, instead of mere inches. *Which one is easier to cut?*

We know that it can feel frustrating when going through this process to feel better, than feel ill again, sometimes it can seem never ending. But we promise you that it is well worth it and it will pay off. Think about it, you have only been doing this intensive daily work for six months, which isn't much comparative to the years that you accumulated it. As you release more and more, you will feel better, feel less rundown, and start to have less and less times where you feel like this. Be kind and patient with yourself. Don't get angry at yourself. You told yourself yesterday that it was OK to release that junk, now nurture you until you feel better. You wouldn't tell your loved one that you will take care of them because they have the flu, then the next morning get angry at them because they are still sick. You would make them a soothing light meal and prop them up and give them the space to rest. Do the same for you! *Why would you think you were less deserving?* Love you my dear.

You did not do anything wrong at all. You opened yourself up and gave yourself permission to feel and release old stuck sadness. That is a gift, a beautiful one. You are equating feeling tired and under the weather as doing something wrong, just as you've equated your feeling sick for so many years with you having done something wrong. **Release the word 'wrong' from your vocabulary**. Because you did not know better, you did the best you knew how. You tried to the best of your ability at that time. You tried. It may have not given you the outcome you were hoping for but that doesn't mean you were 'wrong,' it just meant it wasn't the choice for you. Now you've chosen again, and now you've chosen in an awakened state not to hide from yourself or your pain. You are welcoming it, hearing it, releasing it and healing. How perfect. You know no one, not even sweet perfect babies always make the 'right' choices. For the most part, *do you notice that they usually pick incorrectly for the outcome they are wanting*? But that is how we learn.

Although perfectionism can be motivating and at times can yield astonishing results, it can be very depilating. **You are not perfect, no one is. You were not meant to be perfect. You were born to see, experience, and learn what it is that works for you**. No matter if that is what your parents, teachers, religion, or peers think, you are here to conjure joy based on what makes you feel good as long as it is not harming another.

So let go and relax. Rest. You are not lazy you are taking care of you. You are honoring yourself and what you told yourself yesterday that it could do and how you would support it. So do it with a smile and before you know it, you will feel wonderful.

Now go rest as we see you are exhausted and it is hard to even type.

Love you, we do.

After the exhaustion, came a shingles outbreak.

Q: *Today I would really like to know why it is that I continuously have shingles outbreaks and how specifically, I can go about deactivating the virus permanently. And any viruses for that matter, like Epstein Barr. Thank you for your help.*

A: A human body carries many viruses, but it does not mean because there is one that you have to suffer from symptoms. We know that you do not like the idea of suppression through drugs as you innately know that suppression is not the answer. That is why you used the word deactivate.

As you know, your immune system correlates to your stress load and specifically how you allow or disallow the stress to affect your system. **Your suppressing yourself is a catalyst to exhibiting symptoms—suppressing your release of grief and suppression of your joy and goodness to yourself.** Yes, this can be exacerbated by certain foods high in arginine, but *why is it that your partner eats that and does not suffer?*

He does not expect it. He does not suppress his happiness or well-being. He does not feel unworthy of feeling good. You do. You feel that you do not deserve to feel good, look good, or have joy. This is from self-loathing, a lack of self-love.

You do not need to fight them, suppress them, outwit them, or do something to stop them. **You merely need to turn into what you do want and the rest will fall away.** Overcoming illness or having remission or healing and never experiencing that thing again is not done with force, brain power, or unknown knowledge. It is from surrendering to a better and healthier way. It is allowing the good. See you don't need to fight for or earn this goodness, happiness, or joy. It simply is there. You just have to open your arms, heart, and mind to this fact. You have to step into the lovely current and allow it to carry you to all that you are wanting.

There are two big obstacles that although we have explained them many different ways, you still haven't fully understood. **One, that self-love, kindness to yourself, self-acceptance, and knowing that you are a beautiful perfect being no matter what, is the key to your finding peace.** As very simple as it sounds, you are profoundly aware of just how elusive this can be to an adult who has never found or better yet recognized their beauty within. It is elusive because it is hard for you to see, and sometimes difficult to stay focused on the small steps that will allow this to become your predominant feeling daily.

Secondly, and the only other thing you need to do is allow. **Love yourself and allow joy to flow to you. That is it.** Yes, again simple. Yet you've found it difficult to let go of your survival mentality, merely existing and trying to do everything with tenacity instead of allowance.

Think about it, how hard is it to hold an umbrella open against whipping rain and wind? Merely impossible right? You try hard, it seems that you may have found the way to hold it to protect yourself, but then snap, your umbrella is broken and hanging by your side.

Fighting against life does not usher in what you are wanting. Standing against the current or the wind does not work. But if you merely turn yourself so that the wind is at your back, you will feel supported and gently moved along instead of gritting your teeth, putting your head down and trying to walk against the wind.

Stop thinking that fighting will yield you the results you are wanting. It has been shown to you over and over again that all that you get or 'earn' is exhaustion and feeling unwell. Then you lie down and rest and feel like giving up. You let go, feel better, and then come back refreshed and ready to try again. But instead of walking with the wind at your back you turn against the wind again and repeat your fight. It will never change, there is no treasure chest waiting on the other side that you have to fight to earn.

You already have the treasure inside. You were given the wind and the current to carry you, not for you to fight against. **Allow the universe to support you, guide you, and help you along your path.** That is what we want, that is what you want, you just have skewed and misguided thinking that allowing is giving up or that allowing good is not earning it. You earned it by coming here and experiencing life. Don't shun your gifts that you were given, that are shown to you each day.

Now step into the breeze, allow it to gently meet your back, supporting you and guiding you. Trust the love we have for you. Trust the guidance that flows to you through love, nature, and spirit. It is there to help you not trick you or fight against you.

You deserve to enjoy life, feel that blessings and joy come easily, and that love, especially your self-love is full and infinite. You are here to learn to love yourself, not because you are to learn what you think is selfishness, but to learn what it is that supports everything. Once you know self-love, all the rest will fall into place perfectly, effortlessly, and more fulfilling then you could ever imagine.

Now go feel all of the love, joy, and support that exist for you today and every day. Look at yourself in the mirror, meditate, exercise and enjoy feeling alive. It is the homeostasis that you've been searching for. **You have not been sad because it doesn't exist, but because you haven't allowed yourself to bask in your own love.** You've missed it terribly. Now go and love you, love life, love all that is.

We like rose colored glasses, it is the best way to see.

I think I've figured out that the reason I have a problem with trusting is because just when I feel like I'm improving, bam, I'm hit with something else that makes me question that.

Q: *I have noticed a big improvement in my ability to take things in stride and stay calm when something unexpected or bothersome pops up. But, I had it brought to my attention by my daughter this morning that I have not yet become good at remaining calm and unaffected when someone I love is being rude and disrespectful because they are* upset. I did as you've suggested before to calmly state that I'm happy to help but that I will not be spoken to that way. I also have found on many occasions when she was grumpy or coming off as being rude that I would get off of the call. Today, I had to be on the call because she needed a new phone. I was upset that I was buying her another phone since her father broke it. It isn't like he can't afford to replace it and what really upset me was that instead of being rude to him, she was being rude to me and wanting me to pay for it. I don't know if I need to learn to separate my feelings about things from the situation at hand? How can I stay calm and kind, yet stand my ground with not being treated rudely especially when it is undeserved? Thank you so much.

A: **First of all, there is no time when you are deserving of being mistreated. No matter what.** You are still second guessing or feeling guilty for choices that you did or didn't make regarding raising your daughter. You did the best that you could, and you did a wonderful job. Just because she is telling you she is not happy with the choices that she made, doesn't mean you need to feel so bad for her that you compromise your own integrity. What we mean is, you can have compassion that she is not happy about a situation, but do not feel that you had any bearing on it. You advised strongly against it and fought her making this choice for over a year. Eventually, you let her and now she struggles with regretting it. Not your fault.

See as parents, we think that it is our job to give our kids the best life there is. **What we really are motivated by is to give them all of the things we did not have.** Although you may think that this is a gift, you can now see it can have a different outcome. You wanted your daughter to have a magical childhood, filled with love, attention, extravagant birthday parties, a great education, time with mom, and support for anything she wanted to try. You did all of that and more. There is nothing for you to feel guilty about.

As you were told by her therapist, in her twenty years of being a therapist she had never seen someone try so hard to be a good mother.

That in fact you had actually given her too much which caused her to be spoiled and entitled. But, you did and it cannot be undone, however, you can begin teaching her a new way now. **You can show her how to have respect for herself by requiring nothing less from her during your interactions.**

Your biggest pitfall is your unresolved feelings regarding your own childhood and choices that you made during hers. There is that little voice in you that says that you could have done just a little better if only you had done this or that. It is over, you cannot change it. Let go of it. You did the very best you were capable of and by no stretch of the imagination did you do a horrible job. You did a wonderful job. So, tell yourself that and release that so you can get onto a new chapter where you teach her that you do not overextend, do without, or take abuse from anyone because you love yourself and you do not allow this.

What you really feel guilty about is usually how you get angry and raise your voice when you get upset. Then you go against how you want to be treated because you feel bad and think that you need to make up for your behavior. Stop doing this! Even if you raise your voice, cuss, or whatever, this does not mean that you compromise your requirements of being treated with respect. **You are not treating yourself or her with respect when you act from your anger.** Therefore you don't require to be treated properly in return. It is a sick cycle that you keep allowing yourself to ride on. Get off of the ride!

Promise yourself and make it a priority that no matter what, who, when, or where that you will not disrespect yourself or others by speaking in a manner that is mean, rude, or argumentative. Regardless of what your ex has done, your daughter has done, or the fast food worker, you are not getting them back, making them understand, or 'showing them' by getting loud or cursing at them. The only person you are hurting is you. **A person who loves theirself does not continuously and unconsciously hurt theirself.**

This means that you have to become aware, you can't react unconsciously or just act without forethought. At least until you no longer feel the need to be led by the past or someone else's behaviors.

Think about it, you have been divorced for eleven years, *do you really want to keep getting angry at your ex?* No. If he mistreats your daughter, she is an adult now and she needs to deal with him, not you. You can help her but not by making up for his slack, talking bad about him, or getting angry at him and raising your voice with your daughter when she expects you to clean up his mess with her.

Here is how it should have gone down. You bought her a phone, you pay for the phone every month, and you also advised her on numerous occasions that you were not going to pay for a replacement and that she should get a strong case to ensure that it was protected. She disregarded your advice because she did not find those particular cases attractive. Then her father dropped the phone on concrete, breaking it and promised to buy her another one. Then he did not. None of this has any bearing on you. You forewarned her, you gave her advice on how to avoid this situation, and then her father retracted on his promise to replace what he broke.

This should have nothing to do with you and you know it. That is why you are so upset. You know that you did your due diligence and you resent having to make up for both her and her father's shortcomings. You should have patted her on the back and told her you were sorry she learned this lesson the hard way. That you will continue to offer her advice and hopefully she will heed it more in the future. If her father refuses to replace it, then she can be mad at him and deal with that.

Stop thinking that you have to protect her from him. You do not. All that you can do is continue to offer your time, energy, and insight to help her make the best decisions she can. She is an adult now and thus will learn lessons just as you did. **You are not a 'bad mom'**

because you don't pick up the pieces every time her decision results in an undesirable outcome.

When you stop thinking that you are required to do this, you will no longer feel resentment or anger that you are being ignored and then disrespected. You will no longer feel a need to feel vested in what she or anyone else does or does not do. She is no longer a child that relies on you to take care of her. All that you can do now is to love her unconditionally and share with her your experiences so that she can gain insight. Whether she takes it or disregards it or even shuns you because you are not giving into her childish demands of entitlement, will not affect your love for her or most importantly how you respond to her. Only you can set your parameters for how you require that you be treated, and only you have control over how you respond to those who do not respect that.

Give her the best and most important gift, that of demonstrating self-love so that she may learn that for herself.

You are not here to buy or fix every whim in her life, you *are* here to love, model, and share insight from your experiences. What she does with the information is her choice and her consequence to deal with.

Now love you and promise yourself that you will no longer disrespect yourself or others, for once you do this the 'problem' of getting angry and raising your voice will not exist. You like to get to the root, there it is my dear, there it is.

Now go enjoy nature, sit in the grass, feel the sun warm you, feel the love that all things, in all ways have for you, and know that they are always there for you.

With infinite love.

19

Resolving Pain

SADLY, I'M FRUSTRATED ABOUT INTERACTIONS with loved ones, feeling less than wonderful, and trying so hard and having learned so much, yet still in a space that I don't want to be. It feels like I don't have anything left to try with. I'm tired.

Q: *I'm depressed. I'm not happy at all. I have no motivation to do anything not even brush my hair. I don't enjoy anything. I'm even starting to not even enjoy this writing. I'm just continuing with the hope that something will help. I have no interest in friends, activities, nothing. I'm tired of coming back to this low place. I hurt, I ache, I'm tired, and I don't feel any interest in anything. I don't know if it is impossible for my body to make these happy chemicals in my brain, but I'm starting to not care. I try to eat healthy, exercise as much as I can, take supplements, meditate, read, etcetera, but nothing seems to help. Please help me. Thank you.*

A: Release all of those feelings you are clenching on to, the ones where you feel the pain. They are knots of what you think you should be, what you should have done, and your wish that things were a certain way.

Release each one and repeat—*I let go of all that I had planned and thought was what should have happened. I release all that I wish I would or would not have done. I release all of the feelings I have about what a perfect life would be. I let go of all past, present and future scenarios in my head for what would be better or happier. I release any type of regret from the past and I release any wishing for the future.*

Yes, you feel the tears rise because you harbor pain from what you wish would have been with your daughter, your family. How it looked or felt or turned out.

Continue repeating—*I release what I think I should have been, what I should have or have not done. I release any and all judgments of myself and others. I did not make a mistake, I am not a mistake, I merely made the best decision I could with the information I had at the time. I let go of judging myself based on what I have been taught is right or wrong. There is no right or wrong, just choices. I tried to make the best choice possible for myself and my loved ones and did the very best I could. I congratulate myself for always trying to do the best I could, no matter if I or anyone else thought it was good or bad. I accept that there is no good and bad, only choices and consequences. I am not good nor bad, I just am. I am part of all that is. I am no better or worse than anyone or anything. I am just as worthy of feeling self-love as a newborn baby, a beloved rock star, a pope, or a billionaire. I am perfect, whole, and intelligent and I let go of all that does not serve me, and I know that I'm worthy and welcome all of the joy, happiness, and contentment that I deserve.*

Amy: *I still don't feel better.*

You read the words but didn't mean them or feel them. You didn't visualize releasing them and letting go. Although you hate how you feel, you do not believe that it will get any better. You do not believe there is anything better than what you wish would have happened.

If you do not leave a window open and ask *what better can there be?* You will not know. Ask...

Amy: *I did and afterwards had many signs from number sequences to picking something to read or watch and it was just what I wanted to hear. Why is it that I have to get so low to hear or get it?*

You don't. You just have to learn how to 'get' to that place of letting go and allowing, asking, and having your eyes open to receive. Because this has not been your approach, you wear yourself out and get to the point of completely giving up for you to allow it in. It does not have to be this way, you can do this each day from the start instead of going through the old way of trying to squeeze it out or hold on so tightly. It really is about letting go and allowing, believing, and receiving. It is that simple.

What is not simple is the 'letting go' for you. As you've seen it feels better and is the place you want to be. So if you need to be so vigilant about something, don't be so vigilant about trying too hard to do the right thing or trying so hard that you are in pain, or exhausted. **Simply, dedicate yourself to letting go, relaxing, and allowing.** Then you will have the ability to see the synchronicities everywhere in everything.

I'm excited that I found a quick and easy solution to my back pain!

Q: *I'm confused about how to go about determining the best approach to fixing something. For example, I've had hip, lower back and sacrum issues for years now. Lately, I've suffered for months and have not found a permanent fix for it. I tried just letting go last time and relaxing, even taking pharmaceutical drugs to help. Then I tried* chiropractors, massage, heat, stretching, yoga, swimming, resting it and so on. Nothing really seemed to help fully. Then during a session with Mary Ellen, she told me to watch a video on GaiamTV by Gay Hendricks called Liberating Your Full Orgasm Reflex. It isn't about sex, but about releasing old injuries—emotional or sexual abuse—by utilizing breath and little tiny movements. It felt so easy that I was sure it was old people exercises. But to my amazement, I noticed relief immediately. It has only been three days, but I've noticed a huge improvement in that it feels freer, and there is hardly any pain. I almost can't believe how simple it is.

My question is why did it take me so long to find the simplest solution? And how do I know what the right or best approach is to healing something? And how do I determine whether something needs a physical approach, emotional release or whatever. It just seems so confusing. Thank you for your help.

A: **The best approach is to ask.** Yes, ask yourself and ask for help from those who help you that you do not see—angels, ascended masters, the universe, or whatever works for you, even all of them. Ask them to help bring to your awareness the way or ways to help resolve the issue.

See your issue or root cause of the hip, sacrum, lower back pain was about stuck trauma. You ask and want to 'clear' the gunk out so that you see clearly, so that you have openness to living in the now. You want to get rid of the pain so that you can live your best life. Some of our most deep-seated pain is related to this area. As we said before this is the base of your spiritual nature and an important area to be clear in.

This can be the most difficult to let go of because we work so hard to block out these deeply painful memories of childhood sexual abuse, shame, and so on. As Gay Hendricks explains in his video, traumas from these types of events get stuck there causing physical responses of tightness and tension which will manifest physically.

As we have said before, most physical maladies are a result of unresolved or stuck emotional turmoil.

We need to kindly and gently release these blocks. The physical help that Gay demonstrates may look very simple but is very powerful in letting go of past pain and ushering in healing energy via breath and subtle movements. It is wonderful.

Yes, it is very simple but very effective just as letting go and allowing yourself to see, hear, experience, and feel all of the beauty around you. When you are retracting in pain and ignoring your body's signals that something needs to be released, you are holding onto and impeding the resolution of the pain. When you open up and let go, it subsides. This is the way with all things.

Good for you reaching out and creating the opportunity to work with someone like Mary Ellen who shared this video with you. Good for you for being open and willing to try it no matter how silly you thought it sounded. And good for you for doing the gentle and easy work to release this junk. We said 'gentle and easy' because we want you to truly absorb the fact that work, learning, releasing, and growing does not have to be so very difficult as you have imagined and created for your previous learning.

Anything can be as hard or as easy as you imagine. Easy does not mean a copout, the easy way, or the lazy way. These are words you've heard that made you feel ashamed. They were said to you by people who had the same thing happen to them, and it goes back continuously from scared and asleep people. They did what they could. So can you. **Now that you know differently, do differently and be the change that will affect all that come after you.** What a beautiful gift to give all of your future family, one that is a lasting and life changing gift. *And you thought you didn't do much?*

We see the impact that your awakening has, the ripples that will reverberate for lifetimes to come. We are so excited for you, your drive to be your authentic self, and all that you are accomplishing. We know you look at one question and one answer and one hour as insignificant, but we know how life altering it can be.

We know that you have been feeling sad and felt defeated and useless. Please know that every action of learning, letting go, growing, and sharing has meaning beyond your comprehension right now. What you are doing is not 'useless' so stop thinking that way. What you are, what you are doing, what you are sharing is everything.

With admiration and respect we leave you now. Let go and allow all of the beauty you want to wash over you today. **Notice the little things and watch as they weave a tapestry of miracles that you can behold as the sun sets.**

Amen

It is amazing to me that from day to day how different things can be. One day I can feel really sad and low and with a few words or exercise feel like a new person. As I let go more, trust more, and go deeper into meditation, I am beginning to experience some amazing things!

Q: *As I was meditating I had an epiphany. I felt for a minute what it was like to stand up and leave my body…kind of like you see on TV when someone dies and their spirit gets up and walks out of their body. It was during this that I realized, not just heard your words or as an abstract thought, but really felt that the spirit holds pain, not the body. When I stood up I wasn't in my body anymore and although my spirit felt lighter, I could still feel the tugs of aches here and there. Now I finally get that all pain begins emotionally and spiritually. I also know that when these become ingrained enough or held onto long enough, they manifest in the body and I can feel that pain greatly on a physical level.*

I guess we get the physical pain as a last resort screaming to us that we are ignoring the emotional and spiritual pain that we need to release. Now I also understand what Robert Taub was explaining to me when he said that he wasn't a fan of many supplements because with the change of energy in the body, the deficit or need for something can change overnight. I understand that now because just within meditation the intense pain I felt just minutes before went away.

I know that much of the previous questions have explained this and how loving myself and releasing misconceptions of regret, sadness, and anger will release me from this physical pain that I've been suffering from for many years. I guess today I'm looking for more guidance on how to listen to the more subtle pulls to do this instead of waiting until I feel unbearable physical pain that forces me to act. Also, I wonder why I find it so difficult to maintain the bliss throughout the day that I feel while meditating. I know you've probably spoken about both of these things, I guess I'm just looking for more insight or another way of looking at it so it becomes easier or clearer for me. Thank you for your help and patience with teaching me.

A : When you are meditating, you are suspending any thoughts, therefore, you are not thinking of past regrets or future anxiety. You are simply bathing in the perfection of your light. This is why you feel so at peace and feel your pain dissipate because you are not feeding the pain that you harbor for 'mistakes' or regrets from your past. You are also not stressing about making another mistake or thinking about what things could go wrong in the future.

The only way to maintain this bliss is to be in that state continuously, to be in the now or in the present moment like you are while meditating. See, you feel like this is so difficult because while you are meditating you feel it is OK to let go and let it flow. You feel that is how you are during that meditative state and you know that you can't control it. That meditating and allowing the flow of universal energy is the complete opposite of control and trying to force something to be how you want. You know that it is relaxing, opening up, and allowing yourself to come into alignment with all that is.

But when you leave the meditation, you feel that you must leave that allowing state as well. You try to control your behaviors and your environment so that it doesn't upset you because if you are not upset, you will not act in ways that disappoint yourself. Inevitably you have to interact with others and have situations arise that cause you not to have control of your environment. Then you get anxious and feel out of control and you fight against what is. When you do this you have anxiety, pain, anger and so on.

It is a sick cycle that will not end until you embrace what you know that works during meditation and put it into practice as your way of being. You will never be able to control others or situations. You can only control you but as you've seen, trying to control yourself doesn't work either. **The only control you have is whether you align your energy with the flow of life, that of nature, love, and the universe.** When you do this you feel joy, peace, calm and the way you want to be. This is when you will find peace no matter who is around you, what they are doing, or how they act or feel about you. **None of that will matter because when you are aligned with your true self and with the love of the universe, you will not have any judgment or feeling about what anyone else is doing.**

Think of it like you are outside looking into a world where people are going about their days. Think of shutting down the thought that it is real life. Think of it like a play on a stage. So you are watching these people happy, sad, abusive, laughing, crying and so on. If you think of it like it is a play you are not as vested in their actions. So you look at what is going on with no emotional charge. It is not right, wrong, good, or bad, you are just watching actions and consequences. This is how the universe looks at us. The only difference is that they care and love deeply. It is not an emotionless, detached feeling but a non-judgmental accepting watching. And the really big difference is that the universe offers love in many ways whether it is through animals, nature, people, songs and so on.

We walked you through separating out feeling so you could really experience the non-judgment that there is for you and your actions. But then we want to stress that the love that is felt for you, for everyone and everything is beyond belief. Combine the love you have for your daughter, your family, your friends, and for your beloved pets and multiply that times a million and that is the love that is sent to you, felt for you, and frankly is you. You are a part of that. We are not separate.

When we say that, we don't mean just that we as people are not separate and are all one, but also that we are not separate from the universal love, God, or however you want to label the collective force that we are a part of. **You have the divinity in you that is as majestic as mountains, as beautiful as the sea, and as perfect as every sunset and sunrise.** You are all of those things.

One of the biggest problems or misconceptions that cause us to feel pain and sadness is that we feel separate. We feel separated from source, God, love, and nature. The fact that our spirit or energy is cloaked by water, skin, and bones, we forget that we are one with all that is. Imagine that you are not your body but the light that is inside. Now imagine that that light is the same source that lights the earth, illuminates the night sky, that beauty that decorates the earth, that makes you fall in love with babies and puppies, and takes your breath away when you see something beautiful for the first time. Now feel your spirit and reach out and feel the spirit of those things. It is the same, it is one.

When you find the joy in every moment because you focus on this connection, and only act with love towards all things then you will realize that you are a piece of all that is beautiful

and perfect. And when you know this, there is nothing to mourn and nothing to fear. That is when you will truly live in peace at all times, in all ways, always.

Do not focus on why you haven't been able to maintain your bliss, but feel the bliss and practice being there in all that you do. Practice seeing the truth, that you are one with all there is. When you do, you will no longer suffer from unnecessary self-inflicted pain—emotionally, spiritually or physically. You will only see love in everyone and everything including yourself.

Beautiful isn't it?

Have a lovely day.

Q: *I am proud of myself today. I woke up not feeling well with shingles. Ricky was not in a great mood, thus he did not extend any affection or interaction. Then my feeling not-good-enough because I don't make enough money, I don't feel well a lot so I'm useless, and Ricky doesn't like or respect me because I don't contribute much financially went into high gear as usual. Instead of allowing it to run rampant and making myself feel worse, I took a deep breath and told those feelings that they weren't true. I reminded myself that how Ricky feels in the morning is about him not about me. I reminded myself that getting upset and down about the shingles and not feeling well would just feed into it and make me feel worse.*

Then I put my shoes on and went for a walk to sweat and just be. I did not think of anything or repeat any mantras; I just looked at all of the beauty in nature and enjoyed feeling my body move. Then I came in and meditated with the sole purpose of feeling the good in me. It felt wonderful and I even near the end had a vision. I'm not sure what it meant, but it was a lady who although she didn't look just like me, she reminded me of myself. I watched her walk unwaveringly as she took off her robe and dove out of a window. Then I was her and I was falling and I was scared. I landed in a pool of pure water. It felt like it washed all of my pain away and I was happier than ever. Then I was on the ledge as myself and I jumped and figured out how to float gently down into the pool of water.

I guess the only little tug I feel in my state of bliss is am I doing all that I need to do to manifest what I'm wanting? I would love to have more money at least enough to pay my bills. I would love to wake up feeling better and stop getting shingles outbreaks. I'm not asking these things out of fear, well maybe a touch that I don't want to keep living this way, but I want to get to that which I'm wanting on the shortest path possible. I've applied for a few jobs to make some money and did not get them. I let it go knowing that the right one had not appeared yet. I've rested when tired and have been eating well and doing all of the things to feel healthy. Yet, I still have not seen either thing change yet. Do you have any advice? Thank you.

A: When you let go in your meditation and in changing those things that you did not like in the morning, you allowed yourself to be free of those things and reach a place of healing where you felt better. This vision was a visual story if you will for that. You let go even though it was scary for you, it was not your norm, but when you reached the pool, you felt joy, peace, and all that you were craving. This is a great lesson for you to remember when you find yourself straying from this path. Remember that trusting, believing, and letting go will get you there.

This is one of your biggest struggles—letting go. When you do you find happiness, but the fear creeps back up and causes you to retract once again. The good news is that the more you practice the letting go as you did this morning and the more that you embrace that feeling when you were jumping from the window, the more you will find what you are wanting.

It is just a muscle that needs to be strengthened. Do not beat yourself up if some days you just need to rest. Do not beat yourself up when you feel yourself contracted back to a state of fear. Be patient and kind and understanding. You are not stupid or dense as you think of yourself when you do not get something right away. You are a sweet soul who reacts from her wounds. Know that getting angry, frustrated, or giving up will not change your situation.

Think of yourself as a little girl that you are teaching to tie her shoes. You do not show her once or even five times and then bam she is a pro. No, you model it for her a few times while she tries mostly unsuccessfully. But you praise her for her effort. Then you get behind her and take her hands and walk her through the steps and praise her when they are tied as if she did it alone. You laugh and celebrate this small feat as though she won an Olympic gold medal. Then you give her tips and pointers as she tries on her own. And when she gets frustrated and says that she can't do it, you tell her that she can and you help her again. And this goes on until after a while she gets it, after she has practiced many times.

Is she stupid or dense because she didn't get it the first few times? Do you scold, reprimand, or call her names? No, you are patient, and gentle, and supportive. You praise her when she tries and you keep supporting her until she can do it.

This is how you need to treat yourself during this process. You are learning a new way of being and it can be much more trying then learning to tie shoelaces. You took a huge step today by not feeding into your typical patterns of self-abuse. Bravo, you did the next thing and chose differently. What a joyous day! You should celebrate yourself! We are so very proud of you.

As you continue to make this choice each day, you will find that you get to a point where they are fewer and farther between the days when you recognize that joy and self-love are your norm. You are manifesting what you are wanting. You wanted to stop beating yourself up so much and calmly and kindly recognize when you weren't choosing that. You did that today. Be patient our friend, it will become second nature sooner than you think.

Although you know and appreciate all of this, we can feel that little pull underneath to hear why you haven't seen an increase in your financial situation and great improvements in your health. You have seen it in your household as bills have gotten paid a lot more lately. Yes, by Ricky but it is happening. You do have to detach yourself from the judgment you are still heaping upon yourself. Instead of rejoicing in the fact that more money has come into your home, you are still beating yourself up by the fact that you think you didn't bring it.

Why is it so hard for you to appreciate the fact that we all work together? Look at all that you do for Ricky, your home, his business, and for yourself. You may not have people handing you the money, but you are assisting him in doing what he does so he gets the money. Taking care of him, his clothes, bedding, cleaning his home, grocery shopping, cooking meals and cleaning them up, writing blogs for him, and all of the work and writing you are doing for you is work. You know that but doubt it when you don't see your hand collecting the money.

You are working towards bringing your own money into your life and his. And it is coming, just believe this and continue to do what you do. You are creating avenues. Be patient, all will be evident soon. All that you need to do is to continue to allow, do the next thing, be in your joy, and let go. It will come.

We are so proud. See us clapping and celebrating your learning to tie bunny ears on your sneakers. No they are not lopsided, they are perfect. So are you.

With so much love and adoration.

20

Trusting My Intuition

Q: *I had an amazing akashic reading session with Karen Adams of AkashicJourney.com yesterday in which she accesses the akashic records to offer guidance. It was enlightening and helped me to feel that I was on the right path with my spiritual learning and writing. She also offered advice with specifics on how to accomplish what I was wanting. I am grateful for the direction and look forward to my future. It is funny, although I feel relief in knowing that I'm not just spinning my wheels, I feel a bit uneasy today. Everything seemed so crystal clear yesterday when she was talking to me. Today, I feel less clear and like I remember bits and pieces about what to do, like the haze is settling in around me again. She said that feeling of searching in the dark for the door knob that I have is because I'm forging new territory. I also feel now like somehow I have to live up to what I'm supposed to do and feel some anxiety to do it 'right.' I also don't want to be paralyzed by fear because I know from past projects that if I don't allow them to flow and do it, that someone else will, which also creates anxiety for me. How can I put all of this stuff aside so that I can just do the next thing to the best of my ability?*

A: People like Karen who have accessed their abilities and share them with others are there to help when someone feels a bit lost. They 'turn on the light' so to speak so that you can see the room that you've been in that has appeared dark to you. This allows you to have some verification that you are doing the right thing for you and heading in the right direction.

It is not there to foreshadow everything for you because *how much fun would life be if you were told everything that was going to happen, when, and how to do it?* It would get pretty boring pretty fast. **You may not think so right now, but when there is no surprise, no magic, eventually it would get monotonous and there would be no mystery to keep you engaged.** It is not a penance that you are paying or a test that you don't see everything clearly before it happens. It is life. It is the way things are set up so you try, learn, and grow. It is supposed to be fun, not scary.

Think about it. *Remember playing "Pin the Tail on the Donkey" when you were a kid?* The premise being that you were blind folded and spun until you were dizzy and then let go to try to pin the tail in the correct place on the donkey. Well most of the time you did not get it on the backside area but on the face or nowhere near the donkey. *And what did you do?* Everyone laughed. You did not get mad or feel less than or think there was something wrong with you. You laughed and had fun. And remember when you tried to cheat if you could see out of the handkerchief over your eyes…you did better because you knew what you were doing, but it wasn't as fun at all.

That is kind of how guidance is. It is great from time to time to show you other perspectives or to think along pathways that you may have not previously to help you out. But it is not there to tell you exactly how it should or will be because you always have choice. So instead of being upset that you can't remember every detail and it doesn't feel clear, celebrate that you were happy with where you were when the light came on, be happy that you're heading down the right path for you, and rejoice in the great hint that you would find more joy and success than you even fathomed.

Do not feel that you have to do something 'right' or in a certain way or in a certain amount of time. This is the opposite of what was intended for you when this gift was sent your way. There is no time frame. There is no fear of someone else doing it first because no one is you, and no one can do it like you. **You cannot do it wrong, because as long as you put in the effort, open your heart, and allow it to flow, you will get there.**

You know the statements you see and hear a lot that the prize is not the gift but the journey, well it is true. You are supposed to be having fun and enjoying your learning and journey. You can't do it wrong, you don't have a time frame like you are being tested on multiplication, and you are not being judged. You are being applauded, cheered on, helped up, and thrown encouragement, light and help from guides, loved ones and the entire universe.

So, stop walking stiffly and put your hands in the air and shake it like you just don't care. We will turn the music up, just listen!

It is a game, not a test. It is fun, not scary. Embrace joy, not anxiety. We love being a part of your journey. Join us in celebrating every moment!

With love and booty shaking,
Us

Q: *I have this issue I was hoping you could help shed some light on for me. I don't have very good eyesight and I find myself straining*

a lot to see. But it is more than my eyesight; my eyes get so blurry sometimes that I can't see well even with glasses. When I wear glasses for too long I get a headache so I only wear them when driving and when I have to. I also have sinus pressure and pain above my eyes that runs along my eyebrows and past my temples to the side of my head. It is always tender there and I feel like my forehead is hanging over my eyes. I'm always wrinkling up my forehead trying to see well. It is strange. Is there something causing this pain/pressure? I do notice that when I'm watching TV if I notice that my eyes are blurry and I relax my neck, shoulders, and eyes that I can see so much better. Is stress or straining causing some of my blurred vision? Thank you for any advice in letting go of this problem.

A: You don't trust that you can 'see' what you are wanting, and you are worried that you will miss something so your norm is hypervigilance. This is so you are ready for whatever comes your way at any time. Part of this was ingrained in you when you didn't know what was coming next as a little girl. It is part of the stress that is labeled post-traumatic stress disorder. It is an inability to relax because your body and mind are stuck in a hyper alert state and ready for a life-and-death situation at any time.

Yours is compounded by the fact that you try so hard. You want so bad to heal, get better, and not miss any signs that you are in a hyper aware state most of the time. This state has you constantly looking for a sign and you don't want to miss it, kind of like your eyes are peeled open 24/7 even when you are trying to relax.

The issue here is that the signs or synchronicities that you've experienced have come in the complete opposite way. They happen when you are relaxed or immersed in something else. **They are carried on the wings of gentle breezes, floating down and landing softly next to you.** They are not something that you stand guard to see or experience, they cannot be forced, and you cannot stop life to wait for them. **They come when you are in alignment with allowing and letting it flow.**

Think about the ones that you've experienced lately. You saw the special session for an akashic reading while merely browsing Facebook. The pull you felt was gentle and almost fleeting. You saw it, felt it, but wanted to confirm with Ricky because you didn't fully trust that the message you got was for you. But as you think back you realize that it was clear, it was just in a delicate manner almost like a whisper. *Why do you think meditation is such a great tool?* Because when you quiet your mind, body, and surroundings you can get in touch with that gentleness that delivers the connection to all that you are wanting.

This is how you get information, by letting go, by going with the flow and allowing yourself to align with this energy that delivers the reminders that you are connected to all that is.

The eye strain issue is just another example of your trying too hard, so hard in fact that it keeps you from what you are wanting. Again there is no hard fast quick fix. It is merely going to be gentle reminders when you become aware of this state that you don't want to be in. Don't get mad that you are straining again, simply look at it as a pointer.

Repeat—*Wow, I'm trying too hard to see. I will take a deep breath and close my eyes for a moment and relax. I know that I will come into alignment with intuition and synchronicities easily and effortlessly by letting go. I trust that I am safe and watched over, therefore, I do not need to fear what is coming next. I am the creator of my life and I choose joy. I choose to welcome to myself a life full of happiness, relaxation, fun, abundance, and all of the things that I am wanting. All that I need to do is think of that which makes me happy and think about all that I am grateful for. I am so lucky to have the freedom, abundance, love, learning, and peace that I do. I love it and welcome more of it into my life.*

There is no point in getting frustrated because it will only give you more frustration. When you are feeling this tightness do not get upset or fight against it. Simply sit back, take a deep breath, feel the tension dissipating and refocus on the things in your life that you love. Feel gratitude and imagine only those things that make you smile.

Do you notice that your forehead feels lighter already? You are not straining to see or hear, you are just allowing this energy to come. You trust that it will and you do not have any preconceived expectations about whether it is good info, or that it will give you anything, you are just allowing it to come. It is almost as if you don't comprehend these words and as you've noticed you get so much more out of it when rereading it. When you are typing these words you are opening yourself up and allowing. When you go back to it, you can then relax and allow them to 'sink in' as you say.

Healing is not about figuring out the right protocol, doing something in a certain fashion or order, or finding a miracle action or thing to take to find relief. It is merely aligning yourself with universal life force energy. In this energy you are allowing and when you are open and allowing this pure love to flow through you, there is harmony. This harmony allows your cells to vibrate and be as they are intended. This place of being is where all well-being is. In well-being and peace there is no sickness, pain, or distress. This is how you heal, by choosing this. It cannot be tricked into, forced by supplements into changing, and no amount of straining, reading, or trying will force it to be. It is simply allowing and letting go of that which doesn't serve you.

Remember jumping out of the window that you spoke of during a previous writing? You let go and you not only landed safely but you reached complete bliss in a pool of pure water that washed away all that you didn't want. It really is that simple. The only thing that doesn't feel simple is the doing it part. **The fear that we build up**

against something is the true obstacle, not anything else. *What is the saying you've heard a lot? "There is nothing to fear except fear itself."* That is so true because nothing can hurt you more, impede your progression, or stop you from allowing all that you are wanting except fear.

If you have to choose one thing that you can 'do' to change the direction of your ill health, it is to realize that **fear is not real. It is a manmade illusion that we create to impede our success.** *Why would we want to impede our own success you ask?* Because our ego, the collective shadow of our pain, wants us to believe that we are not worthy of the perfection that lies within. Do not listen to or acknowledge this thing you call fear, it is merely a roadblock to your bliss. Do what you have to do, ignore it, pat it on its head and walk past it, or whatever action you deem necessary to continue on your path of discovering joy. That is one of the biggest things that those who pass away realize is that all that they thought was so important or scary or blocking their earthly happiness was merely their own manmade junk.

There is nothing blocking the life you want except your collective pain whose name is fear.

Outsmart fear and let go of associating with pain. You are not your pain. You do not deserve your pain. You did not do anything wrong so that you need to suffer. You are merely blinded by pain and fear. Straining harder to see around or through it will not help. Relax, zoom out, sit back and see the big picture. They are just little sad guys that are trying to get you to relate to them. You are not them, they are not you. You are love, energy, and all that is beautiful. Don't fight them, instead lead by example and show them what is true—that you are joy.

We love you so very much.

Amen

When I learn something new, along with the understanding comes a 'test' if you will to see if I've really understood or let it go. Which is OK, it just seems to bring up more questions and things I don't know what to do with.

Q: *Wow, I'm so enthralled with how the universe works. I had an akashic reading the other day and it was fabulous. I was told that I was blocking my own abundance, good health, and success because I had not let go of the situation with my daughter having moved in with her father and all of the emotions surrounding that. It seemed so clear and easy to understand during the reading that it all happened to teach us each our lessons and I was good with it. And of course, within a week my resolve was tested. To sum it up, basically my daughter spent last year's Christmas holiday with her dad because we had just moved here. She offered unprompted that she wanted to spend a few weeks over Christmas here with me this year. However, I believe she doesn't want to because she gets spoiled at her dad's and she is afraid that if she is not there over the actual holiday, she will not get it all. I know that she is a teen who is wrapped up in what she can get, but my feelings are hurt especially with the way she was handling it. I got upset because I don't want my feelings to be hurt, and I don't want to care so much. But they are and I do. I was calm, did not let her disrespect me or use me as a scapegoat and told her I would let her know when she could come after the holidays. So, I'm not upset with my reaction to her, just that it hurt me. And that I feel like I don't know how to respond. Do I put the money aside to fly her out after the holidays to spend time or do I use that money and go on a vacation with Ricky over the holiday itself? I don't want to react out of hurt and angry emotions, but I also don't want to just allow her to choose so she* *gets what she wants from both sides. I'm not sure what to do. Thank you for any advice.*

A: First things first, instead of being upset at yourself, pat yourself on the back. You did better with this conversation than ever before. You were calm, respectful, and kind. Second, stop beating yourself up or 'feeling bad' because you are sad. **There is nothing wrong with feeling sad or angry or any emotion. This is where your problem lies. You think that to be strong you do not need to or should not feel any emotions.** Even when you have reached a point where you don't react from any of them, you still will feel hurt if you think someone that you love is choosing money over time with you. There is nothing weak about you for feeling.

You also reacted kindly yet were honest and voiced your outlook on the situation. Notice she did not correct you or deny that you accurately pinpointed her reasons for not choosing to be with you. It is good that you calmly expressed your awareness of her behavior. And although you and she both know that her behavior was monetarily motivated and she was making excuses for it, you did not make judgments against her behaviors, you merely let her know that you recognized them.

This is all great progress! We think you should be celebrating instead of feeling torn. You were able to love her, teach her, and speak your truth calmly, kindly, and non-judgmentally. This is leagues beyond your reactions just a month ago. So take a deep breath and smile, you've done well!

Now as far as how to proceed for your holiday, it has nothing to do with Cassandra. She chose to stay at her father's. There is nothing wrong with that. So your planning for what you do over your holiday is not impacted by her presence or not. It is a non-issue. If you have the money to go somewhere for you and Ricky to celebrate and you want to, her attendance should have nothing to do with your decision.

You are feeling guilty because you think it is wrong for you to go do something fun. *Why?* If you would have offered her a Christmas vacation, she may have come then, but only for the trip. Or she may not have come anyway. But either way, she is not coming so take her out of the equation.

What you are really upset about is not having the family Christmas you wish for. Your little girl there making cookies with you, spending time together, and being the family you want. You are missing what was when she was a little girl. But if you remember correctly, you were usually sad because she was only with you for part of the holiday and the other part she wasn't there.

Did you ever look at maybe this is a gift to just enjoy your holiday this year? No, we are not saying that not having her around is a gift, but not having the sad, tugging emotion of splitting the time is a gift. Maybe you can relax and enjoy time with Ricky. Making yourself happy should be a priority that you've long forgotten about—one that you really don't think of because you were always worried if Cassandra had enough, or if she was happy. *What would make you happy?* Make that little girl inside happy; enjoy a holiday doing what you would like. Give yourself a gift.

As we've spoken of before, it is not selfish to love yourself, give to yourself, and think of yourself, it is called self-love. This is a demonstration for your daughter as well. That is what she is choosing. She wants what she wants, and she chose it—right, wrong, or indifferent. She is not apologizing for her choice. *Why would you apologize if you choose doing something for you?* Because you are sad that spending time with you was not her choice. That was her choice this year. Honor that and choose to spend your time making yourself happy doing what you would like.

See we put so much credence in our happiness based on others choices, reactions, or if they are shunning us. When really they are doing what works for them at the time. Yes, a mother may be sad that her daughter doesn't choose her during a holiday. But now let it go and choose to give to you what you would have given her. *Why are you less important? Why do you have to change your holiday?* Make it fun, doing whatever makes you guys feel great. Then everybody wins.

And maybe one day, she will crave the bonding you do over the holidays and you can share the love with her and her family that you have because you gave to yourself. **You will have shown her that you do not base your happiness on her actions or anyone else's. You will have taught her that only you and you alone can love you whole.**

You are still struggling with whether you save the money and don't go on a trip so she can visit after the holidays. We say, worry about you, take care of you, and plan your holiday. Somehow she may still be able to come after you return. Maybe it will be much cheaper because it was after the holiday. Maybe it is postponed until a month or two later.

You are not being a bad mother by not bending to her requirements for her holiday. Wish her well, be happy for her, call her on Christmas and listen to her tell you about her presents, send her a present or card, and then share your happiness of what you are doing. Do not punish her for her choice, but do not punish yourself either and hold onto the resentment that you didn't do what you wanted because you were trying to recreate another Christmas for her after the fact. That is teaching her that she can get whatever, whenever, regardless of your wants and needs.

No go look at holiday getaways and put the intent out there! Celebrate you. Get excited for you. The holiday is special for you and for Ricky. Stop allowing there to be a cloud over it of sadness and wishing, it is only hurting you. Love you. Celebrate you. Give yourself the gift of love, peace, acceptance, and self-care.

Be Merry!

We love you so.

Sometimes it still seems so hard for me to understand, trust, or feel my own guidance system.

Q: *I would really like to learn to trust my own gut instincts in my life. Sometimes I don't even have a gut instinct, I just don't know what to do at all. Then when I do get a gut instinct, I question it and second guess it. It can be about something as silly as what to order off of a menu at a restaurant to something more important like what to do or say to someone in a situation where I'm uncomfortable. I don't think that I'm not intelligent enough to make a decision, I just get so afraid that I'm going to make the wrong one. Not that I don't think it is OK to make a mistake, I just want to choose correctly the first time to avoid having to do it again.*

I also recently learned a lesson about listening to my gut. I had a type of reading with someone and I found it very helpful. So, I struggled with one piece of information she gave me that didn't sit right. I couldn't stop thinking about it over the next couple of months because although it was the opposite of how I wanted to proceed, I kept thinking that what if she was right and my gut was wrong and what would happen if I didn't listen. Then, recently I had an akashic reading and she told me what my gut had been telling me about this one thing. I told her that I had felt that way but was told differently by someone else. She assured me that my gut was the path and to listen to it.

I understand that we all have our own filters that can affect the information we give. So, I guess my question is how do I deepen my own self-trust so that I don't discount my path regardless of what others share with me. I want to listen to guidance and be open to suggestions as to not cut off avenues of receiving information, but I want to more easily be able to discern what is best for me. Do you have any advice? Thank you.

A: You stated one of the reasons that you struggle is because you are afraid of choosing incorrectly and having to not only go through the process again but clean up the mess from the incorrect choice. **Your fear is what is interfering with your ability to 'hear' your gut.** The gut instincts are being drowned out by the voices of fear. If you let go of the fear, quiet it, ask it to leave, or whatever way works for you to visualize the release of it, then you will be able to be clear enough to feel the path to follow.

See how that works? It is funny or ironic as you say that the very thing that you are 'afraid' of is the very thing that is causing the 'issue' you have. **Your fear of messing up or having more work is what is impeding your ability to use your intuition to help you navigate the road you want to travel.** No matter what you choose it is not wrong. It may be a detour and it may lead you down a path that you have to turn around, come back, and go down the other one. But even if you do this, it is never wrong. Each choice leads you to learn something and then you can choose again.

It sounds like your biggest issue is fear of creating roadblocks or more work for yourself because you want to travel a straight shot to where you are wanting. This can be good because you want to be in the place where you are really living your purpose. **However, sometimes the small pit stops or detours are where we learn the most, have the most fun, and meet some great people.** So stop fearing that these small curves in your path are bad or a waste of time.

As we have spoken of before, it is not what is at the end, it is the journey—the joy, fun, and learning along the way. It is not a race that you will win a bigger better prize if you finish first. We see you relaxing already when you view it from this way. There is no time crunch or better reward if you do it as quickly as you can with the least bumps as possible. Think about it, when you are driving along in your car and you come across those areas where the road dips down and you get that fluttery feeling in your stomach. *What do you do when those happen?* You smile. And you may not have smiled at that moment and felt that fluttering if the road was just straight.

There is not a straight road that shortens the distance; they are winding back country roads with beautiful views. So take it easy, enjoy it. Approach life like you are enjoying a Sunday ride in that 1972 convertible Stingray Corvette. *Sounds a lot more fun huh?* You know that is the beauty of life that you get to choose. That choice is not about how quickly you can choose and how fast you can get there. It is about enjoying it. We would choose the Corvette as long as it was a Sunday stroll. See Corvettes aren't very smooth when you are rushed or taking the shortcuts over bumpy terrain.

Lastly, yes we are all here to help guide one another, help one another, give joy, hugs and smiles to one another along our journeys. But yes, humanness comes with filters that no matter how enlightened you are, you may bring your own 'stuff' into a session. Even in your own words you said you enjoyed the session, you felt uplifted, and you were happy with it. *So why would you discount an hour of great insight for one inaccurate sentence that she shared because of her own issue?* You shouldn't. And you didn't, which is great. But know that ultimately, if it doesn't resonate with you than that is OK. Let it go. Do not try to mull it over a million times as you do to try and see how it could fit. Put it aside, and if one day it comes up you may see how it does fit. If not, then it wasn't yours.

You do not give yourself enough credit. Each and every person is a piece of the divine. Each holds all of the answers and knowledge in them. **Life is about remembering these things, or recognizing them and your intuition through gut instincts, mother's intuition, or however you want to label your guidance system.** It is there to help you navigate your journey through your life. Do not feel scared of it in any way, whether that is your inability to hear it or whatever 'issue' you have.

It is a gift, an intrinsic part of the beauty of you. You are not any better or worse than anyone else. Do not think that you are wrong for embracing who you are. You and only you have the most clear, pure connection with you and to all that is. Embrace it and use it for the betterment of yourself, your journey, and what you can offer to others. And you are not perfect, no one is, so don't ever be afraid that you are wrong or that someone else is right. **All that you are to do is honor that voice inside, do what you feel is best in your heart, and offer what you are guided to give knowing that you are doing it with the best intentions.** Nothing else is yours to be concerned with.

Enjoy it, enjoy living. When you do you will find it is beautiful, magical, and so much fun!

Even with all that I've learned, I still find myself struggling with things.

Q: *I'm feeling down today. I didn't have the best weekend and once again I'm here not happy with much. I have come at least far enough over the last eight months that I'm not blaming anyone else for how I feel or thinking that any external factors would change anything. I'm also trying not to beat myself up for feeling this way. I'm just feeling hopeless as I'm not feeling well, I'm depressed, and I wonder if it will ever change. I tried laying in the sun, saying positive feelings or statements so that instead of saying, "I'm tired," I said, "I feel energized and happy," etcetera. I meditated, ate a fruit and vegetable smoothie, I took it easy and for some reason I still don't feel well. I'm confused about why using the tools isn't working and why even though I use them and don't get so upset my immune system is still is so affected. I feel so run down. Please help, thank you.*

A: Depression, sadness, and hopelessness are directly linked to expecting or wanting something different than what is or what happened. This thinking is the cause of you not feeling well. Now it may be 'true' to you that you wished something or most things were different this weekend. And there is nothing wrong with wanting something different for the future. The problem lies in the fact that you are still sad or thinking about the weekend and how it disappointed you. You are focused on what you did not get that you wanted or how you envisioned it being the perfect weekend. Feeling bad or rundown is from putting your energy into being angry, sad, mad, or disappointed in what is or what was. This will never make you happy or get you what you are wanting.

See these disappointments happen to show you things. They show you what you like or enjoy, or conversely what you do not like or do not enjoy. They are not happening to you because you or something you did was wrong. It is not a punishment. You are not less than or paying a penance for something you did. It merely is an experience.

A healthy way of changing this is to merely look at things differently. It may seem so difficult but it really is just choosing a different way to view these things. Don't label them as disappointments or an awful weekend, merely observe them. When you see from the observation that you did not enjoy them, simply recognize this and make the statement, *"That is not what I choose, I choose to feel happy, free, have fun,"* or whatever it is that you are wanting.

You will not get the experience you want by focusing on what it is that you did not like on the weekend. *See?* Simple, yet it may seem difficult because this is not your 'normal' or typical way of observing and reacting to things. You did have some joyous times this weekend, *did you not?* Yes, once you think about it and ask yourself what you did enjoy, you remember three things that you did that were wonderful, made you smile, and where you had fun. But your focus was that the weekend was awful because of the other three things that did not make you feel this way.

Why would you choose to ignore the good that was just as prevalent as the bad? It is like you take a broom and sweep the weekend into one pile. Yes, you had some unpleasantness but that doesn't mean you disregard all that you did enjoy. If you did this every time something that you did not prefer happened you would be sweeping away all of your joy because everything wasn't always joyful. *Seems silly now that you look at it from this perspective huh?*

See, you want a life where nothing ever happens that you do not like, that you never have problems or issues come up, and that everything is always perfect. But that is not how life is. And even if it was like it is in your fantasy, realize that without the issues, the joys may not feel half as good. We know that you have had more than your share of sadness, pain, issues, and disappointments. When we say this we are not negating that these things happened to you. We do say however, that for the most part you have a great life, with many blessings, and love sent your way. You no longer have to wonder when the next awful thing is going to happen. You are not a helpless little girl who doesn't know what to do. You are not powerless.

You have all of the power of the universe inside of you. You have all that you ever need inside of you. You have all of the love that you've ever wanted inside of you. You do not need to brace or protect yourself from those you love or the outside world. They can't hurt you anymore because you know now that others actions have no effect on your bliss. No one can give or take away love because you are already full. You know that we are all one, we are all connected and that anything that you've viewed in the past as unloving or hurtful is merely a human learning experience. **You are here to act, observe, learn, feel, see, be, mess up, make mistakes, find joy, experience pain and through it all remember the biggest**

truth there is—that you already have all that you ever wanted inside of you.

So, we say when someone you love disappoints you—tell them kindly and gently. And if they continuously hurt you, look at your reaction to their humanness. *Is there something that you can do to help them or can changing your perspective alleviate your pain?* If not, make a different choice. And talk to them again about what you've discovered about yourself and their actions. Express your love, not your disappointment with them or their actions. Together choose differently. Eventually, the issue will resolve because they changed, you changed, or the relationship changes.

Nothing is concrete, we are here to learn, grow, change and remember who we are. **Most 'problems' or issues that we have on earth are merely the absence of inner sight because if we really saw the perfection inside, we would have nothing to be upset about.**

Celebrate the joys, take note of what bothers you for it points to something you need to look at inside, and hold onto gratitude. Being grateful for each and every joy will keep you focused on what makes you feel good. Love you, love life, love everything and everyone because each is just as important and profound as the next thing.

Choose joy, choose love, and choose feeling good no matter what. *See how you feel like a new person in just a half hour of focusing on what you do have?*

Isn't really 'seeing' grand?

We love you.

Q: *I was so happy that the pain in my right hip went away after doing the exercise from Gay Hendricks I mentioned in an earlier*

writing. Now, I'm having problems in the left sciatica and the exercises don't seem to be working. I assume that means it is something different. Could it just be physical or does every pain have an emotional base? Also, I would like to ask my left sciatica pain what it is trying to tell me. I appreciate your help because it hurts so bad it is hard for me to feel good to be in meditation and in receiving mode. Thank you.

(I could not get into mode and stepped away. I went to the chiropractor and the pain resolved for a few hours. Then it came back, so I sat down and meditated until I was in mode so I could resolve this.)

A: Physical misuse or alignment can be a reason for a pain or physical issue. Usually though the original weakness or predisposition is rooted in an emotional cause. *Haven't you ever noticed that people tend to have 'issues' throughout their life with either their back or hips or sinuses or what have you?* Generally that is because of a weakness there related to an unresolved emotional pattern or issue.

We see the frustration that you have let go of the right hip issue and now you are dealing with the sciatic pain on the left. Unfortunately sometimes, clearing out old wounds, or patterns can seem cumbersome and annoying as you say. These are big issues for you with the previous being sexual and physical abuse in this area. This is wonderful that you were able to release stuff there. Do not discount the paramount importance of what you did because you are now seeing another one. You did not fail because you have pain again; you succeeded and have moved onto another area. This is cause for celebration.

Not every pattern or pain will be so acute with such a huge emotional base that you will need to work on it individually. We see you looking ahead about how many more of these can you deal with. It can be a lot quicker than your previous one, it is just really getting down to the core and letting it go without resistance, without anger, and without ignoring what it is trying to tell you.

Now ask—*Left sciatic pain, I hear you, I feel you, I know that you have brought up something for me to look at and clear out. What is it; tell me what it is that you are trying to have me look at?*

Amy: *While meditating on this question I saw myself drawn down into a fetal position in which I drew my left hip up to shield me from stuff coming at me. That stuff was past sadness, abuse, and pain. I could feel that my body, especially my left side was tired—tired of shielding me, tired of being ready to recoil to protect me, and tired of living in fear. I felt tears well up for feeling sad that I've lived this way for so long. That I've spent so many years on guard to get in the impact ready position. I felt the tears carry with it the old wounds and the exhaustion from being in the position for so long. I really want to release this feeling like I flinch every time I may feel that something could go wrong or I suspect there is danger to my well-being. I want to release the patterns that a therapist labeled as PTSD. I no longer want fear to control me. I want to relax into the flow of life. I want to trust that no matter what happens I will be OK and that I will be supported. I want to release this heaviness I feel on my left side. I no longer want the old movie clips to continue to play on silent in the background of my life. I want to turn the TV off and feel free to breathe in life now. I no longer want to define myself by what I've survived but by what I am in this moment. I really want to let this go, do you have any advice on how to go about this? Thank you.*

Everything begins with your intention, which you just stated so beautifully. The only thing we suggest is to change your statement from *'I no longer want,'* or the *'I want,'* statements from this longing to an action. So we would say instead of, *"I no longer want fear to control me,"* to *"I freely flow with what is."* Eliminate the word fear because just by saying it you contract. Say it and feel that. All that you stated was what you want to get rid of or don't like and which is causing you pain. Notice that when we give you statements that focus on what you **do** want, the positive is drawn to you. If you would like an example of a way to word your wishes above, this is an example of aligning yourself with what you are wanting.

Repeat—I am free. I breathe in deeply the joy of now and the love and energy that fills me from inside. I gently release any memories, stories, or patterns from the past that I no longer wish to keep relieving. I choose to live in the now fully alive and aware of the grandness and perfection that I am part of. I open my arms, soul, and heart to life and I know that I am safe and cared for by myself and the limitless love of all that exists. I align myself with this beautiful energy and feel supported, guided, loved and embraced in all that I do. I know that all that I need is myself because all of the love, guidance, and all that I'm wanting has always existed inside of me. I gladly open up so that I may bask in this every day and that I may share it with the world. I need not concern myself with how it is accepted by anyone, because all that matters is that I live from my heart. Others reactions are about what is going on with them, not me. I am excited and grateful to live every moment from this bliss that I've discovered inside. I am free.

Amen

Now how do you feel? Lighter, the left and right side both feel equally relaxed and open to what is. *Right?* Remember, if you feel the pain returning you may need to say and allow this to wash over you again. The muscle and fear memory may need to be worked with more than once. Do not look at it as a chore, but a gift. *What is greater than speaking to you with love to give yourself this gift?* Remember how great you feel right now. Remember how the pain left. Be patient with yourself and kindly and calmly repeat as necessary until it becomes your natural nature. Remember…you are that little girl inside learning to tie her laces. Give her the loving care that she deserves.

We love you so.

21

Unexpected Surprises

Q: *Oh how I've missed this. I haven't written in a few weeks because I went back east to visit family and friends. It was wonderful because I experienced just letting go and allowing, and I had so many lovely unexpected surprises come up.*

I heard from my deceased (as we call it) brother and mother during a 'Dinner with a Medium' that I had nothing to do with planning. I had almost declined the invitation. Then I had a session with Mary Ellen where I declared that if I was meant to go to Drunvalo Melchizedek's "Awakening the Illuminated Heart" workshop that an opening from the waiting list would open up. Twenty minutes later, I received an email that a spot opened up. The whole two weeks were filled with joy and unexpected surprises.

Now that I'm back and settled in, I still have a problem trusting myself and feeling confident in my decisions. Although I've seen firsthand how relaxing and welcoming the synchronicities of the universe brings to me more than I could imagine, I still feel myself tense up and feel afraid that I won't succeed. That if I am not diligent enough or disciplined enough that I will let the opportunities pass me by. Maybe because I was out of my element and didn't have anything to accomplish or do, I allowed more? I didn't feel any need to perform, create, accomplish, I was just there to visit and enjoy people that I love. I really want to feel that freedom and allowing every day in my life, not just when I'm on vacation. How can I incorporate this into my daily life even when I have a to-do list, work, cooking, cleaning and life?

A: *What was different while you were away?* You trusted. You trusted that your family and friends would house you and feed you, and that you did not have anything that you had to do other than enjoy yourself. You unplugged from feeling that you were not good enough and you chose to just be. Be there and enjoy a meal, a cup of tea, or holding your Nana's hand. You did not feel that you had to be anything other than what you were—a friend, a daughter, a mother, and a granddaughter. You believed that you already were those things and you trusted and believed that you were good enough in those roles. That love, caring, and thoughtfulness were the only things that you had to do, and when you came from your heart they came naturally. They did not cause you any stress, concern or strain because you are very comfortable in that way of being. You know how to love, show caring, express these feelings and enjoy the company of those you care about. When you didn't have to clean, cook, and do all of the stuff that you do at home, you were able to relax and enjoy just being in the moment.

We are given these opportunities to experience a different perspective and allow ourselves to incorporate this into our daily lives. There is no reason that you can't experience this same peace and serenity in your daily life. Yes, there will be times that things come up but when you are in this place of trust and knowing that all will be OK no matter what, you will find joy being and you will see life this way no matter if you are working, cleaning, dealing with a 'crisis' or whatever.

Once you let go of the fear that you are not good enough and once you release judgment of yourself, you will see that how you felt on vacation is how you will feel every day. There is still a part of you, even after all of the miracles that you've experienced, that is waiting for the track to run out if you will. You gain momentum and are riding along happily on a train and then you suddenly become fearful and start looking out the window to make sure the track is still there, that it isn't going to just stop abruptly. This is impeding your ability to keep going, flowing, and winding through the hills and valleys of your life.

You want to know how you can just know that the track is always there so you don't have to fear its disappearance. It is called faith, a concept that you have always struggled with. You want to believe, you have believed, but you feel that you have been burned when you weren't expecting or deserving of it. So now when you feel yourself flowing along, before you completely let go, you slow down, stop the train and get out to survey the track. You have grown weary of this stopping and starting and want to just continue on without second guessing this anymore.

You can change this fear by knowing that you lay the track. Your belief, faith, and expectations are what lays the track before you. There is not a big scary angry God that reaches down and picks up a piece of track so that you crash. There is no evil entity or energy that has control over you as the train or the track itself. No it is not an old track in certain areas where it could just break. See you are not an old rusty train riding on an old dilapidated track. You are a new state-of-the-art silver aerodynamic train like you've never seen before. Think of it like the sci-fi movies of the future. Better yet, get rid of the track. You could imagine that it appears in front of you, as it does. Wherever your life goes, it will appear. But we can feel you straining to think of ways that it may not.

So why not think of it like star trek? There are no tracks for them to beam from one space ship to another. They simply are on their ship, step inside the transporter, and then they are on the other ship. Omit the travel track and the time and just be where you want.

You know, being in the moment of each thing does not mean that you have to go painfully slow and analyze each step or each piece of the track. It doesn't mean slowing down to an excruciatingly slow pace. It means awareness. When you have heard about and practiced mindfulness from reading Eckhart Tolle's books, it doesn't mean that you need to live a life in slow motion. It is just a way, a pointer, a lesson to understand the concept of being present, being in the fullness of your miraculous self no matter how trivial the task at hand. It does not mean that being a monk, or living without modern technology is more sacred or the correct way. It is just how you learn to feel that which you are, because if you can feel the aliveness and perfection in washing a dish, then you've truly gotten in touch with the immense beauty and perfection that you are.

See the dichotomy comes up again. **The simplicity of a seemingly meaningless task can awaken you to the whole universe.** *Remember as an older child and teenager that you wanted to go faster and faster and experience more and more like you couldn't do it fast enough?* During this time you were focused on fulfilling impulses and feeling the power to experience being alive. You were tired of the slow, mundane, and repetitive aspects of learning as a child. This rush to experience can take you away from feeling the greatness inside. *Why do you think elderly people are content with sitting and being?* They've experienced it all. They know what it is like to learn slowly, experience wildly, and know love, heartbreak, joy, and loss. And when you sit there having experienced so much, you get to know that you are all that and so much more inside. That no matter what your body is doing on the outside, you are so alive on the inside.

We are here to learn to be in our infinite awareness while synching this up with our bodies and minds. When we combine them with complete faith and trust, we are whole. That is what you crave, that is what you are wanting. Do not look outside of you for what already exists inside. This is the ultimate dog-chasing-his-tail scenario. Be aware and tuned into who you truly are and allow it to guide you. Trust that it is wise and infinite and know that you are always safe and loved. You are not on a runaway train that you need to slow. You are a part of all that is and it all exists within you. **You do not need to control it, you merely need to learn to feel comfortable being in it, coming from it, and allowing yourself to trust that all is well.** It always has been, it always will be.

Sometimes unexpected surprises are the most powerful eye-opening experiences. For me, at the *Dinner with a Medium* with Psychic Medium Nellie Walter, some epiphanies were born. I had an amazing life-changing reconnection with my brother through Psychic Medium Ricky Wood over twelve years prior, and this recent connection reminded me and further helped me to see things differently.

Q: *I'm starting to realize that a lot of the fear that I've viewed my life through was just a misperception of how things really are. The pain that I felt with the loss of my brother and mother was superficial. Not that I don't still miss them, but the medium connection that I had reinforced that they are still very much around me. They didn't die, they just changed forms. I still think there would be a feeling of loss because of their physical departure but if I had seen that they still existed then, maybe I wouldn't have suffered for so long. It is like the more I get in touch with feeling and perceiving from beyond my physical senses, the more I realize that not only are they still there but we are all connected and part of the same energy source. The separateness I thought existed is just a very temporary state to learn things for our soul's growth. When I step away, kind of like I'm sitting in the audience of a play and I'm watching my life and those around me, the charge that I used to get has diminished so much. Like most of what we bitch about, worry about, and judge each other about is so very trivial when you look at it from this perspective.*

I really prefer being or seeing things from this vantage point because I don't get so offended or worry about things when people are angry or whatever. I guess my question is then, I want to see from here, to take things in stride more, but I also don't want to withdraw from life, relationships, and the lessons I'm here to learn. When I'm sitting far away from it though, most things seem so trivial. I don't want people to think I don't care, but most things seem so petty and not worth the energy. How do I balance this perspective and remain involved and present in life at the same time?

A: It seems you are looking at this as a choice of whether you sit back in your audience seat or not. *Why not sit in your audience seat until your character is on stage? Or if you really want to stretch your perception, why not sit in your audience seat and when you are in a scene, maintain your seat and go on stage at the same time?* Your soul is capable of so much that you are unaware of. You think that you are one with your body and that it is like you are confined. If your spirit is still in your body, yet you connect with the spirit realm while you sleep, *why not while you are awake?*

You know many teachers have explained this in many different ways. A very good visual for you is when Eckhart Tolle described, in his book *A New Earth,* the 'pain-body' as an entity that you can separate from. You can use this as an example of your ability to be in the audience and on stage simultaneously. But you don't have to only separate the awareness and the pain-body or ego. **You can split the huge amount of consciousness to be aware in both places**

at once. You may become so engrossed in the stage scene that you are not aware of the part of you in the audience, but that is good. You do want to be present in what you are experiencing, but having the aware part of you watching and there if you need to take a breath and act mindfully can be very helpful.

You have heard before that your soul can be in a different life at the same time you are here, or that only a certain percentage of your soul is in this life. That seemed too far out for you to really think about. But to help you out here, think of it like the TV's that allow you to have multiple stations up on one screen. You've seen commercials where the die-hard sports fan wants to watch three different games at once. Well this is similar. Your infinite soul can be on stage experiencing, in the audience seeing the bigger picture, and in a higher spiritual dimension all at the same time.

We see that you are already trying it out while typing. Trying to disprove or find a flaw in it. It does feel much different, we know. It is a whole different way of seeing then you are used to that is why it can leave you feeling a bit loopy. You are used to straining to see through your physical eyes. Now you seem to be more centered in your mind's eye or near the top of your head, not just seeing through your physical eyes.

This is like most 'problems' that you encounter or face in your life. You tend to think that there is a yes or no, a right or wrong, or only this or that. When in actuality the views or perspectives are endless. Pretend that your eyesight has been upgraded from an old Polaroid camera to a high-definition new model that can see multiple angles at once while zooming in and out with ease.

Growth is not about becoming someone else, it is not about acquiring enough knowledge so that you know everything, and it isn't even about being enlightened enough to remain unbothered. It is about the ability to change your perspective, your view, and the limiting beliefs that you've always held.

Step back and let your soul lead the way, you will be amazed at how high-tech it is. Allow yourself to use all of the tools, gifts, and joys of being aligned with the awesomeness of your infinite soul. It is a part of all that is. If the world, the universe, and the creator are unimaginably intelligent and grand, then so are you.

These gifts have been sitting under your Christmas tree for a long time. Unwrap them and play little girl, play. We love watching your joy.

Q: *As a continuation of the previous question, I've begun to feel like I'm in meditation even when I'm not. I really like feeling like this because I'm able to separate myself from many pain-induced reactions from myself or others and feel like I can see the beauty in many things I did not before. Do you have advice besides seeing things simultaneously from different perspectives to be like this more? Also when faced with strong anger or surrounded by people who are not like this, it tends feel like I'm being pulled from this place I like to be. And when yesterday you spoke of being on stage and farther away in the audience at the same time, I feel like when I'm really emotionally invested or emotions become heightened, that I am all on stage and can't see the big picture as I do when I'm in the audience. Any advice on maintaining that meditative Zen while surrounded by chaos?*

A: It's kind of like a dance with the ebb and flow of the music that you feel naturally inclined to pull back at moments or sway into it depending on the speed and strength of the notes that are sweeping you along. Think of your perspectives and consciousness as this ebb and flow instead of trying to visualize it as choosing one seat or another. This is the next step. As we said yesterday there are multiple perspectives and you can be a part of each all of the time. And when you feel the anger or chaos infecting or affecting your mood, simply ebb back to the back row of the audience.

Others anger, chaos, or raging energy has nothing to do with you, even if it is directed at you or a situation that you are a part of. See so many times we place the blame with someone else, someone else's situation or actions as the cause for our discomfort. When someone is angry and yells and blames you for making them do it, you know that is incorrect. They are responsible for themselves and nothing that you do is the cause of their anger and their inability to separate from that long enough to look at the situation calmly.

The same goes for you on the other end. If someone is angry and yelling at you, only you have control over how you respond. You cannot follow the logic that you were Zen-like and happy and calm until they brought their anger into your world. That is blaming them for your reaction, just as they are blaming someone for their anger. *See?* It is no better to think that someone else has any control over your peace.

This is where ebbing and flowing will take you to the next level. You will have interaction and come into contact with anger, angry people, chaos, asleep people and so on. You cannot quarantine yourself to avoid this. You are not that delicate. Only your inability to ebb and flow is delicate because you have not practiced it. *Why do you think that you are still being challenged with these behaviors and people?* Because you need the practice my dear. You do not become good at something by avoiding anything that impedes it. **You become good at something by learning and practicing it regardless of the conditions.**

Think about it, when you've watched say a sporting event. *Do you have more respect and find it more inspirational when someone is tested, pushed beyond limitations and they overcome them? Or when it is a perfectly sunny day, and they are perfectly healthy, and they throw many perfect passes and easily win?*

Right! You see the beauty and the sacredness in those who face the chaos, opposition, and turmoil head on in a calm collected manner and they get the job done better than if they had no struggle. **You know adversity stirs a fire within so that you want to dig deep and find the best parts of you. Without these trying times, you may have never been motivated to do what you do.** You may have never found what you are finding and you may have been wishing for a situation that you could triumph in.

Do not look at problems, chaos, or trying times as bad luck or a road block. Look at them as gifts so that you may really experience the depth of beauty that your soul contains. **You are not a prisoner of hardship, but a master of learning who you truly are.**

Do you think you went through all of the things you did just to be punished? No you asked for these experiences before you came here so that you would truly experience the most beautiful sacred parts of you. Yes, it brings tears to your eyes, because you did it. You lived through them. You tried with all that you had and knew. **And now you know that you've seen holiness in sadness, exquisite joy in discovering the truth, and were pushed to reach depths of love and understanding that you could have never imagined.**

Bravo our friend, bravo.

We are so proud and we hope that you learn to bask more in these realizations than frustration at what you have yet to achieve. It is all perfect and so are you. No matter what.

Even when I've seen the difference that operating from a higher perspective yields, I still find myself second-guessing or trusting myself.

Q: *How do you decipher if what you want or are being pulled to do is the best choice for you? I think part of my problem of being so indecisive is because I want to make a good choice or the best choice for me from the beginning. Notice I didn't say the 'right' choice, since I know that there really isn't a right or wrong now, just choices and consequences. I know that by making a choice, there is a consequence that I may or may not like but I will learn from. I guess because I've made choices that weren't the best in the past, I feel like I've learned a lot. However, I want to make better choices now from the get go. Not because I fear being 'wrong,' but I fear all of the work or stuff I have to go through to get back to making a better choice. Kind of like I don't want to waste time and just get right to the best choice so I can experience a smoother ride or more joy and less 'tough learning.' A lot of the time I get so uncomfortable when I have to make a choice, even in a restaurant looking at a menu, because I fear that I will choose something that isn't the best or most fulfilling. So maybe I've graduated from thinking I will make a 'wrong' choice, but I still fear that I don't have a clear enough connection to intuitively know the best choice for me. Please help me see this more clearly and how I may overcome it. Thank you so much.*

A: It seems that you have moved your fear of being 'wrong' junk over to the fear of 'making more work for yourself' category. Which you should be commended that you no longer fear that choices will be wrong. Now we will address your fear of making a less pleasing outcome for yourself or creating more lessons.

First, you are placing an amount of disdain upon learning. This is because you still equate learning with pain or disappointment. You know that all learning or realizing that a different choice may have been better is not a punishment or has to carry a painful lesson for you. Yes, many of your life lessons were born from pain or discomfort. This is what motivated you to choose differently, to get back up, dust yourself off, and choose again. Pain, discomfort, or feeling unfulfilled can and has been a great catalyst to change in your life.

What you would want to look at then is *was it worth it in the end?* Think about it. When your daughter was diagnosed with rheumatoid arthritis as a child, it caused you both pain that motivated you to look into healing. Now you would not have wished this or chose this to come into your lives, but it did. And you know that if it had not, you would not be who you are now. *Would you give back all that you learned about holistic healing modalities, organic food, and the awe inspiring healing abilities the mind, body, and spirit possess?* No.

That was the beginning of your journey to change. The love you had for your daughter. The drive it gave you to research ways to heal the immune system rather than treating her symptoms with drugs. You benefited so much too because if it weren't for your love as a mother, you would probably have not sought out ways to help heal yourself. Her healing is a living embodiment of the potential that exists when faced with a situation you do not want. How love, commitment, and determination can lead you on a journey of discovery that can completely transform your life, the person you love's life, as well as countless people who read you and your daughter's journey of healing. You have no idea how this may have ignited this searching for many other parents and their children. It was not just a gift to your daughter and yourself, but a gift to the world. We are all connected. **Everything you do will touch the life of someone else, who will touch the life of someone else. The ripples are infinite**.

So no, not all learning even if it is born out of discomfort or a seemingly negative situation is painful. It was for moments, but this time in your life is such a great example of how worth it it was so that you could be who you are today. And she healed, and you began healing, and others healed and so *was it really that awful? Would you live through it again? Was your life positively affected by this less than joyful event and learning experience?*

You have surprised yourself to say that you wouldn't change it. It seems that some very deep rooted painful experiences, especially those of the loss or death of your loved ones, has heightened your pain/learning memory to have you think that all things are irreversibly, unresolvedly painful.

Maybe we need to delve deeper into that subject for your next question so we can separate out your fear of learning and situations. And although you have reconciled that they are not gone because their spirits live on, it seems that you still carry unresolved issues surrounding the death of your brother and mother.

To finish speaking about your question today of making the best choice, we also wanted to address your choice of words as the 'best' choice. It sounds as if you want to make that choice to avoid traveling a desolate road that isn't the quickest trail to your happiness or enlightenment. And to this we say, there is never a wrong choice and never a wrong road. All roads contain people, places, and lessons that will teach you. Now we understand that you don't want to choose the road with big potholes that cause it to be unbearably bumpy or slow. But there is not one road that is straight and smooth and the rest are untraveled, long, and never ending. *Did you ever think that maybe there is more than one smooth, short road? And why is one the best? Do you know that one road you may meet Jenny who you laugh with, you learn from, and you get what you are needing.* And the other road is where you could meet Nikki, who you like just as much, you learn so much from, and it is straight and smooth. Neither is better, shorter, smoother, or the 'best' choice. Both are great choices and both will lead you to the destination you are wanting.

Part of the misperception you are experiencing is based on the fact that you think that you have to reach a final destination, in a certain amount of time, and less rumpled than everyone else. This is where you could stand to go back to the concept that the road or journey is the fun part—the people you meet are gifts and the pit stops may be lots of fun. *I mean if you saw a tire swing, wouldn't you want to stop and take a ride?*

When you feel this pressure creep up on you to stay the course of least resistance to your destination of bliss, remember that your joy is not a destination. It is the now. It is in the journey. It is in the experiences. You may always have to 'work' on something or learn something new, or side step a bump. But these are not obstacles, they are the goldmines, the gifts to you.

There is no pot of gold at the end. The gold is in the joy you feel while sliding on the rainbow. It is in the giggles that dance through the air and the twinkling in your eyes as you behold the beauty of the path. By the time you land on the other side, you are full of the gold you acquired during the ride. And as you lay there recalling the stunning beauty of the melding of the colors contained in the rainbow you were just a part of, if you could see yourself, you would behold magnificent reverberations of gold and silver waves that decorate your soul.

Ride the rainbow our friend, with no hands!

With admiration and reverence.

Q: *I'm taking your advice from yesterday and asking for further clarification about anything I have not resolved in regards to my brother and mother's deaths. I really felt twelve years ago when I had a mediumship session with Psychic Medium Ricky Wood, that I instantly healed so much pain. I no longer questioned if he or my mom were still 'alive.' This amazing reconnection really opened up my spiritual curiosity because I no longer equated spirituality with religious teachings that I felt where narrow-minded and exclusionary. Both of which didn't*

add up to me on how an all-loving, all-forgiving, and infinite God would want to be modeled after.

Hearing from my brother again gave me a peace that I had never experienced before. I really thought that I had released the pain of loss that I clung to for so many years. A much better understanding of the world, physical death, and the continued existence of our spirits was born for me that day. It wasn't until an unexpected second mediumship reconnection recently that made me realize I still harbored intense sadness and pain surrounding the death of my brother and mother. How is it that I know definitively that they are still 'alive,' yet I still carry a sadness in my soul for losing them? How can I rectify and release this pain? I do know that this is the greatest gift I could give myself and what they really want for me. I just can't see what it is and how to let go of it. Your insight is greatly appreciated. Thank you so much.

A: It may seem difficult for you to see in a haze of sadness, but it is really a clear answer. As you have stated you know that they are still alive. You know in moments when you feel connected to the lyrics of a song that you feel like you can almost touch your brother because he seems so close. You've had experiences where you've heard from your mom in dreams and you've felt her on this physical plane. And although these encounters are outside of the norm of your physical senses, you are sensitive enough that you know that they are around and with you. You are confused because you do not question this yet your heart aches.

This is not because you crave to know they are here, you do. This is not because you wonder if you will ever see them again, you know you do now in different forms. **What you really suffer from is an inability to let go of what you wish had happened.** If you know that your brother and mom are around you, communicate with you, and are there with you, you are not aching for them now. What you are wishing for and living with is the disappointment that the relationship with them on the physical realm was somehow different.

These are for different reasons. Let's start with your mom. And let us begin by saying that this is a 'normal' instinct so do not beat yourself up for having an issue with releasing this. Your mom, even when around you in your first five years of life was unavailable to you. She was in pain and medicating it with alcohol. She did not give you the affection, attention, time, love, and care that any young child wants from their mother. This is where your pain lies. This is what causes the tears to well up in your eyes and the sadness to come to the forefront in your heart. **You have not let go wishing that your young years were different.**

Although this is understandable, this is the crux of your problem. Not because you didn't deserve these things. Oh you did dear little one. You were beautiful and perfect and deserved this attention. And although she couldn't give it to you, she gave what she could at that time. And how lucky were you to have your brother to hold you when you were scared at night. What a wonderful comfort he was to you when you were confused, sad, or needed a tender arm around your shoulders. He was your comfort and this is why his leaving was so painful for you because he was not just your brother. He was the one who showed you love as a little tiny girl. He was so much more, thus his passing cut even deeper.

We know that you know all of these things, we just wanted to acknowledge the pain that we know you felt. The unworthiness, sadness, and how unloved you felt during that time. You know she knows and is regretful that she had to be this role in your life. She wishes that she could have been what you wanted and needed. You are so loved Amy and we know that you know this when you feel her now.

To finally allow yourself to move on from this pain, you need to let go of wishing that it was any different. Although we know that you wouldn't choose it or wish it on anyone else, holding onto that as a way of validating your pain is a self-fulfilling prophecy. You do not feel worthy, loved, beautiful, perfect and OK to be you, and to feed this you think of those times as a child and revisit those negative feelings. You think back to those times and feel the pain again and again so that you can prove that your inaccurate feelings of yourself today are validated. **You can stop it now by letting go of any wishes for it to have been any different than it was.**

Look at it this way. You survived. You had angels that stepped in and helped you. You had an immense amount of love from your brother in her absence. And although you think that it was another awful and hurtful step, your mom knew she was harming you. She knew she wasn't capable and stepped away and gave you to your father and step-mother. Not because of a lack of love, but a lack of her own self-love at the time. She was not able to love herself and therefore she couldn't treat you and your brother as you deserved to be treated. This is why she left. Not because she wanted to abandon you, but because she knew that you deserved better than she had to give at that time. Imagine that. Put yourself in her shoes having raised your own daughter. *How much pain would you have to be in to know that you were not capable of being a good mom?* Devastating. She did not leave you or throw you out like trash. She did that to herself and wanted better for you.

Now, here is some help in releasing this, repeat—*I give myself this gift today to take a deep breath in and with my outward breath release all feelings of unworthiness and being unlovable. I am love. I am worthy. And I deserve to be free to bask in the beauty of my soul each and every day. I release all sadness, resentment, and wishes to change how I lived as a little girl. That pain is long gone and over with. I no longer need to keep revisiting that time for it was just a blink of an eye in my soul's journey. I take that little girl in my arms and love her without expectation or judgment. She is perfect and loving and I will show her this each and every day. I no longer hold resentment towards my mother for the* choices she did or did not make. I release her from those chains of regret so that her spirit may soar to new heights. No matter what mistakes she made, I love her and allow myself to feel her love today and always. I am happy with who I am, who I was, and who I am becoming. I release any need to relive any times in my life as I do not need to go back, only forward. I lovingly take my mom's hand and tell her that I will no longer hold her hostage of judgment. I'm sorry for holding onto that for so long and I with a sigh of freedom release any old pain or patterns related to this time of my life.

As for your brother and what you hold onto regarding him is multi-faceted as well. **First, you should release any feelings of guilt or beliefs that you could have done anymore to change whether he took his own life or not.** That was his choice, his hand, and no one else's. You've spent so long trying to convince your Dad that he should let go of any guilt he feels when you harbor your own. You were a teenage girl. You heard him, you acted the best you knew how, and you did what you knew at the time. Ultimately, it may not have made any difference no matter what action you took. It was his choice, his action, and his consequence. As he told you in the mediumship session, *'let go of the guilt.'* That is what he wants for you. He feels badly enough for all of the pain that you have felt for him over the years, and he wants more than anything for you to let go of any strands of guilt that you still feel. In the name of his love, give him that gift. That is what he wants for you.

Secondly, you also hold onto wishing for a different outcome because you dream of him being in your physical life and those you love, like your daughter. He is, just not in the physical realm. It is easy to let things go when you come from a perspective of gratitude. Be grateful he was there for you as you were growing up. Be grateful that he was there to take care of you as a young girl. Be grateful that he was there as your friend, playmate, brother, and role model. He did those things extremely well. Being grateful for those things and remembering them keeps his love in your awareness. Do not worry or fret that you don't see him physically, he is around you more than you know.

And one last thing to ponder. Sometimes wishing or fantasizing about a person or relationship when it is no longer possible can be unrealistic. Think about how much support, love, and guidance your brother and mom provide you from the spirit realm. *Who is to say that if they were here, that it may not be anything like your fantasy? What if your mom was still in pain, still self-medicating and looking to you to mother her? What if she was alive and wasn't part of your life? What if Craig was depressed, unhappy, self-medicating or not really a part of your life?* Those scenarios are probabilities and would be even more painful that having lost them. **In death they may be much more of a positive and loving part of your life than they could ever be in physical form.**

So take joy in the fact that you feel them. Enjoy that you have them around you in such a loving and protective way. Consider yourself lucky that you know that they are there, you are open enough to receive so many wonderful messages from them, and that you are able to know that they share in your joys.

Today be so grateful that you have chosen to let go of what was and what could have been, and embrace the beauty that surrounds you. Embrace you and the beauty of your soul. Get excited for all that you are learning and all of the joy you have in your life. You my dear are a lucky, loved, protected, and watched over soul that is surrounded by so much love and support. That is what family is for, isn't it.

We love when we watch your energy transform during these writings…**when you see things a different way and you are able to bask in the gloriousness of the truth unhindered by the blinders of self-imposed sadness.**

Above the clouds there is always sunshine!

Unwrapping Me

Having so much peace and a broader perspective has really begun to change my life from how I act, speak, react and so forth. I do believe that I'm on a good path and that I'm doing what I'm supposed to be doing. I wonder though why I don't see these changes monetarily yet?

Q: *I feel myself less involved in things that aren't important and I'm intent on keeping my focus on being in my heart. I get less offended and less upset about things and I'm really starting to believe that I have a bigger purpose here to learn and share that through writing. I'm also trying to be open to abundance and the financial success that I'm wanting coming in any form. I guess what I'm struggling with is that I've applied for supplemental jobs, and I continue to promote what I have written as well as the fact that I can be hired to write. I have not been hired for anything. Why not? Am I missing something? I would really like to usher in much more money as quickly as possible yet I don't seem to know why it isn't lining up or why I'm not seeing the money?*

A: Money is not what you are lacking, belief is. *Why don't you believe that your prayers are being answered? Why don't you believe that the money is on its way?* You think that you've asked and your prayers have been unanswered. Yet they have been heard.

Just because you snap your fingers and the stack of money doesn't appear in your palm does not mean that it isn't on its way. See oh impatient one. You've written about it, you know it, yet you have not fully embraced the belief aspect of ask, release, believe, and receive.

Yes, you have gotten over the aspect of thinking that you have to do something that doesn't resonate with you. You've given up on demanding how it will come and in what form, but you have not given up or relinquished the reins to knowing when. We hear you cry out but *"I have bills due." "I'm paying such high interest on money*

I've borrowed," and so on. We say, it will all be OK. And no we do not say that as pacification, we say it because we mean it.

You have given your all to this learning and growth process. You have put yourself out there to learn, change, and share with others so they may find some information or inspiration to help them on their way. You are dedicated to working on this and you have done an amazing job. Keep it up. You are not quite finished yet. And even when you think you're finished with this aspect, you know that you will have more work on the road of having it in your hand and others in a book format.

Do not be impatient and give up, you are in the final stretch. You are on the right path. **You have asked, now let go and just believe.** We know this is the hardest part of this because *'letting go and letting God'* feels like you are jumping off of a cliff blind-folded and with no parachute. You may feel that way, you may feel naked and vulnerable, but you are protected, you are watched over, you are guided, and all of the ease and joy you are craving is just waiting for this belief from you.

We've said this so many times, but as a reminder—be grateful. Say thank you every day for everything. We know you do it, but do it more. Instead of feeding into your fears when you see bills in your mailbox, smile, and say, *"Thank you for all of the money that I have to pay these in full."* And most importantly, mean it. Faking it or going through the motions will not deliver the goods. Feel it, even if it takes you twenty minutes of sitting there with your eyes closed visualizing it, do it.

Breathe in belief and blow out your fears, apprehension and the tension you hold in your shoulders. It is not doing you any good to hold onto it, hold your breath, or worry. Know that all is well.

We want to stress that you have been doing a wonderful job with believing that this is what you are supposed to be doing, doing it with an open heart, and trusting this path even though you may feel that you are doing it blindly. It may feel that way, but it is not. The way is being led by beautiful beings of light. You are the conduit for the energy that makes up everything. You are not alone trying to climb without assistance. This is a façade. So add that to your visualizing because it is so.

And finally, even in this lean time as you think of it, know that you live, eat, breathe, and sleep like a queen compared to most of the world. Put aside the bills, put aside that you can't buy what you want when you want it. You always have healthy delicious food to eat. You have clean comfortable clothes to put on. You have shoes, and a lovely car, and a beautiful home. You are so blessed. Stop comparing yourself to the extravagance you see around you. You know very well that you do not need to have expensive clothes to look nice. You do not need to live in a mansion to live like a queen. You do not need unlimited funds to buy fresh and varied foods each week.

Many in this world would look at you as literally living like the rich and powerful of their country. So what that you have some bills. So what that your clothes are years old. So what that you can't go to get your hair done. Feel that richness as you sit and do what makes your heart sing. Revel in the peace that fills your home. Be grateful for each and every little thing for the rest of the day. Every time you touch something, look at something, or do any of your regular tasks notice the conveniences that you have that so many do not.

Gratitude is a powerful tool. Let go and believe that you are worthy of that which you ask for. Know that you are bettering yourself with the explicit intent of creating more joy in your life so that you can help others see their own, this is your path. Do not waste one more minute looking at anything that you think isn't perfect about you, your life, or the world. See only the beauty, see only the divine and you will see all that there really is. Everything else you've created to distract yourself from this fact. **Your drive to fulfill the lie that you believe that you aren't worthy is merely**

a self-imposed distraction so that you do not have to embrace your perfection, your power, and your destiny.

You are not being more holy or God-like by belittling yourself. You are not making Christ proud that you suffer. You are not more Zen and Buddha-like because you deprive yourself of self-love or fulfillment. Anything that you still feel in your body that is not complete joy is your attempt to create pain. Not because you do it purposely but because you are misguided. You do not need to suffer to gain the love of others. You do not need to be less than so that you do not outshine others. **Anything other than complete love and cherishment of yourself is a disservice to you and all of humanity.**

When you believe that you deserve to revel in the perfection of all that is, you will believe that you are worthy. And when you believe that you are worthy just for being you, you will see all that you are wanting and more coming to you with ease and abundance. The universe wants you to love yourself and wants you to be kind, caring, and nurturing to yourself and others. There is no separation between how you treat others and how you treat yourself. We are all connected and it affects everyone and everything every time you make a choice.

So today and forward, choose to love you. Choose to embrace your perfection. Choose to be the shining light that you are. It is not only your right, but what you have been searching for in regards to what you should be 'doing.' **Self-deprivation is a man-made attempt to punish the 'bad' out in the name of all that is good and holy. It is not sacrificing or noble, it is actually the opposite of what is wanted for you.**

And the big question that will stop all of this...*Who said that you not getting another job isn't all divine and that your full-time job right now was to put one hundred percent of yourself only into this?*

After believing comes receiving.

We love you.

22

The Magic Continues

AFTER PACKING ALL OF MY clothes, food, and toiletries for the week, I laid down and tried to get in sleep-mode earlier than normal. Tomorrow morning I will be leaving at 5:15 a.m. to go to the "Awakening the Illuminated Heart" workshop with Drunvalo Melchizedek in Sedona.

Luckily, I'd found a house share where a person offers a room in their home for the week at about a third of the price of a hotel room. This is so out of my comfort zone—staying in someone's home that I didn't know, going to a workshop for the first time for five days, alone, and not knowing anyone, let alone what to expect. Taking a deep breath I went into meditation to relax. Just before falling asleep I laughed remembering the Native American putting sage under my nose to wake me up before my last trip to Sedona. I wondered if it would happen again and welcomed it if they wanted to.

My alarm woke me up with no hint of any sage in the air. I wasn't disappointed for long because my excitement took over for what the week held for me. It was still dark out as I began the two and a half hour drive to the *Creative Life Center* where the workshop was being held. With cruise control set to 75 mph and the roads still pretty empty, I was suddenly snapped out of it. *Had I heard that correctly?* As always it was such a quiet and gentle message that I wasn't sure if I'd really gotten one. Then I thought better of questioning it and filed it away, grateful for the guidance. The message had simply been, "When you get there, sit in the left front of the room."

That was it. Not why or anything else. But I knew by now just to go with it. So I did, just after being met by another attendee in the parking lot. Within two minutes of meeting her she shared a story about a friend who discovered that a lover was reptilian when she saw him in bed. Not quite the first encounter I'd expected, but hey, I didn't have the slightest knowledge or thoughts about whether such a thing existed so I brushed it off. Pleasantly surprised by the warm smiles and greetings I was met with by quite a few of the other 125 people surprised me. I was still nervous and a bit overwhelmed since it was usually just me and my computer most days.

I made my way to the front left of the room. Thinking it would be a bit ambitious or teacher's pet-like to sit in the very first row, I chose the second row, end seat, all the way to the left. As I sat down and took a few deep breaths, I wondered why I was supposed to sit here. I could see behind the stage and watched as Drunvalo, who I recognized from the internet, spoke with people. As I looked through the one window where the blinds were pulled up in the front left corner of the room, I noticed a bronze figure amidst the lush garden scenery. Looking harder at the figure, I realized it was a statue. A woman statue that reminded me of the Changing Woman one in town. Although it felt familiar, it was different. For a moment, I could swear she was looking back at me.

That was it! My Native American statue friends were at it again. I couldn't help but smile and let out a little chuckle. When I returned from the lunch break, the blind was closed as it remained for the rest of the five-day workshop.

The Magic Continues

Two lovely ladies named Ann-Marie and Sylvia introduced themselves to me and the people sitting around us. They were from the UK, Ann Marie grew up in the U.S. but relocated, and Sylvia was born and raised there. I'm not sure if it was Sylvia's accent and the way she used words that we don't like "cheeky" that I loved, or Ann Marie's direct but kind way of speaking to you as if she was really hearing what you were saying. Either way, I felt instantly at home with them.

I felt the urge again on the second day to go to the front left of the room when it was time to choose a group for a rebirthing exercise. To my delight, there in the front left of the room were Ann Marie and Sylvia. After each group assembled into six or seven people, we began by all sitting around one of us lying in the middle on a mat. I felt strongly that I did not want to go first, but just as strongly that I did want to go second. Again, I wasn't sure why, but I went with it. With meditation music reverberating and our collective humming, it was easy to get over feeling strange about the exercise. The theory was that we were allowing our group to support us as we were reborn or awakened to being in our hearts instead of our heads.

With a mask over my eyes, five pairs of hands supporting me, music lolling me, and in meditation, I began to feel as if I was floating a bit. It was quite amazing the images I saw in my mind's eye. From flashes of my own mother and family, to being at a huge celebration where everyone was dressed in white, to seeing myself confidently descend the stairs as a little girl to join the party, I was pretty blown away by the experience. At the end of the exercise, the group was surrounding me and Ann Marie took my mask off and welcomed me back. Looking at the floor I saw a four inch mini rainbow to the right of me. It was very dark in the room, but I assumed it was coming from the stained glass ceiling in the center of the room. I thought it to be good luck and pointed it out. Anne Marie then told me what she witnessed during the exercise.

Shortly after my turn began, she saw the rainbow appear on my throat. Then it moved down and sat right on top of my heart for the remainder of the twenty-minute exercise. I peeked during every remaining person's turn and never saw this happen again. I felt honored although I wasn't sure why. I mean it could have been complete coincidence, but I couldn't shake that it was a message for me somehow.

Surprisingly, after sitting for so long, I was completely wiped out at the end of the day. I was in bed and asleep shortly after 9:00 p.m. At first I thought that maybe I was awake at 3:00 a.m. because I went to bed so early, but I'm never wide awake after only six hours of sleep. Whatever the reason, I picked up my Kindle and felt the urge to read. Again, I felt that quiet knowing guiding me. I hadn't gone behind the building to look at the statue I'd seen on the first day, but I felt the urge to learn more about "Changing Woman."

I googled it and read a few different accounts of the Native American Indian Legend. To sum up the story, a baby girl was found on top of a mountain under a rainbow. First Man and First Woman raised her, but she grew from infancy to puberty and thus menstruation in just four days. She is seen by Native Americans as the embodiment of the Earth and the changing seasons as she is said to have been born in the spring, matured in the summer, grown old in the fall, and died in the winter. No worries though, for she is reborn every spring.

After reading a few slightly different accounts of this story, I couldn't help feel I was living this journey during the workshop. Like I was putting all of my learning, growing, desire to die to my previous life, and to be reborn to living through my heart into action. It gave me peace that this was possible. I embraced this week, the process, the discomfort of doing something new, and was open to the miracles of the universe.

The continued knowing's, messages, synchronicities, and unexpected surprises filled every day of the week. This pattern of happenings, going to sleep early, waking up and reading something that helped it all make sense continued throughout the week as well. My wonderfully kind roommate, Sandra from Germany, calmly shared with me one evening that it was a good luck omen after spotting a huge spider in the kitchen. When I saw one on the ceiling in my bedroom shortly after, I was still freaked out. Only pure exhaustion allowed me to fall asleep. In the middle of the night, I felt compelled to look up the spider's metaphysical meaning which I found to be explained as 'grandmother energy and protection.' That didn't seem to make much sense to me until the second to last day at the workshop.

During a break I walked around the building to verify that I'd seen a statue that first day outside the window that had since been constantly covered by a closed blind. I came upon her and felt some relief that I hadn't made it up. As I came closer I drew in a breath. She was a grandmother in prayer. Her name plate read, "Trail of Tears." I knew definitively at that moment that I was guided, protected, and loved. Unsure of how, but confident in my belief that there was a knowing there, for what I'd been through, for how much I wanted to get through it, and how I felt like a trail of tears had carried me to this very place, at this very moment in time.

Gratefully and in reverence I stood before her for a long while before thanking her and rejoining the workshop.

Back to Reality

Q: *So, it has been a couple of weeks since I asked a question and wrote because of being at the "Awakening the Illuminated Heart," Workshop by Drunvalo Melchizedek in Sedona. It was amazing and I felt so at peace and really felt complete love for myself there. Surrounded by people that seemed like-minded, I could speak freely without feeling judged and it was a wonderful experience. I came home feeling like a different person and like I was floating. Even in midst of a crisis with Ricky's family, the following week I still felt centered and as if I was 'seeing' from my heart and without much judgment.*

Now, after entering my second week I feel kind of sad. I know that I didn't lose all of what I learned, I do feel different. There is definitely a feeling a self-love that I didn't have before going, and a broader perspective on many things. I guess I miss the high I felt when I got home. It was almost as if the mortal problems didn't really affect me. Now I feel like I've floated down like a deflated helium balloon. It's as if I was up there with all of my friends, full and shining, and now I'm barely floating any more like a sad little balloon days after the birthday party is over.

Part of me feels like I failed, like I wasn't able to maintain that elation or perspective for long. And although I know logically that the changes that took place for me that week can't be unlearned, I just want to feel as great as I did then. Why is it that I can't live in that place? Why do I have to come back down and feel the pangs of frustration and shortsightedness again? And although you probably know, yes, I have continued the meditations and exercises every day since coming home, so I'm not neglecting the work. Thank you for your insight.

A: Again we must begin by reminding you that you should be celebrating not feeling deflated. You went out of your comfort zone and found a treasure chest of love for yourself and others, amazing tools to use at home, and were lucky enough to immerse yourself in that energy, learning, and comradery for a week. That is truly a blessing that has irreversibly changed how you think of yourself and others, and how you will approach life from here on out. **We remind you to be grateful for what you did get, what you do have, and not to dwell on what you don't have.**

You know by now that learning and changing is a progression. Each step, each day, each experience is a step towards living the life that you want. Being there for five days in a row was a type of rapid change that many don't have the luxury to experience. You packed years of change into one work week. Wow, that is something!

So now that you are in a place of gratitude for what you received, you see that the sadness and deflation is but a distance glimmer now, *is it not?* This is another example of **what you focus on becomes your reality.** All that this means is that you've made great progress and still have some more things to look at. Not that you've failed, you have not. You just need to continue to gently remind yourself when you become aware that you've fallen back into old patterns of focusing on what you do *not* want rather than what you do want.

And if you really think about it, it is not much different than when you come back from a vacation. You wish it didn't end. You wish it had been longer. There is a sort of letdown in the fact that you are back to your 'regular life.'

But dear one, we want you to know that it is not a punishment. It is an honor that you have been given the opportunity to learn and grow and share this with people. *What would be so great about sharing what you learned with those that you learned it with?* Not much, because they get it, they know, they were there. But to come home, and be different, act different, and shine this on those in your life is where change happens. They will see that you changed. **They will see that you approach life differently and it will spark that yearning in them to seek what can change in their own life.**

What is that message that you heard about lighthouses from Lee Carroll's Kryon Channeling? You do not see a group of lighthouses together, it is unnecessary and repetitive. You see a shining lighthouse in the darkest areas, standing strong and lighting the way for those who cannot see. Be a lighthouse. Shine light for those who are in the dark. That is all that you need do with what you've learned.

Part of the sadness you feel is not because you feel that you've sank back down into the darkness, you have not. Part of the sadness is a bit of loneliness again. When you see other lighthouses and are surrounded by them at the conference as you were, you felt at home, you felt alike, you saw that you were with family. But when you are a lone lighthouse standing in a very dark, stormy sea, it can feel lonely. The conference was a reminder for you that you are not alone.

You have an important job being the lighthouse. Think about all of the ships that may sink without your light. **Remember, do not attach yourself to where your light shines. Shine it freely, with love, and without discretion.** It does not matter whether people use it, like it, turn the other way, or yell that your light is bothering them. All that you need to know is that you are doing your job by lighting the way. What others do is their job, life choice, and part to work out. Their choice is not a reflection of you. You are merely a night light. So whether they welcome your shine or shun it, do not let this affect your resolve to keep on standing strong and illuminating around you. Anything else is ego. Taking credit for helping or not helping is merely your ego, not your soul's response.

When you go into your heart and meditate, feel that oneness and complete love and peace that you brought home with you, and carry that through each day. You did not lose any of it, you merely have let ego and wounds that you've yet to completely shed to cloud your vision. Do not let others pain poke your pain so that you can both fall prey to avoidance and distracting yourselves from what you really are—divine, perfect, loving beings that merely need to let go of everything else.

Again, celebrate, rejoice, and feel immense gratitude for what you received and continue to receive every day. The more you are grateful, the more you will recognize all that you have to be grateful for. Continue to use the tools that you received to center yourself in your heart each day. When you approach everything in life this way, you will always see the beauty in everything.

We love you. We are so proud that you love you. And never forget that we are all one.

Amen

Even after the transformation I've experienced, I still find myself discovering there is more work to do.

Q: *It has been yet another few weeks since my last question. Although I know that I no longer see things with the blinders on that I used to wear, I found yet again yesterday that there is always more to do. I thought that my ability to mean it when I say that I love myself meant that the 'work' on learning to love myself was complete. Not that it doesn't need to be nurtured but that since I had discovered it, I no longer needed to heal the part of me that felt unloved. During a recent session with Mary Ellen, I realized that I still wasn't loving the little girl in me. That in certain situations I was avoiding, swallowing, or just going back into surviving mode. At first I thought this was a failure, but then I realized that if I didn't love me, I wouldn't be able to pick up that little girl and hold her, love her, and teach her that it is safe to be me. That it is OK to want the things I want and be who I want to be, without apology or the need to defend myself, be mean to or get angry with those who do not. I now realize that discovering and working on ourselves is never really finished and that I don't need to look at it like it is a constant battle. Discovering the healed and the still raw, the content and the yearning, the knowing and the searching is a part of everyday here. It is not a test, it is not a race, but simply the gift of life. Thank you for helping to remind me of this.*

I also must say that as I sit here now, I'm starting to lose the separateness I felt when I started asking questions. Then it was little-old-hurt me striving to hear how I could heal. Although I'm still sure that there is always something else for me to reach for and to discover in me, I somehow feel that I've melded with you that has answered me. Like I'm not separate from the knowing or the answers. They may not always be clear at first, but I feel like the sunrise has shown itself in the corner of my windowsill. I am so grateful for you, for whoever you are that has patiently sat with my repetitive questions because I couldn't see through the pain. Please let me know of anything I can do, share, offer, and be to honor all that you have given me.

A: You have let go of your separateness enough to understand that we are all one. You are able to feel what it means and that is gift enough. We are all here to learn, grow, realize, and awaken to this truth. Whatever words, feelings, situations, and other pointers that you need to see will appear. It is not the wishing that those will stop or change that will allow for you to see and know this. As you have experienced, it is the river that smooth's the rock.

We hope for you that you will remember or remind yourself when you forget the things that you have learned. Always honor your spirit by feeding it nourishing thoughts, feelings, activities, and surroundings. It is alive always and in all ways. It does not go anywhere, you just lose sight of it. You see this physically with the care of the body. Just because the physical senses do not tangibly behold the spirit, forsake it not, for it has existed and will exist long after the body you occupy.

There is no grand gift to honor all that it is. **The grandest gifts are the simplest ones.** A smile, a hug, a kind word, generosity of spirit, honoring yourself so you may honor others, thoughtfulness in acts, and most of all start with you. **For once you have found the fountain of unconditional love flowing forth unhindered inside, everything else will come naturally and effortlessly. Love you so you may love another.**

Discover how to clear the path to living life from your heart, for it is the greatest gift to you, to those you love, and to all of humanity.

In love and admiration,

Your Friends.

As I'm taking the time to go back and edit the formatting and grammatical mistakes so I can present this in book format, I'm still discovering more about myself.

Q: *Rick said something to me the other day and I can't get it out of my mind. I really thought about it and realized that it was a message. I won't go into all the details about what I was talking about* *but his response to me was, "You are human Amy. You don't like that you are, but you are."*

And after pondering it for a couple of days I know that it is true. Part of my disdain within myself I believe is because I highly regard the spirit and the spirit world, but I feel that somehow being human is less than. Like it has brought my spirit down. I even have anger like this human body and mind is impeding my spiritual self. I do not feel this as much anymore but this may explain why I've been so hard on myself for not knowing better and making human mistakes. I find the spirit and the unseen and unheard beautiful, but I see the human body as less than. Like the lowly acts of excretion and the weakness of the body and mind as pathetic. I feel like this may be the big issue that fueled my self-loathing. I feel like this body and this place is a step down from the spirit world and I don't find much joy in it. The most joy I feel is when I'm reading, writing, or learning about the spirit. I'm pretty sure you will say that I should love this body and that it is an invaluable vehicle in my journey here on earth. I want to feel this way so how can I see the holiness in my body, its imperfections, and the human experience?

A: As with anything that you wish to change, you simply start by recognizing that which you want to change. Congratulations that you heard the whisperings of spirit through another. *See how we are all angels for one another?* You did not disregard the statement although it felt uncomfortable. You did not brush it under the rug even though it is a part of you that you do not like about yourself. You looked at it and felt it to be true, pondered how it is creating that which you do *not* want in your life, and made a decision to try to find an answer to changing how you see.

That is usually the biggest obstacle so take a breath and know that the hard part is over. For when you really truly want to grow, it will be brought into your life. Also, know that if it comes in such a way that may not be comfortable, *do you not want to retreat? Was it not uncomfortable to look within yourself and see that you feel this way? Did it not bring up sadness for you that you feel this way towards yourself?* Towards this beautiful physical manifestation that provides you with the opportunity to learn and grow. Without which, your spirit may not have the ability to understand things so clearly. That my dear, is a human mistake. It is not ugly, disgusting, or less than. It is a beautiful miraculous gift.

Gifts are not always shiny and new and cost money. Some of the most beautiful, holy, and life-altering gifts are those that have come to you in your darkest hour. They may be as quick as a passing sentence. They may be so quiet that you almost missed it. **But the fact that you are given messages, guidance, comfort, and love through one another is one of the most spectacular gifts there is.**

Speaking of gifts. Do not fret that you do not have the many commercialized trappings of the typical holiday celebration surrounding you. Pretty lights, shiny paper, bows, and breakable gadgets are not the essence of what this holiday was created for. A gift is given to honor and give thanks to those who have been there for you throughout the year. It matters not what that gift is, whether it is expensive or free, big or little, extensive or simple. **Simply what matters is giving from the heart.**

And you will find that the most memorable moments, gifts, and joyous times are not from what you were given monetarily, but the feelings that surrounded you. *Did you feel loved? Did you give a hug and mean it? Did you share something you learned this year? Did you ask how someone is and really give them your full time and attention and hold space for them?*

Stop often and feel gratitude. Enjoy the quiet moments between the hustle and bustle. Appreciate the time and effort put into the meal that you eat. Be grateful for what you have already, each day, and all year. There is always someone worse off than you. Do not get angry at the person rushing or cutting you off, step back and send them love. Realize that each day is holy, not just the day of birth. But every day, good and bad, sunshine or rain, cold or hot, each and every moment.

Then you will see that there is holiness in the hands that prepare food, wipe tears, hold doors, type words, and holds hands and reminds you that you are loved. Then you will see that spirit is part of the human form while on this earth. There is not a separation. Yes, when the body dies the spirit will live on, but in no way does that mean that the body is less than. Yes, from our side, we see it as a vehicle to learn, grow, and experience. Imagine when you see your daughter, friend, or loved one and you hug them. The feelings become tangible in the hug. *So which is holier? The feeling or the hug?* From our perspective, they are as equally as holy.

You are not impeded by your body. You are not impeded by your mind. What you are impeded by is seeing them as separate from your soul. Because on this earth when you are born you become one, you merge into one being of higher knowledge and a physical being that can take that knowledge and use it in conjunction with your physical ability to make things. We see beautiful colors, but oh how satisfying to take them and meld them together to create a beautiful painting that you can enjoy each day. We can hear music, but how beautiful it is to channel that through your body, your fingers, and your voice to create a unique song that people can enjoy. And oh dear one, how truly inspiring is it to take the depths of your soul and put it into words so that those who read them may be uplifted, transformed, or see a piece of their divinity that they could not before.

Rejoice in the beauty of your aliveness in physical form. Be grateful for each thing that you can do with it. Cherish it, use it, and love it, for it will bring you closer to your spiritual realm that you are devoted to more than you know.

Embrace all, be all, and love all. It is all one, we are all one.

Hallelujah

I know without a doubt that I'm supposed to share my story and these messages, but I worry too.

Q: *I know that this year of work, learning to love myself, and this time is coming to an end. I really feel like I'm supposed to put this out in book form with the hopes that it could help others with their healing and discovering their own self-love. I have one major concern that is holding me back, which is hurting those that I love. Yes, I feel vulnerable putting my deepest darkest feelings out there for the whole world to see and although it scares me, I can get over that. What I'm really struggling with is sharing information about my partner and daughter. They didn't ask for me to share this information and I feel like it may be intrusive in their lives. I love them both more than anyone or anything and would hate to cause them any embarrassment or pain. I can't see another way to share my story without giving details about our interactions because that is part of the questions I struggled with. Although ultimately, the answers always came back that the 'issue' was with my perception or reaction, I don't want them to resent me for sharing our interactions. My partner is open to it, but I'm afraid my daughter will end up resenting me for some of the information I shared. Do you have any advice for me? Thank you.*

A: Ultimately the decision is yours. What you shared was your perspective, your feelings about a situation, and you always came from a place of love and wanting to better the relationship. It is not a tell-all or a place where you were bashing them, so you are not "giving the dirt" on them as you say.

Give them the opportunity to read your words, your growth, your understanding and see what they have to say. Maybe you could alter a part of the question if it makes them uncomfortable, but *would you want to bury the project?* We feel that you would not. A wise decision as you do not know how many people you could touch with being brave enough to share your account. **Helping others is your goal and the best way to do so is to share your experience and what you've learned.**

It is wise that you wish to be fair to those you love. It is kind that you want to make sure that they are comfortable with what you want to share. Follow your heart. You wish to get their approval, yet you are afraid to have them read it in case you may not get it. Give it to them to read and allow them to come to you with their truthful reaction. Let them know that you would be happy to work with them on something they feel uncomfortable with, but also let them know that sharing this is important to you.

You are fearing something that hasn't happened. You are afraid to act so you are catastrophizing what might be when you do. Go within your heart. Speak to them from it and share what you have written. When they come to you sit quietly and listen to their input. Work with them and come to an agreement on what if anything they are uncomfortable with. It really will be less painful then you are anticipating.

That is the issue with fear. The pain that you experience from playing out the scenarios in your head is usually much worse than the reality. What is truly painful is the mulling process. Stop doing it. You know that your story and question and answers are good to you. You are confident that this is something you were meant to share. Approach your partner and daughter with what you wrote. Offer them time to read and share their concerns, then go from there.

Do remember when they approach you with their concerns, hear them from your heart and not as an attack on your work. What they may or may not think is based on their perception, their experience, and how comfortable they are with being OK with learning from their choices. Their reaction has nothing to do with what you've learned. Remember we are all in different places and spaces.

If you offer someone a forum to be heard, then hear them. Put aside your ego, judgments, or insecurities about your work. They are not attacking you, they are fearful of judgment from others. Hopefully as they read through what you've learned, they will realize that there are none. And anyone who judges them hasn't stopped judging themselves yet. That is their issue to work through not yours.

Life is a balancing act of facing your feelings, sorting through them, and learning from them. It is very simple when we stop judging. It begins with you.

Namaste

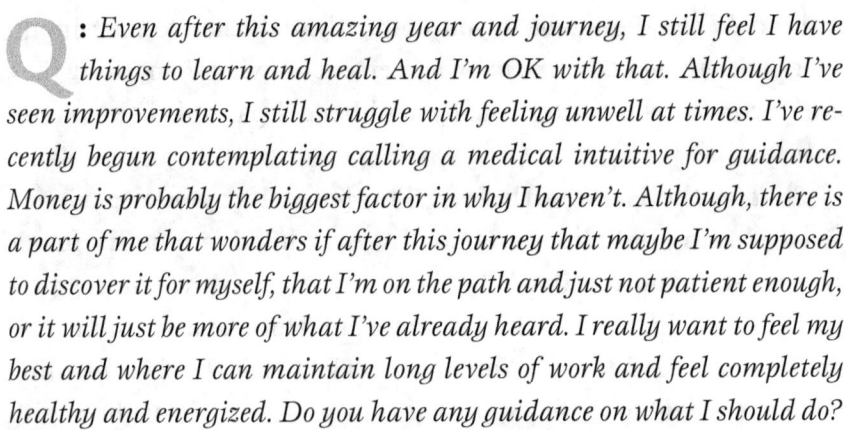

Q: *Even after this amazing year and journey, I still feel I have things to learn and heal. And I'm OK with that. Although I've seen improvements, I still struggle with feeling unwell at times. I've recently begun contemplating calling a medical intuitive for guidance. Money is probably the biggest factor in why I haven't. Although, there is a part of me that wonders if after this journey that maybe I'm supposed to discover it for myself, that I'm on the path and just not patient enough, or it will just be more of what I've already heard. I really want to feel my best and where I can maintain long levels of work and feel completely healthy and energized. Do you have any guidance on what I should do?*

A: You have come so far in the last year and should be so proud of it. You do understand now that you create your life, your joy, as well as your pain. **There is nothing needed other than being in your heart, intention, practicing these things each day, and treating yourself with love and respect.**

Although, when we have been in a pattern for so long it can create something in us that can take a while to transform. Not because you can't do it immediately, but because it will take time and practice to change your approach.

We think you know this deep down and this is why you question whether it is really necessary. Reminders are always good if they help you get on or stay on track. But as you've seen while going through and rereading and editing this work, that you learn something each time you read it again. That is because you are always changing, learning, and becoming. You are remembering the power that you possess.

It is not right or wrong. If you feel he can help you find an approach that may help you to feel physically better while you still work on changing your approach to yourself, then feel free to.

You know how to heal. You know what to do to change your health. Simply, practice each day to feel this and eventually it will be your dominant intent always and in all ways.

With infinite and complete love,

Your Friends

24

One Year Later

HERE I SIT ONE YEAR after shutting the door for the last time in Pennsylvania. What a difference a year can make. I've experienced so many synchronicities, released so much that didn't serve me, went through a ton of ups and downs, and though it seems like more than a year since so much has happened, I wouldn't change a thing. Which is a good thing since I can't. The only thing I can change is how I look at things and I can say that has definitely happened.

I am so happy that I can say that my relationship with my daughter is better than ever. Not because everything is perfect all of the time, I just no longer feel sad, disappointed, used, or unloved in my relationship with her. Quite the opposite, I'm filled with love for her and most surprisingly for myself. I talk to Cassandra almost daily. She calls me a lot and my guess is, she feels it now. It started after the workshop when I acknowledged that I loved myself and actually felt it for real. *Coincidence?* Probably not. She knows that I love her and I'm so happy that I'm teaching her by example how to love and honor oneself. I'm actually full of gratitude for Cassandra doing her thing, so I could do mine. *Who knows?* None of this may have ever happened for me if things didn't go down the way they did.

Throughout the questions and answers in this book, I chose to leave out the details about why Ricky struggled this year. That is his story to tell. What I can comfortably say is that he was extremely worried about and hurt by people in his life. Just as I struggled with things, he did as well. Looking back it is clear to me that he and I were both working things out within ourselves and within our relationships with loved ones. I have also realized that I was so caught up in figuring things out that I probably wasn't as patient and supportive as I would have liked to have been.

What I know now is that I no longer expect anything from Ricky, I'm just grateful for being able to share a life with him. I've always loved and appreciated him, his support, and the love he demonstrates that he has for me. As in any relationship, I'm sure we will continue to be mirrors for one another so that we may always grow individually and subsequently, as a couple. **Love is the most delicate of flowers, yet when watered and fed properly, it can grow more beautiful with every passing year.** Each day I am humbled that he chose to be here, with me, and love me no matter what.

I no longer need to feel sad to feel connected to my brother or mother. Finally, I know that I am honoring them by being happy and loving myself. It took a long time, but it is truly a freeing and wonderful place to be. I've chosen to no longer—wish they were here, wish that I could change what was when they were here, or wish for anything except that they find joy in where they are now. What amazing teachers they were for me and how lucky that I can feel their love today.

I see the world and people differently. I feel so much less judgment for other's actions. Don't get me wrong, I'm still human. I still have times where my feelings can be hurt, or I find myself slipping out of my happy place. But with a few moments, and sometimes a day or so, of breathing and reminding myself that it all begins with me, I remember who I am. I am whole, loved, perfectly imperfect, and full. I discovered the truth, the infinite flow of love that is mine always. I am no longer angry or disappointed in the needy sad little girl I once was. I thank her, for without her I may have never really known me.

Do I feel healthier than I did a year ago? Definitely! *Am I at a 100%?* Not yet, but I know that it takes time and that I'm on my way. I finally understand that living a loving, fulfilling, healthy, happy, and joyous life really begins with a foundation of self-love. Once we understand how to love, honor, and respect ourselves, the rest will fall into place so much more easily. I truly believe that as I become more and more grateful for my body as an extension of my soul, I will find my ultimate health.

I continue to have a monthly BodyTalk session with Mary Ellen over the phone. As much as I've discovered and grown this past year, I'm still constantly learning and growing. I have to say how grateful I am to have the opportunity to have a mentor like her. Watching her learn, grow, and dedicate herself to her own healing so that she can help others is truly awe inspiring.

You know, although I always appreciated a good magic trick, I thought magic was fake or just an illusion. I can say now that I believe in magic. The only illusion is that we think there isn't any. Unwrapping me was quite the journey, which may have never been possible without some help from my friends. To each and every one of you, thank you, thank you, thank you.

A final thought…

Someone asked me at Drunvalo's workshop if maybe I was "Changing Woman?" I didn't know. And my first thought was, how pompous of me to think so or to think that she would be helping little old me. And then I thought better of belittling myself to think that I was not worthy of help, guidance, or had something important to contribute to this world.

I do know that I'm not better than anyone, nor am I less than. Maybe I'm just an example and we are all changing women and men. Maybe this is just another story of a regular girl who became a woman by putting down her self-loathing and picking up her self-love.

Or just maybe, one who loves a good story and found her salvation in one called "Changing Woman."

The End.

Some of the Friends Who've Helped Me Along the Way:

Ricky Wood—Psychic Medium & Intuitive Life Coach- RickyWood.net

Mary Ellen Foust—Healer & Teacher- facebook.com/BeneficialTherapies.com

Drunvalo Melchezidek—Spiritual Scientist, Author & Teacher- www.drunvalo.net

Karen Adams of Akashic Journey—Akashic Reader- akashicjourney.com

Robert Taub—*Healer & Teacher*- awakeninginamerica.com

Nellie Walter—Psychic Medium- nelliewalter.com

Oprah Winfrey—*Visionary, Growth Facilitator and Much More*- oprah.com/own

Lee Carroll Channeling Kyron—Channel, Author & Teacher- kryon.com

Eckhart Tolle—Spiritual Teacher & Author- eckharttolle.com

Gay Hendricks—Psychologist, Writer, Personal Development Coach- hendricks.com

Esther Hicks of Abraham Hicks—*Channel & Author*- abraham-hicks.com

Learn more about specific healers, teachers, and holistic tools that Amy has used at www.intuitivelifestyles.com.

About the Author

A.P. Morris shares her personal experiences with the hope of helping others.

Her first book, They're Not Gone, details fourteen stories including her own about how reconnecting with her deceased brother through Psychic Medium Ricky Wood changed her outlook on life & death.

She lives in Gilbert, Arizona.

You can contact her at amy@apmorris.com

www.apmorris.com

www.ingramcontent.com/pod-product-compliance
Lightning Source LLC
Chambersburg PA
CBHW051417290426
44109CB00016B/1338